VIC AND SADE

VIC AND SADE

The Best Radio Plays of Paul Rhymer

EDITED BY MARY FRANCES RHYMER

FOREWORD BY JEAN SHEPHERD

A Continuum Book

THE SEABURY PRESS · NEW YORK

The Seabury Press, Inc.
815 Second Avenue
New York, New York 10017

Printed in the United States of America

Library of Congress Cataloging in Publication Data

Rhymer, Paul.
 Vic and Sade : the best radio plays of Paul Rhymer.

 (A Continuum book)
 I. Title.
PS3568.H9V5   812'.5'4   75-44426
ISBN 0-8164-9284-0

CONTENTS

FOREWORD

––•–•••–•–

By Jean Shepherd

One day when I had to stay home from the Warren G. Harding
School because of some Kid problem like a sty or a case of diarrhea
and everything was quiet in the house in the Northern Indiana
steel-mill town where we lived, half-way up in the next block on
Cleveland Street, I suddenly heard my mother laughing uproari-
ously in the kitchen. Now, my mother wasn't the kind to laugh
aloud much, especially alone and in the kitchen. I struggled out of
bed to see what was going on. There she was, sitting at our white
enamel kitchen table, wearing her rump-sprung Chinese Red
chenille housecoat, her hair festooned with aluminum rheostats,
laughing her head off.
"What's up, Mom?"
She waved weakly at me. She giggled again.
"What's happening, Mom?"
She wiped tears away from her eyes with a soggy dishtowel.
"Walter's kneecap is acting up again."
"Huh?" I asked in the best Rush Gook style.
"Go back to bed. Can't you see I'm listening to the radio?" She
was indeed. She had a white plastic Sears Roebuck Silvertone radio
with a cracked plastic cabinet, badly repaired with adhesive tape,
on top of our beloved Hotpoint refrigerator. It was her constant
companion. It hummed, and gave her shocks continually, but out of
its imitation gold speaker grill flowed her secret world of fantasy
and entertainment. She was one of millions of lucky and discerning
housewives who had the good fortune to actually hear VIC & SADE.
They are, naturally, a decreasing band, those lucky ones, but they
all, to the last one, remember whole episodes and places, people,
and the Chicago & Alton freight yards. Paul Rhymer was unknown
to most of them, as he is to most of the civilized world today. There

is just no one to compare him with. As far as I know, no one working in mass media has ever created such a complete and flawless world, peopled with characters so fully realized.

Most work done for the mass media is highly perishable by its very nature. Unfortunately, also by the very nature of mass media, the mediocre and the banal tends to outlive the truly creative and original. The "Lone Rangers" and the "Green Hornets" are forever being dredged up as examples of "The Golden Age of Radio," while unfortunately the true gold is mentioned rarely, if at all.

My memory of the actual show as broadcast is episodic because VIC & SADE was a daytime show. Radio, in those days, as television does to this very day, reserved its night-time prime hours for the "important" shows. Daytime hours were packed with things designed for "housewives," usually a term tinged with slight derision in network offices. Therefore, not only was the great work of Paul Rhymer burned up by the nature of mass media itself, it was doubly cursed by being cast among the quicksand shoals of the world of Soap Opera. It's as though "Death of a Salesman" or "Our Town" had debuted on a typical Wednesday afternoon between "As the World Turns" and "Against the Storm," followed by "The Hollywood Squares."

Being a kid at the time, daytime was spent going to school, or outside just fooling around, but on the few times that I did hear VIC & SADE, Blue-tooth Johnson, Rooster Davis, Third-Lieutenant Stanley and Mr. Gumpox's horse Howard became firmly embedded in my subconscious—forever. I remember nothing of "The Lone Ranger" except "Hi Ho, Silver!", which is not much of a line when you think of it. All I remember of Fred Allen is his phony Chinese accent when he was playing a detective, but Smelly Clark's Uncle Strap taking his lady friend to Peoria for a fish dinner somehow got me where I lived. Maybe it was because Paul Rhymer created *true* humor. He did not deal in jokes, but human beings observed by a sardonic, biting, yet loving mind.

Rhymer has been compared to Harold Pinter by some, Mark Twain by others. Personally, I feel that Rhymer was a complete original. Curiously enough, Rhymer *reads* better than any of the so-called "serious" writers of his era. The VIC & SADE scripts are not only still fresh and funny, but are absolutely recognizable as an authentic picture of American life which persists in millions of homes today. Yamilton's Department Store, Peoria, the peanut machine at the Depot, Consolidated Kitchenware, Plant Fourteen, The Sacred Stars of the Milky Way were never touched by Steinbeck or Odets. The Okies are a quaint period piece, but Gloria Golden is still playing at the Bijou. Her name may be Faye Dunaway or Raquel Welch. Rush's complaint "All they ever have in movies is Love, Love, Love. Boy, they sure are boring" could have been said yesterday afternoon.

Another thing that amazes me is Rhymer's wild and subtle imagination. Wild in the sense of being totally unpredictable, and subtle in that he touched at times on the faint vein of madness that runs through all of us. He rarely went for the obvious; hence he preceded the Theater Of The Absurd by decades. In fact, it is my opinion that in some ways he was far closer to Ionesco in spirit than he was to Thornton Wilder, who sentimentalized American life in a way that Rhymer's sense of irony refused to allow. For example, "The Washing Machine Is on the Blink" combines the American Do-It-Yourself syndrome, Masochism, and the continual breakdown of modern technology in such a totally nutty way as to be completely logical in the way a Marx Brothers scene involving a grand piano, a stuffed duck, a bolt of lightning and an out-of-work Fire Chief does. In some twelve minutes of inspired dialog, Rhymer convinces us that two otherwise sane human beings, down in the basement trying to fix the washing machine, begin to enjoy electric shocks, experimenting with various electric shock techniques, finally conspiring to lay one on an unsuspecting mother, all the while cackling maniacally in ecstatic pleasure. There are very few minds that could possibly conceive of the electric shock as pleasure, but that's Rhymer for you. I, personally, am curious just what your average nice, hard-working housewife of the period thought when she heard that one. I suspect more than a few crept down into the basement covertly and tried sticking their fingers into hot AC outlets while standing in puddles.

Another example of Rhymer at his surreal best is the little gem called "Caramels on a Hot Day," in which we find Rush, as he puts it, "stirring up a little excitement" by sitting on the front porch, making round balls out of square three-for-a-penny caramels. Think about that for a moment. A hot day, caramels, and boredom. This is exactly what a kid does do, squatting on a front porch in the heat of summer, but who would think to build a fifteen-minute drama to be broadcast to millions out of that dynamic situation? Better yet, who but Paul Rhymer could pull off such a feat, or would have the courage to do it even if he could? Rhymer obviously was very sure about his work in a medium where that kind of security and self-knowledge is almost non-existent.

In a way it's too bad that Paul Rhymer never wrote for the more recognized media. Great reputations exist in the theater or the novel on far less profound and effective work than Rhymer's. In fact, he probably wrote more funny lines in one month of daily scripts than the combined output of five of the leading playwrights of modern times. Not only that, his characters were truer, more consistent, and far better realized. Remember, reading these scripts in published book form is barely skimming the thinnest surface of the body of VIC & SADE. These works were written to be *performed*, and yet in spite of that they come alive, snapping and crackling, off the page. One reason, technically, is that Rhymer created a vast cast of unseen and unheard people who were every bit as alive and interesting as Vic, Sade, Rush, and Uncle Fletcher. Fred and Ruthie Stembottom and their continual snaillike drives in Fred's old automobile to Chenoa, Illinois, and Ruthie's "scared rabbit" smile; Mr. Ruebush, Vic's boss at the plant; Ike Kneesuffer's indoor horse-shoe set in his basement; Miz Husher's continual peevishness, and, of course, Vic's beloved lodge brothers in the Sacred Stars of the Milky Way—Robert and Slobert Hink, Y. Y. Flirch and H. K. Fleeber, are all part of the well developed cast of millions.

Not all of VIC & SADE's episodes were pure fun and games. In fact, they rarely were. Practically every episode had little shafts of insight, and often sadness, that would come and go like the brief hints of darker things we all have in our own lives. Sade's tenderness over poor old Uncle Fletcher's wandering mind; Vic's understanding of Rush, and his obvious love for Sade, comes through in a beautifully written and subtle episode called "Vic Confides in Rush about Mothers." It contains hints of the inevitability of death, references to the "Empty Nest" syndrome (Rhymer was thirty years ahead of psychiatrists on this one), overlaid with a beautifully realized treatment of masculine relationships. In addition, he managed to be funny. Rhymer must have been a hell of an interesting man to know.

Perhaps one of the things that Rhymer did best was to illuminate and dramatize lightly, effortlessly, and without at any point lecturing, the vast gulf that exists between *types* of people. I have never read a better short story touching on the smothering boredom, yet natural concern we feel in the presence of close relatives than in "Vic Reviews a Vacation Week with Bess and Walter in Carberry." Poor Walter and Bess, trying so hard to entertain Vic, and Vic trying so hard to *be* entertained, while Sade all the while blithely chatters on with her sister Bess, never realizing that Vic's only vacation for the year is going down the drain. This episode, by the way, points out another quality in Rhymer's work. He never ridiculed or put down people merely because they are what they are. However, he is razor-sharp when it comes to blasting the fraudulent and the inane. "Vic Is Elected to the Congress of Distinguished Americans" is a classic example of Rhymer putting another one right in the bull's-eye. This particular con has been around for a long time, and there are countless walls in dens all over the country upon which hang framed scrolls proclaiming "officially" the profound and notable greatness of the yahoo who pays the rent. In fact, it was only last week that I received, personally, three notices in the mail informing me that I had been selected "to be signally honored" by outfits with names very much like The Congress of Distinguished Americans. I remind you that this particular episode was aired 'way back in the Thirties.

Some of Rhymer's funniest stuff dealt with that all-pervasive goofiness of the 20th Century—the movies. Vic, particularly, was great on the subject. In fact, in "Stembottom's Invitation to Drive Thirty-five Miles to a Double Feature" we find Vic emitting "low, painful groans" for three full pages of dialog when faced with the nightmare of attending a double feature of two pictures he had already seen, and hated the first time around, and which he describes as "rotten, rotten, rotten." Nobody in today's situation comedies is ever remotely as honest about a fellow medium. Does Archie Bunker ever blast the movies, or even mention them at all? Does Mary Tyler Moore? Never. That's the thing about the characters in VIC & SADE. They lived in the real world, where people really do say such things as movies are rotten, or Yamilton's Department Store is throwing another one of "them phony Sales."

Judging from his scripts, if Rhymer were alive today he would probably snort in derision at the pompous tone of this foreword, but I also suspect he would secretly have enjoyed it. Rhymer was an artist, and no artist who ever lived ever turned down a tribute to his work. I think I should point out a few techniques that Rhymer used that everybody tries but few master. Most contemporary writers for mass media simply feed a series of one-liners to their characters, go for the cheap laugh, and hope that no one is the wiser. Rhymer, in contrast, wrote *dialog;* succinct, spare, yet with an absolutely true ear for the rhythms and inflections of American speech. This is much easier to talk about, or discuss in class, than to accomplish. Obviously, Rhymer was a very gifted listener. A few brief examples:

SADE: Sounds like somebody's trying to knock our front door in.
RUSH: That stuff cookin' on the gas stove okay, Mom?
SADE: Why?
RUSH: Makin' a gurgling sound like it needed water.

Now that's nice. *People* talk like that. This, if you wish to read the rest of the dialog, which gets better as it goes along, can be found in "Manual for Wives of Sky Brothers in the Sacred Stars of the Milky Way." There is also some very nifty Latin, a language not often heard on mass media. No pun intended.

Finally, I should point out that the announcer was also an integral part of the daily drama. My mother, for one, loved him. I think his name was Bob Brown. His subtle, confidential style set the tone for the daily session of eavesdropping in the small house halfway up in the next block. My mother to this day tells about the time, not more than five minutes into the episode, the cast, including the announcer, got to laughing so hard over some nuttiness that Rhymer had come up with that the entire show was a shambles. They just laughed and chuckled until finally they gave up trying to be Vic and Sade and Rush and Uncle Fletcher and went off the air, hooting and hollering and leaving millions of listeners in kitchens everywhere doing the same thing. When I was just beginning in the business, I

had the rare honor to meet the fine actress who played "Sade." *
She looked just like Sade should look. She looked, well, like *Sade*.
The series was long off the air, but was rapidly growing as a legend.
I asked her what was the hardest thing about playing Sade on a
daily basis, year in and year out. Naturally, I figured she'd say
something like "endless rehearsals," how tough the grind was, and
so on.

"Well, son, I'll tell you," she said, sounding exactly like Sade
about to straighten out Rush on some fine point of life. "The hardest
thing was to keep a straight face. Sometimes those scripts were so
funny that we had to fight all the way through the show just
breaking up. And the more we rehearsed, the funnier it got. Why, I
remember one day having to turn my face to the wall while Uncle
Fletcher was telling me about a trip he took to Cairo, Illinois, in the
company of one of his friends. The engineer was on the floor, the
announcer had to leave the room, and I can tell you it wasn't easy."

What better compliment can an actor pay a writer?

I have one practical suggestion for those of you who have had the
great sense to pick up this volume of scripts. Read them aloud. Get
three or four good friends together and decide who's going to play
Vic, who will be Sade, and finally Rush and poor old Uncle
Fletcher. You can call in your next door neighbor to do the
announcing. Ten to one you'll be doing VIC & SADE episodes until
five in the morning. Have fun. That's what Paul Rhymer and VIC &
SADE are all about.

---

* The same actors played their parts, from 1932 to 1945: Arthur Van Harvey played Vic;
Bernadine Flynn was Sade; William Idelson was Rush; and, Clarence L. Hartzell was Uncle
Fletcher. Announcer Bob Brown's lines appear in italics before and after each radio
script.—M.F.R.

•━━•◆•━━•

The Paul Rhymer Papers, mainly VIC AND SADE scripts, were a gift in 1969 to the State
Historical Society of Wisconsin. They are in the collection of the Mass Communications
History Center, which makes available to serious scholars significant historical records from
all phases of mass media: radio, television, the press, advertising, public relations, theater, and
cinema.

1

—·—◆—·—

The Washing Machine Is
on the Blink

*It is late afternoon as our scene opens now, and here in the living
room we find Victor Gook and his young son Rush. The older
gentleman is looking over the newspaper and the younger gentleman
seems to be occupied with a school-book. And as we draw closer, we
hear this latter individual say:*

RUSH: Gov, wanta take the book now an' see if I know 'em?
VIC: Your definitions?
RUSH: Yeah.
VIC: Shoot.
RUSH: Here's the book.
VIC: I'll just listen.
RUSH: No, take the book. I gotta have 'em word for word.
VIC: Toss it over.
RUSH: [*tosses*] Catch.
VIC: [*catches*] Got 'er.
RUSH: I'll start with "elocution"   . at the top of the page there.
VIC: Uh-huh. Let 'er rip.
RUSH: "Elocution is the art of delivering, written or extemporane-
ous, with force, propriety, and ease."
VIC: Yeah.
RUSH: That got 'er?
VIC: Yeah. Is "rhetoric" next?
RUSH: Uh-huh. "Rhetoric is the science of speaking with elegance
and persuasion."

1

VIC: Emphasis.

RUSH: "Emphasis is a particular stress of the voice on a word or words in reading or speaking." Examples: *I* think I will tie my shoe. I *think* I will tie my shoe. I think *I* will tie my shoe. I think I *will* tie my shoe. I think I will *tie* my . . .

SADE: [*entering*] Vic.

VIC: Uh-huh?

SADE: Whatcha doin'?

VIC: Coaching Mr. Jackson here in his English lesson.

SADE: Well, look, I'm in a little *trouble*.

VIC: Trouble?

SADE: My wash machine's on the blink.

VIC: What ails it?

SADE: It won't *run*. An' the *worst* of it is, it gives a person *shocks*.

VIC: Yeah?

SADE: There's electricity right in the *water*. Stuck my hand in an' little jabs went right up through my arm.

VIC: Prob'ly what's *happened* is the lead wire's had some insulation scraped off an' the current . . .

SADE: Wish you'd come see. I'm scared to death of it.

VIC: How come you're washin' this afternoon?

SADE: Just runnin' a few towels an' a table-cloth through. Will ya run down an' take a look?

VIC: *I* guess so. Any special hurry?

SADE: Yes, there is. The table-cloth is Ruthie's an' I wanta get it washed an' ironed. Fred's stoppin' by for it after supper.

VIC: [*rising*] I can prob'ly wrap some tape around your lead wire an' doctor it up in a jiffy. Guess we'll hafta post-pone our definitions, Ike.

RUSH: O.K. Mom, can you get a *big* shock from the wash-machine?

SADE: Enough of a shock to scare the daylights outa *me*.

RUSH: Guess I'll go along. I haven't had a good shock in I don't know when.

SADE: [*as they go*] Don't fiddle around, son. Electricity is a very dangerous thing.

RUSH: You can just stick your hand in the *water* an' *feel* it, huh?

SADE: Yes. I like to jumped through the *ceiling*.

VIC: Some of the *current* is escaping is all, kiddo. You couldn't get a big enough shock to hurt . . .

SADE: Be careful of the garbage bucket going down cellar. It's on the top step but one.

VIC: *You* don't hafta come along, Sade. I'll just . . .

SADE: Wanta get Ruthie's table-cloth outa the way so ya don't step on it or anything.

RUSH: Next year *I'll* be able to fix stuff for ya, Mom. The freshmen up at high school study electricity second semester an' . . .

SADE: Want me to let the water out, Vic?

VIC: No, don't think ya need to.

SADE: That's good. Got all these nice suds worked up. Stick your hand in there once.

VIC: Get quite a jolt?

SADE: Jolt enough for *me*.

VIC: Well, I don't imagine. . . . [*laughs foolishly*]

SADE: [*giggling*] 'Lectricity all right, huh?

VIC: Yeah. [*laughs*] Help yourself to some voltage, Pete.

RUSH: Think I'll take it kinda easy at the start. Just stick one *finger* in so. . . . [*laughs*]

VIC: [*chuckles*] Hot stuff, huh?

RUSH: It just gives kind of a *tickle*.

VIC: Goes right up your arm though. C'mon, Sade, join the party.

SADE: I *will* not. Scares the livin' life outa me.

RUSH: 'Lectricity is good for ya. They used to have a machine down at Klemm's drug store where ya put in a nickel an' grab a-hold of . . .

SADE: Will ya see if you can fix it, Vic? If I'm gonna get Ruthie's table-cloth washed an' ironed before Fred comes, I'll kinda hafta hurry.

VIC: I *already* see what's the matter. One side, Oliver.

RUSH: I *enjoy* feelin' this good ol' electricity go through my system. Gives me the sensation of. . . .

VIC: Move. [*to Sade*] See here this lead wire?

SADE: Yeah. That what's broke?

VIC: It's not *broke*. The insulation's been scraped off. A piece of tape wrapped around it will do the business. Rush, there's a tin box with tape in it on the shelf there.

RUSH: [*moving off*] I'll get it.

VIC: [*silly laugh*] C'mon, Sade. Put your hand in here.

SADE: Not for forty dollars.

VIC: Won't *hurt* you any.

SADE: Maybe not. But it *scares* me pink.

VIC: Why, there's not enough current here to. . . . Just lay it down, son.

SADE: [*moving off*] Holler soon as it's ready, will ya, Vic?

VIC: Yeah—only be a couple minutes.

RUSH: [*laughs*]

VIC: [*laughs in sympathy*] Quite a kick, ain't it?

RUSH: Wish there was *more* of it. *This* only gives a *tickle*.

VIC: Move over a little. Shucks, I . . . [*laughs foolishly*]

RUSH: [*laughs in sympathy*] Ain't that the doggondest feeling.

VIC: Yeah. [*chuckles*]

RUSH: Hey, I just thought of an *invention*.

VIC: What's that?

RUSH: Well, ya know in depots an' movie shows an' places where they got wash rooms?

VIC: Uh-huh.

RUSH: Why not fix 'em up so when people washed their hands, they get a good healthy shock like *this*.

VIC: Uh-huh. Only trouble is, folks like your mother'd holler for the police.

RUSH: Yeah. Heck, wish we could get *more* good ol' 'lectricity in this wash-machine.

VIC: *I* know how it could be done.

RUSH: How?

VIC: Pour a little *water* on the floor.

RUSH: An' stand in it, ya mean?

VIC: Sure.

RUSH: Let's do it.

VIC: O.K. Dip some outa the washer with that tin cup there.

RUSH: Figure that'll gun up the current?

VIC: You betcha. Water is one of the world's best conductors. Thomas A. Edison himself once declared that. . . . Right around my shoes here.

RUSH: O.K.

VIC: Pour some where *you're* gonna stand now.

RUSH: All right.

VIC: Electricity is a marvelous marvelous thing. Nobody knows what it is. Nobody knows where it comes from. The sum of the knowledge of . . .

RUSH: Shall I stick my hand in the wash-machine now?

VIC: I better do it first. Might give more of a wallop than you can take. However, I'm sure it won't be so much that . . . [*laughs in delight*]

RUSH: How is it?

VIC: Great.

RUSH: Much as I enjoy electricity, I wouldn't wanta . . . [*laughs*]

VIC: How ya like *that*?

RUSH: [*laughing*] Dandy.

VIC: Goes right through ya, don't it?

RUSH: I'll say.

VIC: Here—I'll show ya something. Stand back a little ways.

RUSH: I hate to leave the electricity.

VIC: *You'll* get some electricity.

RUSH: Where ya want me to go?

VIC: Right here.

RUSH: I won't be able to reach the wash-machine.

VIC: That's O.K. Now look: you're Mr. Steve Butler from Des Moines, Iowa. You want to make my acquaintance. See?

RUSH: [*chuckles*] Yeah.

VIC: [*chuckles*] All right. Say somethin'.

RUSH: Ah . . . you're Mr. Gook, I believe?

VIC: Yes, sir.

RUSH: I'm Mr. Steve Butler from Des Moines, Iowa.

VIC: Glad to know you, Mr. Butler.

RUSH: Care to shake hands?

VIC: Be delighted. Put 'er there. [*They both go into ecstasies.*]

RUSH: That's fun.

VIC: Yeah.

RUSH: Let *me* stand in the water this time.

VIC: All right.

RUSH: Ah . . . what was the name?

VIC: Mister Gook.

RUSH: *I'm* Mister Butler from Des Moines, Iowa.

VIC: The heck. Care to shake hands?

RUSH: Sure. [*more laughter*]

VIC: You put out a pretty mean hand-shake, Mr. Butler.

RUSH: Yeah.

VIC: Well, enough of *this*. Hand me that tape an' let's . . .

RUSH: Hey, Gov, whatcha say we pull it on Mom?

VIC: You couldn't get *her* to shake hands.

RUSH: We'll work it *slick*. I'll say, "Mom, feel my hand. It's cold as ice." An' she'll be standin' in this water, an' *you* can be holdin' my *other* hand. Won't that give a shock?

VIC: Yeah, believe it will.

RUSH: I'll holler then, huh?

VIC: Will you shoulder all responsibility?

RUSH: Sure. [*calls*] Mom.

SADE: [*upstairs*] All finished?

RUSH: [*calls*] Not quite. Can ya come down here a minute?

SADE: What's the matter?

RUSH: Wanta show ya somethin'.

VIC: [*to Rush*] I imagine your mother is a little too smooth to fall for . . .

RUSH: *She's* comin'. Whatcha say I stand right here with my left hand behind me? You take a-hold of it?

VIC: O.K. An' ya better face the door.

RUSH: Yeah.

VIC: I'm afraid there won't be much electricity *left* by the time it goes through my body an' yours too.

RUSH: All the better. Wouldn't wanta give Mom a *big* shock. Just wanta . . .

SADE: [*approaching*) What's the matter?

RUSH: I think there's something the matter with my *hand*.

SADE: [*up*] Your hand? Have you been fiddlin' with them wires an' . . .

RUSH: My hand's so darn *cold*.

SADE: Cold?

RUSH: Feel it once.

SADE: Oh, gracious, Rush, did you have me come all the way downstairs just to . . .

RUSH: *Feel* it once.

SADE: An', Vic, you said it'd only take a minute to fix . . . [*little scream*]

VIC AND RUSH: [*laugh*]

SADE: *That* was a smart trick, *wasn't* it?

VIC: The blame rests on other shoulders than mine, kiddo. The whole scheme was hatched up by nobody else than your son here who . . .

SADE: How near are ya done fixin' the washer?

VIC: Why . . . a . . . as a matter of fact, I haven't . . .

SADE: Haven't even *started* to fix it, huh?

SADE: [*moving off*] If either one of ya ever pull *another* stunt like that on me, there's gonna be some fur flyin'.

VIC: [*after her*] Sade, it was only an innocent little prank. We thought you'd enjoy . . .

RUSH: [*to Vic*] Don't believe she can hear ya, Gov. Almost upstairs.

VIC: We didn't come out so *hot* with our bit of horse-play.

RUSH: [*negative*] Uh-uh.

VIC: I was somewhat apprehensive when you *broached* the scheme. Being aware of your mother's ticklishness about electricity I . . .

RUSH: Say, ain't you Mr. Gook?

VIC: Yeah.

RUSH: I'm Mr. Butler from Des Moines, Iowa.

VIC: Well, break my back.

RUSH: Shake hands?

VIC: Why not? [*They both laugh with delight.*]

RUSH: Hey, I got *another* idea. Let's . . .

VIC: Forget your idea. We've raised enough of trouble an' heartbreak. Hand me that tape an' . . .

RUSH: Just wanta *ask* ya somethin'. Look: If I took this piece of wire an' stood in that puddle of water there by the faucets, an' you held the other end of the wire in the wash-machine, would I get a shock?

VIC: Ya might.

RUSH: Let's try it an' see.

VIC: I think we better get to work here an' undo the hard feelings that Mom . . .

RUSH: Only *take* a minute.

VIC: O.K.—but get a move on.

RUSH: [*moving off*] Boy, I can hardly wait till next year when I'm a freshman in high school an' can learn all the electricity . . .

SADE: [*approaching*] Vic.

VIC: Yeah?

SADE: [*closer*] Got it fixed?

VIC: Why . . . a . . . I was just gonna start to . . .

SADE: I didn't think you had. Listen: Mr. Drummond's upstairs. Came over to borrow some butter. *He* knows all about electricity. I asked *him* to step down an' fix the machine.

VIC: Aw, heck, Sade, all I've got to do is wrap a little tape around . . .

SADE: Uh-huh, but you haven't done it an' I'm in a *hurry*. [*calls*] Mr. Drummond, you can come down if you will. I'm just clearing away some of the *rubbish* so you'll have *room*.

VIC: We're *rubbish*, huh?

SADE: [*moving off*] Great big men that'd shock a lady with nasty ol' electricity.

VIC: *We're* not so *popular*, son.

RUSH: Guess not.

VIC: By the way, son, you *know* Mr. Drummond, don't ya?

RUSH: Know him?

VIC: You have the honor of his acquaintance?

RUSH: Whatcha talkin' about, Gov? Heck, I know Mr. Drummond as well as I know . . .

VIC: Forget it. Just occurred to me ya might like to shake hands with him.

RUSH: Shake hands with . . . ? *Oh.* [*laughs*]

VIC: Get the drift?

RUSH: Yeah. Where shall I stand—right here in the water?

VIC: [*affirmative*] Uh-huh. An' hold your left arm behind ya so I can touch it.

RUSH: O.K. [*They both produce a conspiratorial chuckle.*]
VIC AND RUSH: [*call*] Right this way, Mr. Drummond.

There's a couple of gentlemen waiting to see you in the basement, Mr. Drummond, but don't be too shocked.

First broadcast 1934.

2

Vic Breaks in
Mr. Ruebush's Pipe

It is late afternoon as we enter the little house on Virginia Avenue now, and our scene, strangely enough, opens in the basement. A gentleman of our acquaintance, Mr. Victor Gook, is to be seen sitting on a chair with his feet against the furnace. And another gentleman of our acquaintance, Mr. Rush Gook, just arrived from upstairs, surveys his father, and says:

RUSH: Hi, Gov.
VIC: Heigh-ho.
RUSH: Mom *said* you were down here.
VIC: My corporeal presence is living testimony that Mom told you the truth.
RUSH: Huh?
VIC: I *am* down here.
RUSH: Yeah, Mom said you were down here breaking in a new pipe for Mr. Ruebush.
VIC: Mom's reputation for veracity remains unsmirched.
RUSH: Is that the pipe in the package?
VIC: It is.
RUSH: Smoking tobacco in the other package?
VIC: Yes.
RUSH: Gonna smoke up, huh?
VIC: You've put your finger on my plans.
RUSH: Mind if I stick around an' watch you?
VIC: Not at all. Be glad of your company. There's another chair

over there. Pull it up by the furnace here and we'll have a cozy chat.

RUSH: Okay.

VIC: Have a pleasant day at school?

RUSH: So-so. Had a tough geography quiz.

VIC: I hope you emerged unscathed.

RUSH: What?

VIC: I hope you did passing well.

RUSH: I think I did. Knew most of the questions.

VIC: A better report would be that you knew *all* of the questions.

RUSH: Yeah. Want me to open up your tobacco while you're unwrapping the pipe?

VIC: It'd be kind and thoughtful of you.

RUSH: Hand it to me.

VIC: Here.

RUSH: Mom wouldn't let you smoke your pipe upstairs, huh?

VIC: It was deemed best that I come down cellar. Pipe smoke lingers in curtains an' leaves odors offensive to delicate nostrils. Don't spill any of that now. That's expensive tobacco.

RUSH: It's . . . [*reads*] . . . "South Dakota Mine Run Fine Cut."

VIC: Uh-huh. A brand the boss has smoked for thirty years.

RUSH: Picture of a lady *kissin'* a fella on the front.

VIC: Uh-huh.

RUSH: Funny lookin' lady.

VIC: She's supposed to be Nicotine, the Goddess of the Tobacco Harvest.

RUSH: What's the fella?

VIC: He's just a fella. The picture is somewhat allegorical. Represents a pipe-smoker tasting the joys of tobacco.

RUSH: Oh.

VIC: Whatcha think of this pipe?

RUSH: Let me see it.

VIC: You may examine it as it rests in my hand. Don't wanta take chances with it. It set the boss back a good big chunk of money.

RUSH: How much?

VIC: I don't know.

RUSH: Is this silver there in front?

VIC: Yes . . . don't touch it . . .

RUSH: Big baby, ain't it?

VIC: It has a liberal circumference. The bowl itself, however, is small. I'll trouble you for the tobacco.
RUSH: Gonna smoke up?
VIC: With your permission.
RUSH: Go ahead.
VIC: We'll enjoy mutual ecstasy.
RUSH: On the day I'm twenty-one I'm gonna smoke a pipe myself.
VIC: So?
RUSH: Looks like *fun.*
VIC: It's a regular circus.
RUSH: I'm gonna do somethin' *else* when I'm twenty-one too. I'm gonna smoke cigars.
VIC: Uh-huh. Are you sure you haven't done any smoking to date?
RUSH: Huh?
VIC: I don't want to *pry,* but haven't you ever *tried* smokin'?
RUSH: Never.
VIC: A good many boys your age have.
RUSH: Oh, I had a *chance* to smoke once.
VIC: Yeah?
RUSH: Whatcha doin' now, Gov?
VIC: Tamping the tobacco delicately down in the bowl. Watch closely in order to know the procedure when you get to be twenty-one. It's something of an art.
RUSH: You're just pokin' it *down* good an' tight.
VIC: So it appears to the naked eye. *Really* my sensitive finger tips are distributing the tobacco leaves in a counter-clockwise direction, so that each dainty morsel will yield its full fragrance.
RUSH: [*laughs*] Shucks.
VIC: Why the derisive laughter?
RUSH: How ya expect me to understand all them big words?
VIC: I figured that a gentleman of your educational attainments . . . got a match?
RUSH: No.
VIC: I believe there's a few on yonder shelf. I wonder if you'd mind . . .
RUSH: [*getting up*] I'll get 'em.
VIC: Thank you.
RUSH: Gonna smoke up, huh?

VIC: As soon as you hand me a match.

RUSH: I think there's some here. Mom generally keeps a few to . . . here's one on the ledge.

VIC: Present it to your father.

RUSH: Here.

VIC: Thank you.

RUSH: How much did you say that pipe cost, Gov?

VIC: I didn't say. Wanta watch me light this?

RUSH: I'm watchin'.

VIC: First I draw the match briskly across a resisting surface . . . [*strikes match*] See?

RUSH: *I* know how to light a match.

VIC: Does no harm to learn these things thoroughly. Now I apply the flame to the bowl of the pipe. [*puffs*] I puff. [*puffs*] I puff again. [*puffs*] I puff some more . . .

RUSH: You got it lit now.

VIC: [*puffing*] Yes, indeed.

RUSH: It is good?

VIC: Highly enjoyable. How does it smell?

RUSH: All right.

VIC: [*puffing*] Has a fine full-bodied bouquet, don't ya think?

RUSH: Has a what?

VIC: Smells good.

RUSH: I guess so.

VIC: Now I'll settle myself down to an hour of peace an' relaxation.

RUSH: Does it take an hour to break in a new pipe?

VIC: Takes *many* hours to break it in properly. An' it takes a seasoned pipe smoker to *do* it. Mr. Ruebush picked the right man for the job.

RUSH: You *never* smoke a pipe, Gov.

VIC: I know my business about breakin' 'em in nevertheless.

RUSH: Why don't Mr. Ruebush break it in himself?

VIC: He hates to trust himself with such an important job. Might make a failure of it.

RUSH: [*admiringly*] You're sure smokin' up.

VIC: [*smugly*] Thank you.

RUSH: Keep on smokin' *that* fast an' you'll soon have to fill up your good ol' pipe again.

VIC: Yes, indeed.

RUSH: [*laughing*] I don't *blame* Mom for not lettin' you smoke upstairs. You smoke so darn fast.

VIC: I *never* do things by halves.

RUSH: Uh-huh.

VIC: A few minutes ago I believe you said somethin' about havin' had a chance to *smoke* yourself.

RUSH: That was last summer.

VIC: You didn't go through with it though.

RUSH: No. The way it was . . . Elton Rogers had two cigars he swiped from his uncle. An' him an' me an' Clay Morris was ridin' our wheels up to the Lake. Well, when we got there Elton says, "Well, I guess I'll have a cigar. You guys want one?" Clay says, "*I'll* have one." An' Elton says I only got two so I'll throw one of 'em up for grabs. So he done it an' Clay got it.

VIC: Leavin' you out in the cold, huh?

RUSH: I didn't let on but I really wasn't *tryin'* to get it. *You* know how Mom'd be about me smokin'.

VIC: I imagine she'd disapprove.

RUSH: [*laughs*] I'll say. Anyway I made her a *promise* I wouldn't smoke 'til I got to be twenty-one.

VIC: Uh-huh.

RUSH: So I couldn'ta taken Elton's cigar *anyway*. But I didn't want the *other* kids to know. They'd think I was a sissy.

VIC: Uh-huh. How'd your pals come along with their cigars?

RUSH: [*laughs*] Gee whiz, Gov, ya oughta seen 'em.

VIC: They get sick?

RUSH: Not at first. They smoked away an' talked big . . . spit an' cussed like they were forty years old. But pretty soon . . . oh boy!

VIC: Things happened, I presume.

RUSH: Honest, Gov, I never *seen* two fellas so sick. I was scared.

VIC: I hope they recovered.

RUSH: Yeah, but they laid down an' *slept* all afternoon. Had to go swimmin' by myself. An' ya know what *I* done?

VIC: No.

RUSH: I didn't *say* nothin' to nobody but I decided all to myself I'd wait till I was fifty years old before I started to smoke.

VIC: Uh-huh.

RUSH: I never want to get as sick as Elton an' Clay did that afternoon.

VIC: I s'pose not.

RUSH: No, *sir*. They looked like they needed a month in the hospital.

VIC: Well, when you get to be fifty years old come around an' we'll have a pleasant smoke together.

RUSH: I've gone back to twenty-one now. Might as well get a good early start.

VIC: Uh-huh.

RUSH: You're not smokin' up so much now, Gov.

VIC: No.

RUSH: 'Bout out of tobacco?

VIC: I believe I still got a few whiffs left.

RUSH: Why doncha fill up your good ol' pipe again?

VIC: That might be a good idea. Pretty strong down near the bottom.

RUSH: Want me to clean it out for you?

VIC: Wouldn't want to trust you with it.

RUSH: *I* wouldn't hurt it.

VIC: No. A pipe is like a fine violin. The owner should never trust a rank amateur with it. Watch me closely now: I'm gonna knock the ashes out.

RUSH: *That* ain't hard.

VIC: Don't *look* hard, I'll admit. But there's a trick to it.

RUSH: Gee, you sure smoked up, Gov. Look at all the clouds up there.

VIC: Uh-huh.

RUSH: Maybe Mom'd like to watch you break in the pipe.

VIC: I don't think so.

RUSH: She's up in the kitchen . . . I could go call her?

VIC: Don't think she'd be interested.

RUSH: Smokin' is more of a manly vice, ain't it?

VIC: Yeah. *Say,* son.

RUSH: Yeah.

VIC: I think maybe I'll lay my pipe *aside* for a while. No use runnin' it in the ground.

RUSH: You haven't got it broke in *yet*.

VIC: No, but . . . I'm afraid I'll crack the bowl firin' the dickens out of it like this.

RUSH: We got all this *tobacco*.

VIC: Yes, I know, but . . . fact of the matter is, I seem to remember that a pipe should be broke in *gradually*. A pipe is like a fine *horse*. You whip it an' abuse it an' what you got? You got . . .

RUSH: Aw, Gov. You *said* you'd smoke.

VIC: [*resignedly*] Give me the tobacco.

RUSH: Here . . . all open and ready.

VIC: Stuffy down here, don't you think?

RUSH: All that smoke.

VIC: Yeah.

RUSH: It's got a fine full-bodied *bouquet,* though.

VIC: [*gloomily*] Uh-huh.

RUSH: You know who first started smokin'? Sir Albert Raleigh.

VIC: I wish he'd *choke*.

RUSH: He *did* choke. He was in America an' he saw the Indians smokin' an' he said by gosh I guess I'll try that an' . . . aw, Gov . . . is *that* all the tobacco you're gonna put in it?

VIC: This is enough.

RUSH: You filled it up *full* the other time.

VIC: [*uneasily*] Did I?

RUSH: Yeah. Fill up your good ol' pipe.

VIC: Where's the tobacco?

RUSH: Right there in your lap.

VIC: Oh.

RUSH: Want me to tell you some more about Sir Albert Raleigh?

VIC: Um.

RUSH: Do you?

VIC: Yeah, sure.

RUSH: Why doncha smoke?

VIC: I . . . I guess I'm out of matches.

RUSH: Here's one.

VIC: [*miserably*] Thank you.

RUSH: Ain't you gonna light it?

VIC: Sure.

RUSH: [*cheerfully*] You don't need to be afraid if it goes out . . . I got plenty more.

VIC: Yeah.
RUSH: You didn't tamp the tobacco down this time.
VIC: Ah . . . *you* want to do it?
RUSH: Sure.
VIC: Here.
RUSH: I might be a little *slow* doin' it. Never done it before.
VIC: Take plenty of time. Take all the time you need.
RUSH: [*giggles*] I guess I've won your confidence, Gov.
VIC: [*sluggishly*] Huh?
RUSH: I guess I've won your confidence. Little while ago you wouldn't let me *touch* your pipe.
VIC: No. I mean yes.
RUSH: You mean no.
VIC: I mean no?
RUSH: Yes.
VIC: Um. [*expels what amounts to a belch*]
RUSH: Whatcha say?
VIC: Nothin'.
RUSH: I was gonna tell you about Sir Albert Raleigh. Well . . . he saw the Indians smokin' so he decided he'd smoke *himself*, so when he got back to Germany he . . .
VIC: [*gloomily*] Where?
RUSH: Germany. Sir Albert Raleigh lived in Germany.
VIC: Who?
RUSH: Sir Albert Raleigh. He lived in Germany.
VIC: Oh. What time is it?
RUSH: I don't know.
VIC: Go upstairs and find out, will ya?
RUSH: I think it's about a quarter to five.
VIC: What?
RUSH: I think it's about a quarter to five.
VIC: Five?
RUSH: Yeah. *Wait.* Mom's alarm clock's sittin' on the wash-machine. Lean back an' you can see it.
VIC: *You* lean back.
RUSH: *I'd* hafta get *up* to see the alarm clock.
VIC: *You* lean back.
RUSH: What's the matter, Gov?

VIC: [*parroting him*] What's the matter?
RUSH: Doncha feel good?
VIC: Who me? Feel good?
RUSH: Yeah.
VIC: I feel good. What time is it?
RUSH: I'll look and see.
VIC: Find out what time it is.
RUSH: [*getting up*] It's a . . .
VIC: Go upstairs an' ask what time is it.
RUSH: The alarm clock's right here.
VIC: What time is it?
RUSH: It's a . . . twenty minutes to five.
VIC: Go upstairs an' see what time is it.
RUSH: It's twenty minutes to *five*. I said . . .
VIC: Thanks.
RUSH: Now you can smoke up.
VIC: Thanks.
RUSH: Gov, what's the *matter*?
VIC: Matter?
RUSH: *Yeah*. You look like . . . hey, Gov. Gov. [*calls*] Hey Mom, can you come down here a minute? Hurry up!

Which concludes another brief interlude with the folks who live half-way up in the next block.

First broadcast 1934.

3

Melvin Has Landed a Job

*W*ell *sir, it's late afternoon as we enter the small house half-way
up in the next block now, and here in the living room we discover
Mrs. Victor Gook and young Mr. Rush Gook. Young Mr. Rush
Gook—who arrived home from school just a moment ago—still
wears his hat and overcoat, and he regards his mother, who is
sparkling with excitement. Listen:*

RUSH: What *is* this news?
SADE: Wait till your father comes back. I want him to hear it too.
[*calls*] Vic.
VIC: [*off*] Yeah?
SADE: Hurry up.
VIC: I'm hangin' my coat on a hanger.
RUSH: What's the news about?
SADE: Melvin Stembottom.
RUSH: He get a job?
SADE: Yeah.
RUSH: Where?
SADE: Workin' for the city. [*calls*] Vic.
VIC: [*closer*] I'm comin'.
RUSH: What's he *do* for the city?
SADE: Wait till Gov gets here. Then I won't hafta repeat
everything twice. [*giggles*]
RUSH: You're *glad* because Melvin got a job, huh, Mom?
SADE: Oh, *yes.* Makes it so much nicer for everybody over at
Stembottoms'. I talked to Ruthie a long time over the phone a while

ago an' she . . . [*raises voice*] Melvin went to work an' got himself a situation, Vic.

VIC: [*coming up*] That right?

SADE: For the *city*.

VIC: Good for Melvin. What kind of a situation is it?

SADE: Street department. Got the job just last night. He heard they needed a fella an' he went to the man that does the hirin' an' was took on right then an' there.

VIC: Fine.

SADE: Don't that show Melvin's got gumption? See, last night was *Sunday* night. But Sunday or no Sunday he heard they needed a fella an' went right over to this foreman's house an' asked for the position. First thing this morning his name was wrote down on the payroll in letters three feet high.

VIC AND RUSH: [*chuckling*] Oh, come on now. Letters three feet high are . . .

SADE: Go take off your hat an' coat, Rush. What's the *idea* sittin' in the house all bundled up in outdoor clothes? Wanta die?

RUSH: I wanta hear all the dope about Melvin.

SADE: Go take off that overcoat.

RUSH: Shucks, I ask ya the news about Melvin an' you tell me we gotta wait for Gov. Then when Gov comes in an' ya start to whip *out* the news ya make me go out in the hall an' hang up my . . .

SADE: Scoot. [*to Vic*] Ruthie's pleased as punch.

VIC: Is she?

SADE: Oh *my* yes. See, Melvin hasn't earned a nickel since he was Santy Claus there in Yamilton's at Christmastime. An' that only lasted a week or so. An' no big enormous salary to write home about either. But this job with the city oughta be *permanent*. An' very nice pay too, Ruthie says.

RUSH: Mom, will ya hold up the story till I get back from hangin' up my coat?

SADE: [*briefly*] Yeah. Don't *wrinkle* that coat now.

RUSH: [*moving off*] No. Just hold up the story till I return. Naturally I'm interested in all the various details.

SADE: Uh-huh.

VIC: You say Melvin's employed by the street department?

SADE: Big as life.

VIC: What kind of work does he do?

SADE: He tears up the street.

VIC: What street does he tear up?

SADE: Any street that *needs* tearin' up. *You've* seen that crowd of fellas around town with picks an' shovels.

VIC: Yeah. Well . . . a . . . is it a steady job?

SADE: *Sure,* it's a steady job.

VIC: I was just thinkin' dull times might come along when *no* streets needed tearin' up.

SADE: They're busy all the year round, Ruthie says. An' ya know when ya work for the *city* your pay goes right along like . . .

RUSH: [*off*] You're not holdin' up that story, Mom.

SADE: [*to Vic*] What?

VIC: [*to Sade*] "You're not holdin' up that story, Mom."

RUSH: [*approaching*] You said you'd wait till I got back before you went on with the story about Melvin an' as soon as I turn my back you go ahead an' tell Gov . . .

SADE: [*raises voice*] Come in *here* if ya wanta talk to me. *I'm* not gonna yell all over creation. [*to Vic*] Oh, yes, they're busy all the year round.

VIC: Is there always some street that hasta be torn up?

SADE: I guess so—*sure.* Why, they tore up the street *today.* Melvin helped. Had his nice pick an' shovel an' dug away like a house afire.

RUSH: [*coming up a trifle tough*] All right, where are we?

SADE: [*giggles*] Just more'n dug away with his pick an' shovel.

RUSH: I say *all right, Mom,* where are we?

SADE: Huh?

RUSH: Where are we in the story?

SADE: Whatcha talkin' about?

RUSH: You promised you'd hold up the story about Melvin till I got back from hangin' up my coat, but that promise rolled off a duck's back because I return to find out you've already told Gov several details an' . . .

SADE: Will you save your talky-talk till later, son? I'm tryin' to *tell* Gov something.

RUSH: Yeah, tryin' to tell *Gov* something. *I* don't count. I'm just the little end of nothin' around here an' everybody takes advantage of . . .

SADE: [*elaborate sigh*] Oh, my.

VIC: [*little chuckle*] Pipe down, Sam. [*to Sade*] You say Melvin tore up the street today?

SADE: *Sure* he did. This time yesterday he didn't have any more job than a rabbit. First thing this morning he was out tearin' up the street.

VIC: What street did he tear up?

SADE: The seven hundred block on West Monroe. *Ruthie* was there to watch him.

VIC: Was she?

SADE: You bet. Drove the car over. Parked it in Mr. Hettle's driveway. She sat an' watched Melvin work for several hours. He tore up the street just as nice as you please. 'Course he was puttin' on extra steam because it was his first *day* an' all. He was anxious to make an impression on the foreman, catch on?

VIC: Uh-huh . . . . Well . . . a . . . what was *Ruthie* there for?

SADE: To give him *encouragement*. See, she had the car parked in Mr. Hettle's driveway an' she sat in the front seat an' waved an' winked at Melvin every time he looked up from his shovelin'. Couple times she honked the *horn* . . when he got in an especially good lick with his pick.

VIC: [*chuckles*]

SADE: An' then again she wanted to keep Melvin from feelin' *lonesome* on his first day. Familiar faces around help a person that's startin' a new job.

RUSH: Smelly Clark tells me he was darn lonesome when he started in on *his* new . . .

SADE: But I haven't told you the *best*, Vic.

VIC: What's the best?

SADE: *Doreen* was there.

VIC: Mis' Appelrot's sister?

SADE: Yeah, Doreen Otto.

VIC: Is she Melvin's girl?

SADE: [*giggles*] *Looks* like it. There she was big as life in the seven hundred block on West Monroe Street watchin' him tear up the street. *Ruthie* didn't even know she was in *town*. The way it was she saw this automobile pull up in Mr. Carlock's driveway. She *thought* she knew the lady at the wheel but wasn't *sure*. Pretty soon the lady stuck her head out the car window an' here it was Doreen Otto.

VIC: Come to watch her beloved tear up the street, huh?

SADE: Yeah. She honked *her* horn a couple times *too* when Melvin done something especially clever with his pick an' shovel.

VIC: I think if Melvin wishes to hold on to this fine situation he better tell his sweetheart an' sister-in-law to stay home. No city gang foreman is gonna stand for a bunch of women parked around in automobiles applauding the efforts of his men. After all, Melvin is a *laborer*, not a soprano soloist.

RUSH: I was gonna say that same thing myself, Gov. Them gang foremen are tough guys an' they don't like . . .

SADE: The boss *did* come over an' speak to Ruthie, Vic.

VIC: Yeah?

SADE: [*giggles*] Uh-huh.

VIC: What'd he say?

SADE: He asked her what she wanted.

VIC: What'd *she* say?

SADE: She give him a very cool reception. She said her car was parked in her friend Mr. Hettle's driveway an' wasn't in anybody's road. Looked at him like, "Who are *you* to ask me what I want?"

VIC: She'll *lose* Melvin's job for him.

RUSH: *I'll* say. Shucks, *you* can't . . .

SADE: Oh, she knew she was in the wrong an' left shortly after that. The boss *was* kind of upset about all that horn-honkin', I guess. See, both Ruthie an' Doreen tooted their horns an' it finally made Melvin feel like showin' off a little so he started balancin' his shovel on his chin an' pretendin' to swallow his pick an' comical business like that.

VIC: For gosh sakes.

SADE: But both Ruthie an' Doreen drove away right after that because they could see the foreman wasn't at all pleased.

VIC: You'd of thought he'd of *shot* one of 'em.

SADE: Oh, *they* meant well enough.

RUSH: [*chuckling*] A guy must be a star shoveler that can bring out the *ladies* to see him perform.

SADE: Melvin had quite an audience all right. Oh an' I didn't tell you who *else* was there.

VIC: Who else was there?

SADE: A bunch of men from downtown Melvin's been hangin' around with. *They* drove over to the seven hundred block on West Monroe. Parked their car in Miss Glimpse's driveway an' sat on the running board.

VIC: How many guys were in *that* cheering section?

SADE: Six, Ruthie said.

VIC: Made eight people altogether that come to watch Melvin tear up the street, huh?

SADE: Yeah, eight.

RUSH: Did the men honk their horn when Melvin done fancy stunts with his pick an' shovel?

SADE: Ruthie never said. Oh, but Vic, I haven't told you the best.

VIC: What's the best?

SADE: At *noon* Melvin ate his *lunch.*

VIC: Yeah??

SADE: Sat down on the curbing with the other fellas an' opened his little dinner-bucket an' spread his napkin on-his knee an' just *more'n* ate his lunch. Ruthie said it was the grandest sight she ever saw.

RUSH: What was so grand about it?

SADE: Well, here was poor Melvin . . . been out of work for ages . . . sittin' on the curbing eatin' his lunch he'd bought with his own money. She said you could see the pride stickin' out all over him every time he took a bite of sandwich.

VIC AND RUSH: [*laugh*]

SADE: [*giggling*] No, but *really.* I got a thrill *myself* when Ruthie described it.

VIC: Did any of that big crowd of old pals sittin' around in parked cars invite Melvin over?

SADE: They all honked an' hollered, but Melvin just smiled an' waved 'em away. He *did* step over to see *Ruthie* a minute. She told him to hop in the back seat an' eat his lunch, but he thought his right place was on the curbing with the other men.

RUSH: [*quoting*] "My place is with my buddies. I love the Foreign Legion. I'll die for my dear comrades. An' never quit this . . ."

SADE: Oh an' the didoes he pulled off after he got back on the curbing again.

VIC: What'd he do?

SADE: Just silly little things to make Ruthie an' Doreen an' his men friends laugh. He soaked his sandwich in his thermos-thing full of coffee an' then held it 'way up high an' let the coffee drip in his mouth.

VIC AND RUSH: I bet he got a big hand on *that*.

SADE: What?

VIC: I bet he got a big hand on *that*.

SADE: How ya mean?

VIC: I bet Doreen an' Ruthie laughed at *that* funny stunt.

SADE: Oh, they *did*. An' the foreman *himself* had to smile.

VIC: I'd like to *meet* that foreman.

SADE: Another comical thing he done was pretend to put an olive in one ear an' then pull it out the other.

VIC AND RUSH: [*laugh*]

SADE: An' after that he threw it way up in the air an' caught it in his mouth.

RUSH: He was pullin' off all this funny business while he was sittin' on the curbing, huh?

SADE: Yeah. It just pleased Ruthie to *death* to see him so happy an' gay. See, he's been pretty much down in the mouth since Christmas. No job or spending money or anything. An' *Fred's* been kinda short with him. Now he don't hafta *take* any smartness from Fred. He's earning his *own* lovely salary.

VIC: Uh-huh.

SADE: An' he can entertain *Doreen* a little. Buy her *ice*-cream once in a while.

VIC: Sure.

SADE: Wish *I'd* been there today to see Melvin tear up the street an' eat his lunch.

VIC: Me too.

RUSH: Ya s'pose they'll still be tearin' up the seven hundred block on West Monroe tomorrow?

SADE: I *imagine*.

RUSH: Whatcha say we *go?*

VIC: Let's *do*, Sade. We're generally through dinner by twelve-thirty. We could stroll over to West Monroe Street an' see Melvin eat the tail-end of his lunch an' also watch him tear out a few hunks of concrete.

SADE: All right. An' we can . . . [*thinks of something*] Hey.
VIC AND RUSH: What?
SADE: You fellas don't wanta do that just to laugh at Melvin, do ya?

Which concludes another brief interlude at the small house half-way up in the next block.

First broadcast 1937.

4

Writing to Walter

Well sir, it's early evening now and here in the living room of the small house half-way up in the next block we find our friends abiding quietly at home. Mr. Victor Gook and Mr. Rush Gook are established on opposite sides of the library table, competing briskly at rummy while Sade, in her husband's easy chair, concerns herself with the little daily love story in the newspaper. At this particular moment one of the card players is remarking:

VIC: Here, *here*, my man. There's a *rule* about lookin' at the discards.

RUSH: *You* do it.

VIC: When?

RUSH: *Lots* of times.

VIC: [*mutters ad-lib protests*]

RUSH: Huh?

VIC: You've made a serious accusation. Unless you substantiate that accusation . . .

RUSH: Aw . . . come *on.* Play.

VIC: It's *your* turn.

RUSH: Oh . . . is it?

VIC: *See?* Your poor fuddled brain can't even grasp . . .

SADE: Vic?

VIC: Hello there, Sade. How are ya? By *George*, you're lookin' fine!

SADE: Know what I wish you'd do?

VIC: Go over there and give ya a hug?

SADE: I wish you'd write to Walter.

VIC: [*a chuckling groan*]

SADE: How long's it been since you dropped him a line?

VIC: [*not interested*] I dunno.

SADE: Been *years* and *years*, ain't it?

VIC: Guess so.

SADE: Ain't ya kinda ashamed?

VIC: [*negative*] Uh-uh.

SADE: Oughta be.

VIC: How long has it been since Walter dropped *me* a line?

SADE: That's different.

VIC: Why?

SADE: Walter is not a letter-writin' fella.

VIC: I am, huh?

SADE: Sure. You're down there in your office and rip off letters to people all day *long*.

VIC: Well . . . what the heck would I *say*?

SADE: Oh . . . just some chatty little talky-talk, maybe . . .

RUSH: *Look here!* Excuse me, Mom.

VIC: [*to Rush*] You're *in*?

RUSH: Three sixes . . . three fours, and the ten, jack, queen and king of spades.

VIC: You musta been resortin' to a little cunnin' to accumulate that many spreads so quick.

RUSH: [*chuckles*] Uh . . . your deal this set.

SADE: Why don't you do it right *now*, Vic?

VIC: Write a letter to Walter? [*groans*]

SADE: *Sure* . . . you're just sittin' there idle.

VIC: I'm playin' rummy.

SADE: Ya just finished a game. Go *ahead*. Rush, hand your father your pencil and tablet.

RUSH: Okay.

VIC: Aw . . . I'll dash 'im off a note *tomorrow*.

SADE: Like *fun*. You'd never even *think* of it.

VIC: Well . . . I got nothin' to *say* to Walter.

SADE: He's your brother-in-law.

VIC: I gotta exchange sweet confidences with 'im on that account, huh?

SADE: Well . . . what I'd like to have you do is scribble your note off on that cheap tablet paper and then in the mornin' take it down to the office an' have the girl typewrite it nice.

VIC: Well, what's the idea?

SADE: It'd please Bess.

VIC: I thought it was Walter I'm supposed to write to . . .

SADE: Well, Walter *and* Bess. See, they're good and *proud* of their nice, big, important brother-in-law with his marvelous position. I bet they'd show your letter to everybody in *Carberry* if it was written on a machine by a regular stenographer with her initials at the bottom an' all.

VIC: Um . . .

SADE: Will ya do it?

VIC: [*groans*] I suppose.

SADE: It hit me this afternoon you ought to drop a line to Walter. Bess and I hear from each other almost every week, an' it don't look right for you two men to let whole years go past without . . .

RUSH: [*giggles*]

SADE: [*quickly*] What's the matter, Rush?

RUSH: [*laughing*] Nothin'.

SADE: Why the laughin'?

VIC: [*mock severity*] Get *away* from here, Rush. How can a man write a letter to his brother-in-law with a hyena like you breathin' down his neck?

SADE: [*quickly suspicious*] What's he writin' there? Read me what he's got wrote down there.

VIC: [*mock severity*] Get away from here, Dishwater.

SADE: [*sharply*] Rush . . . you hear what I said?

RUSH: Uh . . . "Dear Walter: How's your kneecap? Does it hurt much? My kneecap jumped out of place last Tuesday at four o'clock while I was swimmin' in the creek. Sadie has been put in jail. Rush was married early this morning [*Rush begins to laugh*]. What time is it? You make me sick. If I had ears like . . ." [*laughter overcomes Rush*]

VIC: [*like a little girl*] You made every word of that up, Rush.

RUSH: I did *not!*

VIC: [*still girlish*] You did *too!*

SADE: That don't strike me so comical, Vic.

VIC: [*pleadingly*] Well . . . I don't know what to *say* to the guy, kiddo.

SADE: [*patiently*] Poor Walter's a guy now . . . huh?

VIC: Well . . . we got nothin' in common.

SADE: [*snappily*] Just married sisters is all . . . got that much in common.

VIC: Won't be news to Walter if I write an' tell 'im we married sisters . . . "Dear Walter: You and I married sisters. I married sister Katie and you married sister Becky. It's great stuff, huh, Walter . . . being married to sisters?"

SADE: You don't seem to have much trouble thinkin' up silliness. Put half that energy into fixin' up a decent letter and you'd get through in five minutes . . .

VIC: Okay. I'll make a *stab* at it.

SADE: Instead a standin' there grinnin' like a chessie cat, Rush, *you* might write a little note.

RUSH: To Uncle Walter?

SADE: *Sure* . . . you're included in the invitation.

RUSH: I'd just as soon drop 'im a line. I'll say: "Dear Uncle Walter: How's your kneecap? Day before yesterday I saw a horse fall down. He got up almost immediately feeling none the wiser. Our garbageman don't wear socks. He claims that . . ."

SADE: [*wearily*] You're a funny man too, aren't ya?

RUSH: Well, maybe . . .

SADE: Who was it gave you a lovely silver dollar on your birthday?

RUSH: [*defensively*] I wasn't allowed to *spend* it. Hadda deposit it in the doggone *bank*.

VIC: Hey Sade . . . *I* can't get anywhere with this.

SADE: Can't ya?

VIC: No.

SADE: All day long ya sit down in your office an' dash off *enormous* big letters to fellas in the kitchenware company. It's peculiar ya can't write a few measly little words to your brother-in-law . . .

VIC: All I got is "Dear Walter: Well, you old horse-thief you. How's tricks?"

SADE: [*quietly*] I wouldn't even say that as a *joke*.

VIC: What . . . "horse-thief"?

SADE: Yeah. Walter might not *understand*.

VIC: All right . . . we'll delete that. *Now* all I got is "Dear Walter:" Not much of a *letter.*

SADE: Put down a little chatty *talky-talk.*

VIC: Such as what?

SADE: Oh . . . "Business is fine . . . I suppose you read in the newspaper about this, that, and the other thing. Looks like big doin's in Washington, D. C., with Congress making different laws . . ." *You* know . . .

VIC: [*affirmative*] Uh-huh.

SADE: Tell 'im about our neighbors that've been livin' next door seven years all of a sudden pullin' up stakes an' movin' . . .

RUSH: [*interrupting*] You wanta hear what I got?

SADE: All right.

RUSH: Uhh . . . "Dear Uncle Walter: Thought I would write an' see how you are feeling. We are fine and Gov's sore throat has let up considerable on the twinges. I expect you people are enjoying the warm weather. A good many of my personal friends have changed into their summer underwear. *I* am still wearin' my *winter* underwear but will probably discontinue the process in the course of the next few weeks. There is only a couple more months of school and then we have vacation."

SADE: Very nice.

RUSH: [*pleased with himself*] I think so. It comes right to the point . . . no beatin' around the bush.

SADE: Say something about how eager your mother's lookin' forward to her visit in Carberry.

RUSH: Okay.

VIC: See how this suits ya. "Dear Walter: Business is fine. I suppose you read in the newspaper about this, that, and the other thing. Looks like big doings in Washington, D. C., with the Congress makin' different laws. Yours truly . . . Vic."

SADE: [*level tones*] Aren't . . . *you* . . . *ashamed?*

VIC: [*defensively*] I put down what ya *told* me to put down.

SADE: *I'd* . . . be . . . ashamed.

VIC: Don't be, Sade. I done the best that I . . .

SADE: [*defeated*] Put your tablet and fountain pen off to one side . . . Go ahead with your rummy.

VIC: Well, shucks . . .

SADE: I guess Walter won't wither away and die just because his wonderful brother-in-law won't take five minutes of his valuable time . . .

VIC: [*sincerely*] Tell me what to *say*, kiddo, and I'll say it.

SADE: Go ahead with your rummy.

VIC: No. By George, I'll do this if it kills me. Tell me what to say.

SADE: What do ya say to your friend Y. Y. Flirch when ya write him letters?

VIC: I say Fraedae saluts quaw sindum clucks agricola punct . . .

SADE: No . . . but what *do* ya say?

VIC: *I* don't know. Generally stuff about the lodge.

SADE: Tell *Walter* about the lodge.

VIC: He don't *belong* to it.

SADE: Well that don't hurt. Tell him you had a meeting.

VIC: Um.

SADE: You sit down and dash off forty pages to Y. Y. Flirch but when it comes to your own brother-in-law you can't think of a word.

RUSH: Um . . . hey listen, Mom . . . "Dear Uncle Walter: Thought I would write and see how you are feeling. We are fine and Gov's sore throat has let up considerable on the twinges. I expect you people . . ."

SADE: [*bluntly*] You already read me that part.

RUSH: Yeah . . . "Mom is looking forward with breathless pleasure to visiting you and Aunt Bess. She anticipates much delight in seeing your faces once again." How d'ya like that?

SADE: [*noncommittal*] It's all right.

RUSH: I think it's dandy.

SADE: A little on the axle-grease and peach-butter side.

RUSH: What d'ya think about that junk about breathless pleasure?

SADE: It's all right.

VIC: [*who is ready to read now*] Okay.

SADE: Got something down?

VIC: Yep . . . listen. "Dear Walter: How are you, old top? . . ."

SADE: I wouldn't call him names.

VIC: "Old top" ain't a very cruel epithet.

SADE: Well, Walter's touchy. Liable to think you're jollyin' him.

VIC: Well . . . just "Dear Walter" then. "Dear Walter: One

hundred alumni of the University of Critton met in the Butler House Hotel yesterday to celebrate the fiftieth anniversary of the University's foundin'. Alumni clubs in 1500 other cities held similar gatherings. The Alumni heard an address by Dr. U. Flossmore Screech depictin' historical events in the University's development and a trombone solo by Miss Edith Klem entitled 'All My Hugs and Kisses, Alma Mater, Belong to Thee.' Yours truly, Vic." [*silence*]

SADE: [*accusingly*] You copied that out of *tonight's newspaper.*

VIC: [*innocently*] What? Do you say I copied it . . .

SADE: [*sharply*] Out of tonight's newspaper, yes! I read it *myself.*

VIC: Kiddo, before you get hot under the collar . . . lemme . . . Where'ya goin'?

SADE: [*short*] Upstairs.

VIC: Not to bed?

SADE: [*short*] I'm goin' to go to bed. Who cares?

VIC: Well . . . it's only ten minutes past eight.

SADE: So?

VIC: Wait now, Sade. Tell you what I'll do . . . I'll write Walter the longest letter . . .

SADE: [*very short*] Lock the door and fix the lights before you come up.

VIC: Aw . . . I've gone to work and made your mother mad. Um . . .

RUSH: Um.

VIC: Now I have to write a letter to ease my conscience. Heck! [*deep sigh*] Well . . . "Dear Walter . . ."

Which concludes another brief interlude at the small house half-way up in the next block.

5

Nicer Scott Has a Ten-Dollar Bill

W*ell sir, it's about nine o'clock as our scene opens now, and here in the living room of the small house half-way up in the next block we find Mr. and Mrs. Victor Gook spending a quiet evening at home. Mr. Victor Gook, in his easy chair beneath the floor lamp, has just exhausted the contents of the daily newspaper and is putting it aside. Mrs. Victor Gook, darning socks on the davenport, has been awaiting this very moment and we hear her remark:*

SADE: I'm gonna need a gunny-sack full of money, Vic.
VIC: Gunny-sack full, huh?
SADE: Rush's clothes.
VIC: Um.
SADE: He leaves for Carberry the end of this week an' that only gives me a few days to buy the stuff he needs.
VIC: What all's he need?
SADE: New *suit* is the *big* item.
VIC: Um.
SADE: Stockings, underwear, shirts, an' wash-pants.
VIC: You'll require a gunny-sack full of money?
SADE: Yeah.
VIC: If I'd been smart enough to stay single I could put all my gunny-sacks full of money in the savings bank an' be rich. Saddled as I am with an extravagant wife an' a profligate son it looks like the alms-house is my . . .
SADE: How'd you like to go *with* me downtown?

VIC: Buy Andy's clothes?

SADE: Yes. Tomorrow or the next day. *Any* afternoon this week. I think we better take care of it early, though, because ready-made suits generally hafta be altered an' if we waited till Thursday or Friday we might be takin' a chance on . . .

VIC: I hear our little curly-headed darling *now*. [*calls*] That you, Rinse-water?

RUSH: [*approaching*] Hi.

SADE: [*to Vic*] Will ya do it?

VIC: Go shoppin' with ya? [*little chuckle*] Oh heck, kiddo, *I'm* no help.

SADE: That's because when we go in department stores together you stand around with your teeth in your mouth an' look bored an' gloomy. You *could* be some help. Clerks are more on their toes to render good service if there's a man supervising . . .

RUSH: [*off a little*] Can I sleep over at Scotts' tonight?

VIC: *Hello* there, Mister Fluke. C'mere an' shake hands an' then go to New York City as my guest an' put up at the finest hotel. I *like* you, Rush. You're a wonderful man. Here's a twenty-dollar bill.

RUSH: [*ignoring this*] Mom, can I sleep over at Scotts' tonight?

SADE: What for?

RUSH: Nicer generously extended a courteous invitation to share his bed.

SADE: You got your *own* bed. Mis' *Scott* don't want neighbor kids clutterin' up her house.

RUSH: She said it was perfectly O. K.

SADE: [*disapproving*] Aw—stay home where ya belong.

RUSH: Nicer slept *here* one night last week.

SADE: That was because his father an' mother had company.

RUSH: Nicer is very anxious to have me. He wants my society. He's completely upset.

SADE: Upset?

RUSH: Upset.

SADE: What's the matter?

RUSH: If I reveal a secret will ya keep it under your hat?

SADE: Yeah.

RUSH: What about you, Gov?

VIC: I usta be the national secret-keeper *champion*.

RUSH: [*after a pause, says impressively*] Nicer Scott . . . [*halts*]

VIC: Yeah?

RUSH: [*brief pause*] Has.

VIC: [*after waiting*] Yeah?

RUSH: [*pause*] In.

VIC: [*after waiting*] Yeah?

RUSH: [*pause*] His.

VIC: [*after waiting*] Yeah?

RUSH: [*pause*] Possession.

VIC: [*after waiting*] Yeah?

RUSH: [*pause*] A.

SADE: [*giggles*] Oh, for lands' sakes, Willie.

RUSH: I wanta impress on ya how *important* this secret is.

SADE: [*giggles*] You're sure doing it. Nicer Scott has in his possession a *what?*

RUSH: [*impressively*] Ten-dollar bill.

SADE: [*not overwhelmed*] Where'd he get it?

RUSH: *Uncle* slipped it to him.

SADE: Fella that drove up around supper-time in the maroon automobile?

RUSH: Yes. He just now left.

VIC: Mr. Scott's brother?

SADE: *Her* brother. Traveling man, ain't he, Rush?

RUSH: Uh-huh. Works outa Des Moines Iowa. He passed through here on his way home from Terre Haute Indiana. Stayed for supper an' sat around most of the evening an' just left about a quarter of an hour ago. Nicer went as far as Oakland Avenue with him for the ride an' when he got outa the car his uncle slipped him a ten-dollar bill.

VIC: A pretty dashing uncle.

RUSH: Chances are forty to one he made a *mistake*. He prob'ly thought it was a *one*-dollar bill he was handing Nicer. See, it was *dark* in the car.

VIC: Um.

RUSH: Nicer said he like to swooned dead away when he got underneath a street light an' examined what he had in his hand. His uncle had been *accustomed* to givin' him money, but he'd never whipped out *that* amount. An' mistake or not, it's his ten-dollar bill to *keep*. Uncle Frank's that kind of a *guy*. A real citified *sport*, doncha know. If he gives somebody a ten-dollar bill for a present it *sticks*. Even if he thought he was givin' 'em a *one*-dollar bill it sticks. *He's* not the kind of a fella that whines an' crawfishes.

VIC AND SADE: Um.

RUSH: So Nicer's got a ten-dollar bill in his possession an' he's completely upset.

VIC: Seems to me he'd be completely *happy*.

RUSH: He's completely *both*: completely happy an' completely upset all at the same time. See, his *folks* don't know he's got that money.

VIC: If they found out they'd confiscate it.

RUSH: Quick as a wink. They'd put it in Nicer's savings account down at the bank. See, that's always been the big *trouble* with sizeable gifts. They're no *good*. Nicer's got a whole slew of uncles an' aunts that send him money every Christmas. He's tough at the ones that send him five- and ten-dollar bills because his folks put 'em in the bank. He likes the ones that send him fifty cents up to three dollars because he gets to spend them kind of amounts without anybody interferin'.

VIC: An interesting slant on the financial problems of our very young. Reminds me of the days when I was a coral-lipped baby, my soft blue eyes an' golden hair . . .

RUSH: Mom, Nicer wants me to stay all night with him. He needs my moral support. After what's happened he's all unstrung. For over a week now he's been flat broke. Hasn't had a nickel to his name. An' right out of a clear sky *this* happens. His Uncle Frank slipped him some money. Not a dime, not a quarter, not four bits. Not a one-dollar bill, not a five-dollar bill. A *ten*-dollar bill. Why, right this minute Nicer Scott's sittin' over on his front steps pale as a ghost. His fingers are twitching an' he's turning alternately hot an' cold. He complains of a buzzing in his skull an' spots before his eyes. Chilly perspiration beads his forehead an' an occasional convulsive shudder racks his frame. He licks his lips with agitation an' . . .

VIC: You're quotin' word for word from Third-Lieutenant Clinton Stanley. I read them same phrases in the book you left in the porch swing s'afternoon. What was it?—*Third-Lieutenant Stanley on the Campus?*

RUSH: Yeah. *Third-Lieutenant Stanley on the Campus* or *The Thrilling Capture of the Bank-robbing Professors of Yale College.*

VIC: In your description of Nicer weren't you quoting word for word from . . .

RUSH: Sure, but them words *fit* Nicer. Can I stay all night over there, Mom?

SADE: [*disapproving*] Aw.

RUSH: He shrinks from the very *thought* of being alone with a ten-dollar bill. He's apprehensive he'll fall into a fitful slumber an' wake up screaming. He's apprehensive he'll . . .

SADE: [*distaste*] You kids read too many of them dime novels. Young lady in Dixon went out of her *head* from doin' that. Bertha Joiner. Ate up cheap story-books by the dozen an' finally turned up dotty one day. Required six months to cure her. An' even after she was *cured* she behaved kinda simple. Only wore one shoe. Remember Bertha Joiner, Vic?

VIC: [*negative*] Uh-uh.

SADE: Very sad case.

RUSH: It's O. K. with Mis' *Scott* if I sleep over there, Mom. Nicer hollered in an' *asked* her. She said fine.

SADE: *You* got your own bed an' your own home. What's the sense of makin' extra work for neighbors by horning in on . . .

RUSH: Think of *Nicer*. Think of Nicer alone in the darkness with his ten-dollar bill.

SADE: Oh, fiddle.

RUSH: He'll have trouble *breathing*. His *scalp* will tingle. His heart will thump like a trip-hammer an' his hands an' feet will turn hot an' then cold an' . . .

SADE: Bet that's just the way Bertha *Joiner* started.

RUSH: Another thing: I owe it to myself to look after my own interests.

SADE: Whatcha mean by that?

RUSH: Nicer owes me *money*. I wanta stick with him an' not leave him outa my sight. Otherwise he's liable to sneak downtown an' *spend* his ten dollars.

VIC: How much does he owe ya?

RUSH: Eleven cents.

VIC: Um.

RUSH: An' that's not the whole *story*. He owes Blue-tooth Johnson a quarter an' Blue-tooth owes me a dime. Transferring the two debts it makes Nicer owe *me* the dime. Also he owes Milton *Welch* a dime. Milton owes me a nickel. Therefore it's the same as *Nicer* owin' me a nickel. So you can see I got quite a chunk of that ten-dollar bill comin'.

VIC: Um.

RUSH: Eleven cents plus two dimes is pretty close to half a dollar. I don't wanta take any chances with *that* much cash.

VIC: Apparently you have interested *motives* for wishing to keep Nicer an' his ten-dollar bill under constant surveillance.

RUSH: Sure. What if he'd suddenly decide to go downtown an' buy a ten-dollar fishing rod or something? It'd leave me right out in the cold.

VIC: You have *other* plans for his fortune, huh?

RUSH: I got *smart* plans. Down at Yamilton's they're havin' a special sale on high-powered squirt-guns.

VIC: Water pistols?

RUSH: Yeah. They'll shoot a stream of water fifteen feet. An individual can buy 'em two for seventy-five cents.

VIC: What would Nicer want with *two?*

RUSH: One for me an' one for himself.

VIC: Oh, I see.

RUSH: Also the Greek is sellin' red bananas three for a dime. I thought Nicer could purchase a couple dozen.

VIC: That's considerable red bananas.

RUSH: Not so many with two guys to eat 'em.

VIC: Um.

RUSH: There's a little store on South Center Street where you can buy a solid hunk of licorice four inches long, four inches wide, an' four inches high for thirty cents. I've always wanted a hunk of licorice like that. Ya carry it around in your pocket an' whenever ya feel like it ya whip out your jack-knife an' hack off a wad.

VIC: You haven't by any chance got Nicer's ten-spot already *spent*, have ya?

RUSH: *Practically*. After he's paid me what he owes me an' makes the purchases I recommend he won't have but about two bits left.

VIC: Don't be too *generous* with Nicer, now. After all, he's not *accustomed* to such rich living.

RUSH: *It's* not such rich living. Ten dollars disappears pretty rapid when two guys are spending it.

VIC: Um.

RUSH: Whatcha say, Mom? . . . Can I stay all night at the Scotts'?

SADE: Aw, I don't like the notion of puttin' neighbors to a lot of bother over . . .

RUSH: *I* won't be any bother. I won't even use their *bathroom*. I'll brush my teeth an' put on my pajamas here at home. All I'll hafta do'll be run across the yard an' climb in bed.

SADE: Um.

RUSH: *I* don't want Nicer runnin' around loose with a ten-dollar bill. He's liable to do something *unwise*.

VIC: Like spending it on *himself*.

RUSH: *Yeah.*

VIC: *Some* people might think Nicer *entitled* to spend his own money on himself. In fact . . .

RUSH: Nicer *wants* me to stay all night with him. I can distract his parents' attention so they won't notice his twitching face an' trembling hands. See, if they had any idea he had a ten-dollar bill in his possession they'd confiscate it in twenty seconds.

VIC: Um.

RUSH: How about it, Mom?

SADE: Oh . . . [*tired of arguing*] . . . *I* don't care.

RUSH: [*with satisfaction*] Fine. I'll go upstairs, put on my pajamas, brush my teeth, bid you folks good-night, an' step across to Scotts'.

SADE: Um.

RUSH: [*complacently*] I feel pretty doggone *wealthy*, by George.

VIC: Why is that?

RUSH: Oh . . . just *do* is all.

VIC: Um.

RUSH: Wish I had another *dresser* up in my bedroom.

SADE: What for?

RUSH: Tomorrow I'll need extra *drawer*-space.

SADE: Why?

RUSH: To put various articles in.

SADE: *What* various articles?

RUSH: Oh—squirt-gun, hunk of licorice, red bananas, aviator's helmet, couple new Third-Lieutenant Stanley books, lucky finger ring, automatic pencil—*lotsa* stuff.
SADE: Um.
RUSH: Nicer Scott's a mighty fortunate individual.
VIC: [*low tones*] Yeah—to have a friend like *you.*
RUSH: What?
VIC: Nothin'.
RUSH: Yep—Nicer Scott's a mighty fortunate individual. His uncle slipped him a ten-dollar bill.

Which concludes another brief interlude at the small house half-way up in the next block.

First broadcast 1939.

6

Uncle Fletcher, from Dixon, Is a House-Guest

Well sir, it's about the middle of the morning as we approach the small house half-way up in the next block now, and here on the back porch we find young Mr. Rush Gook and his great-uncle Fletcher. The gentlemen are seated side by side on the top step but one, talking casually about this, that, and the other thing. Listen:

FLETCHER: I like a collie myself.
RUSH: I like a bulldog better.
FLETCHER: Yes, a bulldog makes a good dog. It's like anything else. Some people like one thing, some like the other. I've always liked blunt-toed shoes. Well, I know fellas that like *pointed*-toed shoes.
RUSH: Don't make much *difference* to *me* about my shoes.
FLETCHER: You're like me with coffee.
RUSH: [*little chuckle*] Am I?
FLETCHER: With coffee I can take it *with* cream or *without* cream. *With* sugar or *without* sugar. Six of one, half a dozen of the other. I could name you off a *dozen* folks it makes plenty of difference to about whether they take cream an' sugar in their coffee or not. But not *me*. Put sugar in my coffee or *don't* put sugar in my coffee. *I'll* drink it.
RUSH: Uh-huh.
FLETCHER: Been that way all my life.
RUSH: Uh-huh. No, but about dogs I think a bulldog's got more *pep* than a collie. A bulldog'd just as soon bite your leg off as *look* at ya.

42

What I'd like to have is a *mean* bulldog. Lead him around on a chain.

SADE: [*off a little, in the doorway*] Rush.

RUSH: Oh, hello, Mom.

SADE: Can I see you a minute?

RUSH: Sure.

SADE: Come on inside. *You* makin' out all right, Uncle Fletcher?

FLETCHER: Fine, Sadie, fine. Wonderful day.

SADE: Yes, it is.

FLETCHER: Looked like *rain* when I got *up* this morning.

SADE: Did it?

FLETCHER: Quite a few dark clouds in the west.

SADE: [*who is now up to microphone*] Uh-huh.

RUSH: Whatcha want, Mom?

SADE: [*low tones*] Come in the house a minute. [*to Fletcher*] He'll be out again directly.

FLETCHER: [*who is now off microphone a little*] All right.

SADE: [*to Rush*] Let's go to the living room.

RUSH: You wanta talk to me about . . .

FLETCHER: [*off a ways*] Garbage wagon in the alley, Sadie.

SADE: [*raises voice*] All right.

RUSH: [*to Sade*] You wanta talk to me about . . .

FLETCHER: [*calling*] *Morning*, Gumpox, how are *you* this morning?

SADE: [*to Rush*] Oh, there he *goes* again.

FLETCHER: [*off, calling*] Say, you were all *wrong* in that argument we had yesterday. I looked up the information in the encyclopedia an' it . . .

SADE: [*calls*] Uncle Fletcher.

FLETCHER: [*calling*] . . . said rutabagas had just as much nourishment any day in the *week* as parsnips.

SADE: [*calls*] Uncle *Fletcher.*

FLETCHER: [*off*] Yes, Sadie?

SADE: [*calls*] Would you mind not yelling, please?

FLETCHER: [*off*] Railroad engineer next door still asleep?

SADE: [*calls*] Yes, I believe he is.

FLETCHER: [*off*] I'm sorry.

SADE: [*to Rush*] Second time *today* I've told him about yelling. He don't remember stuff a *minute*. Mr. Donahue got in off'n a Saint Louis freight drag at nine o'clock an's tryin' to get some rest. Simply *dead* tired.

RUSH: [*little chuckle*] Who'd Uncle Fletcher yell to *before?*

SADE: The mailman. Yelled to him from his bedroom window. [*quoting*] "Pretty warm day to be trampin' around with that big bag of letters, ain't it? I bet your job's pretty hard on *shoe* leather." [*disgust*] Top of his *lungs* he hollered. Goodness.

RUSH: What'd ya wanta talk to me about, Mom?

SADE: [*briefly*] Uncle Fletcher. He's got to be *spoken* to. An' I think *you're* the one to *do* it.

RUSH: [*reluctant*] Aw.

SADE: [*firmly*] Yes, I do.

RUSH: [*reluctant*] *I* can't bawl out a . . .

SADE: It's not a matter of bawling *out* anybody. But you can kinda halfway *suggest* stuff.

RUSH: [*reluctant*] I should think *you* would . . .

SADE: [*bluntly*] When I make any remarks to him that sounds anything like I'm criticizing, he shuts right up tight an' acts like he's injured. *You* can drop little hints an' insinuations an' he'd never *notice*. For instance, you can say . . .

FLETCHER: [*off*] *Say*-dee. Brick-mush man.

SADE: [*to Rush, distressed*] Oh my.

RUSH: [*little chuckle*] Oh heck, Mom, he don't *mean* anything.

SADE: [*sharply*] 'Course he don't mean anything. Only thing I'm sayin' is . . .

FLETCHER: [*off*] *Say*-dee. Brick-mush man.

SADE: [*to Rush*] I bet Mr. Donahue over next door in bed is fit to be tied.

FLETCHER: [*off*] How we fixed for brick-mush, Sadie? The brick-mush man's out here.

SADE: [*calls*] We got *plenty* brick-mush on hand, Uncle Fletcher.

FLETCHER: [*off*] What?

SADE: [*calls*] Tell the brick-mush man not to bother leavin' any brick-mush. We got all the brick-mush we can . . .

FLETCHER: [*off*] What?

SADE: [*to Rush, unhappily*] *You* yell.

FLETCHER: [*off*] I didn't catch what ya said, Sadie.

RUSH: [*calls*] We got *enough* brick-mush, Uncle Fletcher.

FLETCHER: [*off*] Got enough brick-mush?

RUSH: [*calls*] Yeah.

FLETCHER: [*off*] O. K.

SADE: [*to Rush, unhappily*] Why does he yell when I tell him not to yell?

RUSH: [*little chuckle*] He forgets.

SADE: He's got to be *spoken* to. An' not only just about *yellin'* to people *either*. He's got to be told to leave things *alone*. He put my front doorbell on the blink this morning.

RUSH: Did he?

SADE: Yes. He said it didn't ring loud enough an' went an' got tools from the basement an' disconnected wires an' screwed out screws an' everything else. *Now* the darn bell won't let out a *peep*.

RUSH: [*involuntary chuckle of delight*]

SADE: [*crisply*] It's not funny.

RUSH: No, I know it's not, only . . .

SADE: Also he nailed himself to a kitchen chair.

RUSH: Yeah?

SADE: He said one of the legs was comin' loose an' got hammer an' nails an' started to pound away. He was *sittin'* on the chair while he pounded. Tried to get up an' couldn't. He'd hammered nails right through his pants.

RUSH: [*chuckles*] Shucks.

SADE: Did you see the *address* business he made for the front porch?

RUSH: Was that what he was whittling on after breakfast this morning?

SADE: Yes. He whittled this enormous big *board*. It's as big as a sign. Then he printed *numbers* on it. An' stuck it out on the front porch up above the mailbox.

RUSH: [*little chuckle*] Is it there now?

SADE: Yeah.

RUSH: Guess I'll go look at it.

SADE: You can look at it later.

RUSH: Number plate for the house, huh?

SADE: Yes . . . only he printed the wrong number.

RUSH: [*chuckles*] Yeah?

SADE: No more our address than a rabbit. He's got a seven where there's s'posed to be a four an' a zero where there's s'posed to be an eight.

RUSH: [*chuckles*] By George, Mom, Uncle Fletcher is the darndest . . .

SADE: *I'll* say. I wonder what Mr. Donahue thought of that *pounding*. Uncle Fletcher pounded the kitchen chair an' then pounded his number plate. Person could hear the commotion a mile away. He's got to be *spoken* to.

RUSH: [*reluctant*] I don't think *I* better . . .

SADE: *I* do. *You* can drop little hints an' insinuations. If *I* say anything he thinks he's being criticized an' tightens right up. Why don't you just kinda buttonhole him an' . . .

FLETCHER: [*approaching*] You people in the living room?

RUSH: [*calls cordially*] Hello.

FLETCHER: [*closer*] Sun's gettin' pretty *hot* outside.

RUSH: Yeah.

FLETCHER: [*closer*] I can't *stand* hot sunshine like I *usta* could. Didn't *want* any brick-mush, hey, Sadie?

SADE: Got more on hand now than we can *use*.

FLETCHER: [*almost up*] I *told* the fella ya had plenty.

SADE: Uh-huh.

FLETCHER: [*up*] Seems like a nice sociable fella.

SADE: Yes.

FLETCHER: [*brief pause*] Am I interrupting something here?

RUSH: [*cordially*] Not at *all*. Sit down.

FLETCHER: No, thanks. On my way upstairs.

SADE: [*cordially*] Lay down a little while?

FLETCHER: Oh, no.

SADE: Gettin' up at five o'clock the way you do I wouldn't *blame* ya for feelin' tired.

FLETCHER: No, I'm not tired. Just going to my room an' write a letter.

SADE: Write it here on the library table. Pen an' ink in the drawer an' stuff.

FLETCHER: Believe I'd rather go to my room an' write with a pencil.

SADE: All right.

FLETCHER: Don't *care* much for pen an' ink. When I write I generally chew on the pencil point while I'm thinkin'. Fella chews on a pen an' ink an' he gets ink all over his face an' necktie.

SADE: Uh-huh.

FLETCHER: So if you'll excuse me I'll just stroll on upstairs.

SADE: Anything you like.

FLETCHER: Gonna drop a line to my landlady in Dixon, Mrs. Keller.

SADE: [*nodding approvingly*] Uh-huh.

FLETCHER: Tell her I'm feelin' well an' havin' a good time an' so on.

SADE: Sure.

FLETCHER: Ask her to send me on my rockin' chair.

SADE: [*politely inquiring*] Rocking chair?

FLETCHER: [*chuckles*] Hope ya won't think that's a slam on *your* chairs. Matter of fact it helps me feel at *home* if I got my own rockin' chair to sit in. I wake up in the morning an' if I see my own rockin' chair there by the bed I'm easy an' comfortable. I'd feel at home in *Africa* if I had my own rocking chair along.

SADE: [*politely but without enthusiasm*] Uh-huh.

FLETCHER: Ya don't *mind* if I have Mis' Keller send me on my rockin' chair?

SADE: Oh, no . . . 'course not.

FLETCHER: [*moving off*] Well, I'll go on up an' write my letter.

SADE: All right.

FLETCHER: [*moving off*] *Need* me for anything . . . want anything *fixed*, ya know . . . just holler.

SADE: All right.

FLETCHER: [*moving off*] I like to make myself useful whether I'm company or *not*.

SADE: [*low tones*] Uh-huh.

FLETCHER: [*after a pause, off*] Sadie.

SADE: [*calls*] Yes.

FLETCHER: I say if ya *need* me for anything . . . want anything *fixed* . . . just holler.

SADE: [*calls*] All right.

FLETCHER: [*off*] I like to make myself useful whether I'm company or *not*.

SADE: [*calls*] *All* right. [*to Rush, distressed*] He's sending for *furniture*.

RUSH: Just a *rocking* chair is all.

SADE: A *rocking* chair is furniture. [*distressed*] How long's he intend to stay, ya s'pose?

RUSH: [*I don't know*] Um.

SADE: [*aghast*] Goodness, if he sends for his *rocking* chair, next thing he's liable to send for is his *dresser*. His *bed*. His *trunk*.

RUSH: [*after a pause*] Mom, I *like* Uncle Fletcher around.

SADE: Oh *sure*—person likes him *around* an' all . . . but [*unhappy giggle*] it's so *wearing* on a person. Take this *morning*. All that yelling with Mr. Donahue tryin' to get some sleep next door. The monstrous signboard he whittled out for the front porch with our wrong address on it. Nailing himself to a kitchen chair. Puttin' my bell on the blink.

RUSH: Yeah, but still . . .

SADE: [*unhappy giggle*] It's that gettin' up at five o'clock in the *morning* beats *me*. An' his *talkin'* to himself. Why, I can't sleep *myself* after five o'clock worryin' about what he's *up* to. He might paint the *house*. He might crawl up on the roof an' try to shingle it an' fall off an' break his neck.

RUSH: Um.

SADE: An' now he's sending for his *furniture*.

RUSH: Um.

SADE: [*aghast*] How long's he plan to *stay!* Why, heavens alive, he might . . .

FLETCHER: [*upstairs, yelling*] Good *morning*, Mr. Call.

SADE: . . . even intend to stay . . . [*halts*]

FLETCHER: [*yelling*] How are *you* this morning?

SADE: [*to Rush, unhappily*] Oh my.

RUSH: *Heck*, Mom, *he's* got a right to . .

SADE: Listen.

FLETCHER: [*upstairs, yelling*] Can't kick, thanks. Feelin' fine.

SADE: [*to Rush*] He's hollerin' out the window.

RUSH: Uh-huh.

FLETCHER: [*upstairs, yelling*] Glorious day, *glorious* day.

SADE: [*to Rush, unhappily*] Hollerin' out the *Donahue* side of the house.

RUSH: Yeah.

FLETCHER: [*upstairs, yelling*] We've had a *beautiful* summer in *Dixon*. Not too hot an' not too cold. Thermometer hung around seventy degrees all during June, July an' August.

SADE: [*to Rush, feebly*] Go up an' talk to him, Rush.

RUSH: [*little chuckle*] O. K.

SADE: [*feeble and almost plaintive*] Go up an' talk to him.

Which concludes another brief interlude at the small house half-way up in the next block.

First broadcast 1940.

7

Applying for a $4.80 Refund
from the Lodge

Well sir, Virginia Avenue is shrouded in the pleasant half-light of winter afternoon as our scene opens now, and here in the living room of the house where our friends live are Mr. and Mrs. Victor Gook and their son, young Mr. Rush Gook. Mrs. Victor Gook is darning socks; young Mr. Rush Gook is gazing without enthusiasm at his Latin grammar; and Mr. Victor Gook is unbuttoning his overcoat . . . for he's just this minute arrived home from the office. Let's join the group . . . and listen:

SADE: Gettin' colder out?

VIC: Much. I felt like I was wadin' through ice water on my way home.

SADE: Guess I better bring in my plants tonight.

VIC: Yeah. An' throw a couple extra blankets on our bed.

SADE: They're in the closet if we need 'em.

VIC: [*to Rush*] Ike.

RUSH: Yeah.

VIC: Busy?

RUSH: I'm tryin' to study Latin. Not havin' much luck. My brains wanta wander to *other* stuff.

VIC: You need your brains shook *up* a little. How about doin' somethin' nice for Papa?

RUSH: Huh?

VIC: Take my overcoat out in the hall an' hang it on the hook.

RUSH: [*arising*] O.K. Anything to get away from this.

50

VIC: You're not fallin' *down* in your Latin, are ya?

RUSH: I'll prob'ly get *by*.

VIC: Gettin' by is not enough. Either you bring home a report card with good marks on it or you bid high-school farewell. Trouble with you high school guys is. . . . Hold it by the collar now; there's pencils in the breast pocket.

RUSH: [*moving off*] Yeah.

SADE: Believe that overcoat's gonna do you all right.

VIC: *It's* not in such bad shape.

SADE: No. I watched you an' Mr. Kneesuffer walkin' up the street just now. Your overcoat looked *very* trim an' neat.

VIC: This is the fourth winter for it.

SADE: I think if we have it cleaned an' pressed nice an' . . . What's all that—more Christmas cards?

VIC: Nope. This bulky envelope is a communication from Lodge headquarters in Chicago. I hafta fill out some papers an' send 'em back. *You* do too.

SADE: *I* hafta fill out papers?

VIC: Yep. Gonna be startin' supper very soon?

SADE: In a half hour or so—why?

VIC: We might as well do this right *now* then. Get it over with.

SADE: You say there's papers for *me* to fill out?

VIC: Uh-huh. Do you remember last week when I . . . [*raises voice*] Where ya going, George?

RUSH: [*off a little*] Milton Welch is out on the sidewalk loafin' around. I thought I'd join him an' . . .

VIC: C'mere. I need your cooperation in a matter of official importance.

RUSH: [*closer*] Yeah?

VIC: Your mother an' yourself hafta sign some papers.

RUSH: [*up*] O. K. Gimme a pencil.

VIC: We'll take our *time*, Hank. Just sit down an' make yourself comfortable.

RUSH: But Milton *Welch* is loafin' around outside.

VIC: Let 'im loaf. [*to Sade*] I'll explain what this is all about, kiddo. Remember last week when I sent the lodge dues in to headquarters?

SADE: Yes.

VIC: I discovered the next day I had sent in four dollars an' eighty cents too much.

SADE: Of your own money?

VIC: Of my own money.

SADE: Well, *that* was silly.

VIC: Yes, it was. But no harm's been done. I wrote to Chicago immediately an' *told* 'em about it.

SADE: We haven't got enough four dollars an' eighty centses to be throwin' 'em to the *winds*. Goodness, if *I* . . .

VIC: Don't get worked *up*, Sade. *I'm* gettin' the money back. That's what this *letter* is . . . I told you to stick *around*, Ralph.

RUSH: [*off a little*] Thought I'd step over to the window an' watch Milton Welch loaf. He . . .

VIC: Step right *back*. I need you. [*to Sade*] Kiddo, that's what this *letter* is. Headquarters checked over my figures, found I'd sent in too much dough, an' sent me these *papers* to sign.

SADE: What are the papers?

VIC: Questionnaires an' stuff. There's always a certain amount of red tape in a business like this.

SADE: Where do Rush an' me come in at?

VIC: You an' Rush are members of my family an' . . . Well, *here:* I'll *read* you the letter.

RUSH: If you'll give me a pencil, Gov, I'll write down my John Henry an' . . .

VIC: Aw, sit still. Listenin', Sade?

SADE: Uh-huh.

VIC: [*reads*] "Dear Sky-Brother Gook: Yours of the twenty-sixth last received an' contents noted. Sky-Brother Wilson of our auditing staff has checked your statement an' substantiates your claim of four dollars an' eighty cents in excess of the amount due in this office. The cash will be returned to you in the form of a Post Office money order. Before this is done, however, headquarters requires certain written formalities. Enclosed please find routine questionnaires, et cetera, which you and your family will kindly fill out an' remit. Yours fraternally. L. B. Washman, Secretary."

SADE: Means you get your four-eighty back again, huh?

VIC: Yeah—after I get these papers fixed up.

SADE: Why don't they just *give* you your money back as long as they *know* you sent in too much?

VIC: Can't run a big organization like the Sacred Stars of the Milky Way fast an' *loose*, kiddo. Every detail's got to be handled with *care*.

SADE: Where's the thing you want me to put my name on?

VIC: Believe *this* is . . . Yeah, see up here? Says "Wife."

SADE: Can't understand what *I* got to do with it. Might as well have the *garbage man* sign his . . . Hey, I don't hafta fill in all these *spaces*, do I?

VIC: Sure. They're questions.

SADE: Oh, for land's sakes. There's a *million* of 'em.

VIC: Naw. Won't take you five minutes. Got a pencil?

SADE: [*negative*] Uh-uh.

VIC: Here's one.

SADE: I'll just put Mis' Victor Gook down at the bottom an' *you* can . . .

VIC: *No*, Sade. It's all got to be in your handwriting.

SADE: How foolish.

VIC: We want that four-eighty back, don't we?

SADE: They sure make a person go to a lotta *bother*.

VIC: Can't be helped. Rush, here's *your* thing.

RUSH: O. K. if I use my fountain pen?

VIC: I don't care what . . . . No, maybe you better use a pencil. Might hafta erase somethin'.

RUSH: Got an extra pencil?

VIC: Fish one outa the library table drawer.

SADE: Vic, there's forty of these questions.

VIC: Oh, no.

SADE: Sure. They're numbered.

VIC: Well, heck, what of it? Look at the big long document I got.

SADE: You hafta fill all that in?

VIC: Yeah.

SADE: I never heard of anything so crazy.

VIC: You just don't understand the ins an' outs of operating a large fraternal body.

SADE: Says here "Give name of father an' maiden name of mother."

VIC: Don't you have that information about your parents?

SADE: What business is it of your ol' lodge what my mother's maiden name was?

VIC: Hey, if you'd quit doin' so much belly-achin', you'd be through with that.

SADE: I bet if you'd sent in ten dollars too much they'd of wanted to know what Mis' Fisher's grandfather used to eat for breakfast. [*laughs at this jest*]

VIC: Aw, bunk.

SADE: Rush, hear Mom's funny joke?

RUSH: [*coolly*] About Mis' Fisher's grandfather? Yes. Gimme some room to write, Gov.

SADE: [*laughs*] I thought that was a pretty funny little joke.

RUSH: Uh-huh. [*to Vic*] What's all this carbon paper for?

VIC: You use that to . . . . Wait a minute, Sade, you started to fill in your thing yet?

SADE: No.

VIC: Well, don't. It's got to be in triplicate.

SADE: Huh?

VIC: Ya hafta make three copies.

SADE: [*horrified*] Three *copies!* If you think I'm gonna sit down here an' answer a hundred an' twenty . . .

VIC: *No.* You don't hafta *make* three copies. Ya use carbon paper. Here.

SADE: A person don't need to go to *this* much bother when they make out their *income* tax.

VIC: Don't blame *me*, doggone it. If we want our money back we gotta follow directions.

RUSH: Know how to fix your carbon paper, Mom?

SADE: Yeah.

RUSH: Ya use two sheets of it an' put the shiny sides face down an' . . . Yeah, that's the way.

SADE: Such a nuisance.

VIC: Kiddo, do you recall what our address was when we lived in Dixon?

SADE: West River Street.

VIC: Yeah, but what number?

SADE: Heavens, they wanta know *that?*

VIC: Question reads, "Give the street an' number of residences occupied in any cities in which you've resided prior to 1925."

SADE: *I* don't remember the exact address.

VIC: I'll make one up.

RUSH: [*laughs*] Shucks—"Name five responsible people, exclusive of your parents, who will vouch for your character."

VIC: Can't you name five?

RUSH: No.

VIC: Aw, ya can too.

RUSH: Rooster Davis, an' Milton Welch, an', an' Heinie Call, an' . . .

VIC: They want *grown*-ups.

RUSH: *I* don't know any grown-ups that'd vouch for my character.

VIC: Put down Ike Kneesuffer an' Hank Gutstop, an' Mr. Ruebush an' guys like that.

RUSH: O. K.

VIC: How ya comin' along, Sade?

SADE: I'll *never* be able to wade through all this.

VIC: Stuck on somethin'?

SADE: [*reads*] "Make a list of your brothers, sisters, aunts, uncles, an' cousins, placing an "X" after the names of those deceased."

VIC: I got that question here myself.

RUSH: So have I. Did Cousin Brooks kick the bucket that time he was so sick?

SADE: No, he pulled through.

VIC: How about Uncle *Wolrab?* He passed on, didn't he?

SADE: Yes, but he wasn't any *relation* of ours.

VIC: Thought he was your mother's brother-in-law.

SADE: No, he was brother to my mother's *sister*-in-law.

VIC: He was always hangin' *around.*

SADE: Yes, but he was no relation.

VIC: I won't mention Uncle Wolrab on my thing then.

RUSH: I never even *heard* of him before.

SADE: [*in disgust*] Oh, my.

VIC: What's the matter now?

SADE: [*reads*] "Have your eyes ever been tested for color blindness?"

VIC: Well, have they?

SADE: No.

VIC: Write down "No" then.

SADE: The lodge has got to know if I'm color blind or not before they'll send you your four dollars and eighty cents, huh?

VIC: *I* can't help it, kiddo.

RUSH: This *twelfth* question is a good one: "Have you or have you not ever felt as though a belt were drawn too tight around your waist?"

VIC: They're tryin' to find out if you're *crazy*.

RUSH: Yeah, I know. Thirteenth question is along the same line: "Have you or have you not ever been conscious of jagged splotches before the eyes immediately after retiring?"

VIC: Still tryin' to find out if you're crazy.

RUSH: They owe you your four-eighty whether I'm crazy or not, don't they?

VIC: *It's* just red tape. Go ahead an' *finish*.

RUSH: It'll take me all *night*. Fourth question is, "Give a complete list of hobbies." I got *forty* hobbies.

VIC: Do what it *tells* you to do. I got troubles here of my own. [*reads*] "Enumerate positions held an' salaries paid from first job to present vocation." Shucks, I had nine different jobs before I was fifteen years old.

SADE: "Make a list of surgical operations submitted to within the past ten years."

VIC: "Do you travel by airplane?"

SADE: "Are you an instrument in your husband's decisions on important matters?"

VIC: "Do you entertain political aspirations?"

SADE: "Has there ever been, to your knowledge, any member of your family, immediate or remote, who has been for any reason imprisoned for a crime?"

VIC: "Are you afraid of electrical storms?"

SADE: Vic, is all this worth four dollars an' eighty cents?

VIC: I doubt it.

RUSH: *Here's* something.

VIC: What?

RUSH: Read this business on top of your letter here.

VIC: What's it say?

RUSH: *Read* it once. Read it out loud, so Mom can hear.

VIC: *This* what ya mean?

RUSH: Yeah, the paragraph on top.

VIC: [*reads*] "When the enclosed questionnaires have been duly filled out, please assemble an' mail to J. K. Latimer, Stuckley, Pennsylvania. Mr. Latimer is president of our Congress in Charge of Finance, which meets July 13, 1936. Your claim will have its initial reading at that time. After it has passed through the hands of the Congress, it will be sent to the Grand Tribunal in Chicago for research an' investigation. The Grand Tribunal convenes in September of 1936. If your claim is accepted, it will go into the hands of our exalted Auditor, Clyman Smurch, who passes on monetary matters during the financial session held each year. The next session of this nature is scheduled for January 9, 1937. Unless unforeseen difficulties an' delays arise, you may expect a Post Office money order for the amount of your claim one month from that date."

SADE: One month from *what* date?

VIC: One month from January 9, 1937.

SADE: You mean you get your four dollars an' eighty cents then?

VIC: Yeah.

SADE: Here's my thing.

RUSH: Here's mine.

VIC: Whatcha doin' with 'em?

SADE AND RUSH: Puttin' 'em in the wastebasket.

VIC: O. K. Put mine in too.

Which concludes another brief interlude at the small house half-way up in the next block.

First broadcast 1935.

8

Vic Reviews a Vacation Week with Bess and Walter in Carberry

Well sir, it's early evening as our scene opens now, and here on the front porch of the small house half-way up in the next block we find Mr. Victor Gook all by himself. Mr. Gook is swinging gently in the swing, casually examining the newspaper for stray bits of intelligence he may have missed during the initial reading before supper. And at this moment Sade appears from inside the house. Listen:

SADE: I was waitin' for Rush to go so I could talk to ya.

VIC: Fine. C'mon out an' sit down.

SADE: Paper boy come a little early, didn't he?

VIC: Quite a bit early. I imagine he's routing himself different. Don't generally show up till four-forty-five or so.

SADE: Maybe they got a new kid that's faster.

VIC: No . . . same ol' kid. But I noticed when he got to Kelsey he turned left. He's always turned right before.

SADE: [*up*] Prob'ly found a way to switch his streets around so he gets through his route quicker.

VIC: Yeah. Sit down. What's on your mind?

SADE: [*sitting down*] Slunch over a little.

VIC: [*slunching over a little*] You an' me get any fatter, an' we'll hafta get a bigger porch swing.

SADE: *I'm* not gettin' any fatter.

VIC: No? Thought you said you were.

SADE: *When'd* I say I was gettin' fat?

VIC: At Stembottom's the other evening didn't I hear you tell Ruthie that Yamilton's scales registered . . .

SADE: [*with high contempt*] Oh, Yamilton's scales. They never give a person's right weight in their life. Maybe I've put on a quarter of a pound or so, but I *always* do in the summer time. Don't worry: I'll tell ya when I'm gettin' fat.

VIC: [*chuckles*] O. K. What'd ya wanta talk to me about?

SADE: Is it all cut an' dried your vacation begins the first of August?

VIC: Yep.

SADE: Have you been thinking of any plans in particular?

VIC: For my vacation? No, nothin' definite. I've had a few stray *ideas*. But nothin' special. Why?—you got something in mind?

SADE: Vic, what I want to talk to you about is somethin' you'll holler "no" to first shot outa the box.

VIC: Yeah?

SADE: Yes. Because we've been through it before. *This* time though I wish you'd let me say my little say before you jump through the roof.

VIC: O. K.

SADE: Will ya let me speak my piece an' not bust out a collar button?

VIC: [*brief chuckle*] I'll *try* to, kiddo. 'Course I already know what it is.

SADE: You already know what what is?

VIC: What it is ya wanta talk to me about.

SADE: What is it?

VIC: A trip to Carberry.

SADE: [*silence*]

VIC: Am I right?

SADE: Pretty bright fella, ain't ya?

VIC: [*brief chuckle*] I hit the nail on the head?

SADE: Vic, I got a little letter from Bess today.

VIC: Yes, I saw it in on the library table.

SADE: Read it?

VIC: No, I didn't. Meant to though.

SADE: You *never* read Bess's letters.

VIC: You generally read 'em *to* me. An' besides . . . a . . . [*halts*]

SADE: [*quickly*] Besides what?

VIC: [*lamely*] They . . . a . . . most always have the same stuff in 'em.

SADE: [*as martyr*] Well, it's *me* that Bess is sister to. Guess I can't expect *other* people to like her.

VIC: [*babying her*] Aw, c'mon now, kiddo. You know I like Bess as well as I like anybody.

SADE: Like her as well as just "anybody," huh?

VIC: I like Bess fine.

SADE: When was the last time you *seen* Bess?

VIC: Why . . . a . . . I seen Bess . . . I seen Bess . . .

SADE: You seen Bess three years ago last winter. At Aunt Gully's funeral.

VIC: Was that when?

SADE: That was when. When was the last time you seen *Walter?*

VIC: I seen Walter . . . I seen Walter . . .

SADE: You seen Walter four years ago when you an' Ike Kneesuffer drove through Carberry on that trip.

VIC: Yeah, but I kinda keep *track* of Walter. T. W. Evans from Plant Number 11 makes that Carberry territory all the time an' I run into T. W. every so often an' I always inquire how is my brother-in-law Walter Hemstreet makin' the grade, an' T. W. always gives me the low-down on . . .

SADE: Vic, will ya let me say *my* little say?

VIC: About going to Carberry on my vacation, kiddo, you hafta admit . . .

SADE: Let me speak my little piece first.

VIC: O. K.

SADE: An' then *you* can talk.

VIC: O. K. Shoot.

SADE: To begin with, Bess an' Walter both think a lot of you.

VIC: An' I think a lot of *them*. Walter Hemstreet's the kind of a guy that'd give ya the shirt off his back. An' *naturally* I'm partial to Bess because . . . [*halts*] [*pause*] Excuse me, Sade, go ahead.

SADE: Finish what you were sayin'. Then it can be my turn.

VIC: It's your turn now. I'm sorry I butted in.

SADE: To begin with, Bess an' Walter think a lot of you. They look *up* to you. Why, I've sat in Bess Hemstreet's parlor there in Carberry an' listened to her talk to people an' make you out the biggest biggety-big that ever was. Told about what a monstrous big company Consolidated Kitchenware was, an' how many trillions of dollars they had, an' how you dress up for work every day an' sit in an elegant office an' how we got new furniture cash down just writin' a check, an' about you takin' trips on business every place in creation an' . . . an' all like that.

VIC: Uh-huh.

SADE: An' Walter the same way. They both think you're an enormous big guy.

VIC: *You* give 'em that idea, Sade. You're the one that . . . Ah, go ahead.

SADE: No, I *didn't* give 'em that idea. *I* never brag an' blow to Bess.

VIC: Uh-huh.

SADE: The thing is they know you're a white-collar office fella that never needs to really *stint* on things like *most* of our relations hafta, an' we live in a nice house an' I can buy things to do with an' here's Rush going to high school an' I send pictures of you I've cut out of the Kitchenware Dealers' Quarterly . . . an' . . . oh, a hundred things.

VIC: Uh-huh.

SADE: Why, just look how they carried you around on a chip the times we *have* been to Carberry years ago when *Rush* was little. "Does Victor want fresh strawberries?" "Maybe we ought to let Victor sleep some more." "Keep the kids quiet, Walter, because Victor's laying down in the hammock." "Let *me* do that, Victor, you'll get your hands dirty." Victor this an' Victor that. Remember?

VIC: Yeah.

SADE: Do you realize that you've only been to see your own brother-in-law an' sister-in-law about a half a dozen times in your life?

VIC: *You've* been to see 'em, Sade.

SADE: *Sure. I* have.

VIC: Well, heck, I've been a busy *man* all along. I've hadda hit the ball an' . . .

SADE: Only a half dozen little rotten measly stingy times you been to see my sister an' her husband. An' only once in the last four years.

VIC: I haven't been to see my *own* relatives in . . .

SADE: You an' your relatives weren't ever *close* like me an' Bess.

VIC: No, but . . .

SADE: You *know* you haven't done right steerin' clear of Bess an' Walter Hemstreet.

VIC: *I* haven't been steerin' clear of 'em, doggone it. Like I *say:* I been a busy man.

SADE: [*her closing arguments*] Now I know you don't *like* the idea of going to Carberry. There's inconveniences an' things. I *admit* we've had this same talk summer after summer, an' you've always come out an' said "no" flat-footed. Vic, I don't ask you to do many things. It's what *you* decide we always go by. But *I'd* like to have a say-so for once. Here you got a two-week vacation an' no plans. Why not spend *one* of those weeks with Bess an' Walter? They'd be so glad they wouldn't know what to do. An' it's our downright *duty*.

VIC: [*after a pause*] O. K.

SADE: You'll do it?

VIC: Sure.

SADE: I don't wanta *bull-doze* ya, Vic.

VIC: You're not.

SADE: It's just that I . . . I've thought about it so much . . an' I knew how you felt an' . . . they'd be *so* tickled.

VIC: Uh-huh.

SADE: [*sighs and laughs*] Land, I . . . I thought you'd storm around like a chicken with its head off.

VIC: [*little chuckle*] Oh, I wouldn't do anything like that, kiddo.

SADE: *I* thought you would, an' I was . . . a . . . *determined* to . . . a . . . a . . .

VIC: Fight it out, huh?

SADE: [*giggles*] Yes.

VIC: I never cross you on any *important* issues, do I?

SADE: No . . . but you know how . . . you *are*.

VIC: Yeah. Well, look, kiddo, if I *were* to point out a few reasons why . . .

SADE: [*quickly apprehensive*] You're not gonna start backin' *down* now?

VIC: Not at all.

SADE: You'll go to Carberry for a week of your vacation?

VIC: Sure.

SADE: [*pinning him*] Which week? . . . first or second?

VIC: You can decide yourself.

SADE: All right. [*giggles*] I wanta get your back to the wall so you can't sneak loose.

VIC: [*chuckles*] Uh-huh.

SADE: What'd you start to say?

VIC: I started to say that if I *was* gonna try to talk you outa this business, I *have* got a few fairly good arguments on my side.

SADE: What are they?

VIC: Well . . . in the *first* place I work fifty weeks outa the year. Work good an' hard. Two weeks I get for vacation.

SADE: Yes?

VIC: I could argue that I am reasonably entitled to do with them two weeks whatever I *want* to do?

SADE: [*quickly*] Yes, but there's nothin' you want to do especially. Might as well go visit Bess an' Walter as sit here on the front *porch* all the time.

VIC: I'm not arguin' with ya, kiddo. [*little chuckle*]

SADE: Well, go on.

VIC: You mentioned this front porch. I *like* this front porch.

SADE: Bess an' Walter got a front porch.

VIC: It's not *ours* though.

SADE: What's the matter with their front porch?

VIC: Nothin' at all. Sade, will ya listen a minute while I tell ya what kind of a week I'd have in Carberry?

SADE: [*suspiciously*] You're backin' down. You're tryin' to go back on what ya promised.

VIC: No, I'm not. You set the date an' make the arrangements an' off to Carberry we go. I'd just like to tell ya what kind of a week I'd have.

SADE: [*tight-lipped*] Go ahead.

VIC: O. K., I won't bother if you're gonna be sore.

SADE: No, go ahead.

VIC: Well, say we leave here of a Monday an' get to Bess's Monday night. We sit up late eatin' an' talkin' an' gossipin' about ol' times an' old friends. By bedtime I'll have had my say.

SADE: How ya mean?

VIC: I'll have told Bess an' Walter all I know that could possibly be of any interest to 'em. The rest of the week I'll loaf around more or less tongue-tied.

SADE: [*preparing for battle*] Oh, my my my.

VIC: That's the truth. It's happened before. An' they're exactly the same way with me. As a matter of fact they're both a little *scared* of me.

SADE: Scared of ya?

VIC: Like you said a while ago, they think I'm something of a big-shot. They worry about whether I'm havin' a good time. They ain't *easy* with me. They don't know what to *talk* about. An' it makes *everybody* uncomfortable.

SADE: Go on.

VIC: Well, as I say, by bedtime of the first day we've talked over everything we've got to talk about.

SADE: Oh bosh. Me an' Bess sit an' gab away by the hour.

VIC: You an' Bess, yes. But not *me*. All right, take the *next* day—Tuesday. I get up an' have breakfast. Walter goes to work. I sit around the kitchen watchin' you an' Bess do the dishes. I go sit in the yard an' read the Chicago paper. I play a couple records on the phonograph. I turn on the radio. I don't know what to do with myself. You an' Bess notice this an' say why don't I go over an' see my old friend Whitey Kuhn. I go chew the rag with Whitey a little while. I come back an' sit in the yard. Walter comes home for dinner. We eat an' talk a while. Walter invites me to come down an' see the shop. I go see the shop, stall around till I catch on I'm takin' up too much of his time, stroll back to Bess's an' sit in the yard. I try to take a nap. I sit in the yard some more. I'm gradually going crazy. I know that Wednesday's going to be the same as Tuesday, an' Thursday's gonna be the same as Wednesday, an' Friday's . . .

SADE: [*wry little giggle*] That's enough, Vic.

VIC: What?

SADE: I say that's enough.

VIC: Think I'm a selfish old sorehead?

SADE: No, *I'm* the selfish one. I . . . just never thought of it that way before.

VIC: Wasn't what I said pretty much true?

SADE: Perfectly true.

VIC: Shucks, kiddo, I hate to . . .

SADE: Oh, "shucks, kiddo" yourself. I can run up to Carberry over some Saturday an' Sunday by myself. *Any* Saturday or Sunday I can run up.

VIC: No, *listen* now. *I'm* not sugar or salt. I won't melt. I promised I'd spend a week with . . .

SADE: [*laughs merrily*] Oh, forget it, you ol' honey-bunch you. [*changes subject*] Here's Rush back with your cigars.

VIC: [*calls*] Quit cuttin' across that grass, you monster, or I'll have ya thrown in jail.

Which concludes another brief interlude at the small house half-way up in the next block.

First broadcast 1936.

9

Sade Can Keep a Secret

Well sir, it's late afternoon as we enter the small house half-way up in the next block now, and here in the living room we find Mr. Victor Gook and his son Mr. Rush Gook. Vic is established at the library table, occupied with some work he's brought home from the office, while young Rush, newly arrived home from a session of baseball in Tatman's vacant lot, lounges on the davenport. Listen:

VIC: Hey, hey, hot stuff, bright exultation and beautiful music.

RUSH: All through?

VIC: Yep. An' as soon as I jot down a few notes I'll beat you nine consecutive games of rummy.

RUSH: O. K.

VIC: Are you in dismal spirits?

RUSH: *I* feel all right.

VIC: You sound melancholy as though the sedge were withered from the lake an' no birds sang.

RUSH: I'm kinda tired. Played third base over in Tatman's vacant lot ever since school let out.

VIC: Playing third base is fatiguing. I discovered that to be true when I played third base with the Yukon River Rascals in 1910. I'll never forget how the pretty girls showered me with kisses when I won eleven games singlehanded an' . . .

RUSH: [*sluggishly*] Somebody's in the kitchen.

VIC: Beg pardon?

RUSH: Somebody's in the kitchen.

VIC: Burglars, no doubt. [*calls*] Is somebody in the kitchen?

SADE: [*off*] Hi.

VIC: [*to Rush*] It *is* burglars.

RUSH: Uh-huh. [*sluggishly*] Nicer Scott claims he can unfry an egg.

VIC: I bet he can't.

RUSH: Ain't it ridiculous a guy claimin' junk like that?

VIC: How does he go *about* unfryin' eggs?

RUSH: [*little chuckle*] Yeah, how *does* he? Leland *Richards* told him off. "*Look* Nicer," he says, "*you're* no half-wit. Why do you *talk* like a half-wit? Don't you realize you're . . .

VIC: [*to Sade*] Greetings, Doctor Sleetch.

SADE: [*coming up*] Hello—golly, but it's hot.

VIC: Summertime is on us, I do believe.

SADE: You left your pitcher's mitt out on the garbage box, Rush.

RUSH: Catcher's mitt.

SADE: Cost good money. Why do you leave it out on the garbage box? People could steal it.

RUSH: Ya bring it in the house?

SADE: Yeah. Here, take my hat an' hang it up.

RUSH: Um.

SADE: [*to Vic*] Office work, huh?

VIC: Except for a few annotations an' underdelineations I'm all through.

SADE: Um.

VIC: Been shopping?

SADE: Over to Mis' Trogel's.

VIC: How's she?

SADE: All right.

VIC: You seem depressed.

SADE: [*briefly*] Such warm weather.

VIC: Uncle Fletcher looked in a while ago.

SADE: [*without considerable interest*] Yeah?

VIC: Only stayed about five minutes. He saw I was busy an' took an early departure.

SADE: Um.

RUSH: [*coming up*] Mom, Nicer Scott claims he can unfry an egg.

SADE: [*sluggish*] Fry an egg?

RUSH: [*up*] *Un*-fry an egg.

SADE: [*sluggish*] Didn't your pitcher's mitt cost three dollars?

RUSH: Two an' a half.

SADE: *Garbage* box is a fine place for it.

RUSH: I was out in the alley chattin' with Blue-tooth Johnson. Forgot I *had* the darn mitt. Went away an' left it.

SADE: People could come along an' pick it up easy as anything.

RUSH: Um.

SADE: [*sluggish*] What'd be good for supper?

VIC: [*chuckling*] What's *eatin'* you, kiddo?

SADE: Nothing. Why?

VIC: You're so sad an' forlorn.

SADE: [*after a pause, bluntly*] Mis' Husher's mad at me.

VIC: Really?

SADE: [*little unhappy chuckle*]

VIC: Tell me all 'bout it.

SADE: Oh, nothin' in particular to tell.

VIC: Why is she mad at ya?

SADE: Because certain persons let their tongues waggle.

VIC: Yeah?

SADE: [*heatedly*] I can't make some people *out*. They talk just to hear theirself talk.

RUSH: *That's* Nicer *Scott* for ya. The son-of-a-gun will . . .

SADE: [*briefly*] Trot out in the kitchen an' bring in the grocery pad. We need stuff from the store.

RUSH: Um.

SADE: [*to Vic, idly*] Margaret's got a cold.

VIC: Margaret Trogel?

SADE: Yeah.

VIC: How's Alvy?

SADE: All right.

VIC: [*no comment*]

SADE: [*with some heat*] Yeah, certain parties talk just to hear theirself talk.

VIC: I suppose you have some specific party in mind?

SADE: [*briefly*] Helen Guller.

VIC: What's Helen been up to?

SADE: [*briefly*] Turned out to be a busybody.

VIC: This all connected with Mis' Husher bein' mad at ya?

SADE: [*yes*] Um.

VIC: How'd ya find *out* she was mad at ya?

SADE: Mis' Trogel told me s'afternoon.

VIC: Well, tell *me*.

SADE: Oh, nothin' special to *tell*. [*some heat*] One thing though: Helen Guller gets scratched off *my* list. I know *that* much.

VIC: Um.

SADE: [*after a pause*] Remember one time a long while ago me mentioning Mis' Husher sayin' her husband sends his shirts to Wisconsin for his mother to wash an' iron?

VIC: I have a vague recollection of it.

SADE: [*briefly*] It got *back* to her.

VIC: Mis' Husher?

SADE: Yeah.

VIC: [*after a pause*] I don't believe I quite understand exactly what you mean . . .

SADE: It was a *secret*. Mis' Husher considers herself a fine efficient little wife an' naturally she don't want every Tom, Dick, an' Harry an' their brother to know her private business.

VIC: Her private business in this case, I presume, being that . . .

SADE: . . . Mr. Husher sends his shirts to his mother to be washed an' ironed. Yes.

VIC: Well . . . a . . .

SADE: [*heatedly*] *I* never knew Helen Guller was that kind of a person. I always appreciated she was pretty much on the axle-grease an' peach-butter side but I never realized she'd pull off stunts behind a person's *back*. Well, she's off *my* list.

RUSH: [*up*] Here's your grocery pad, Mom.

SADE: All right.

RUSH: I noticed Nicer Scott out the kitchen window. [*sarcastically*] Prob'ly just got through un-fryin' a couple dozen *eggs*. The big ox. By George, somebody oughta . . .

SADE: [*to Vic*] The next time Helen Guller honeys around me with her wishy-washy talk I'm gonna look her straight in the eye an' no more smile than a rabbit.

VIC: Let me get this picture in proper perspective. Mis' Husher told you a secret. She revealed in confidence that her husband sends his shirts to Wisconsin so his mother can launder 'em.

SADE: [*laconically*] Every week. Parcel post.

VIC: Ah . . . did you relay that information to Helen Guller?

SADE: [*tough*] I—did—not. What do you *take* me for, Vic?

VIC: Well . . . a . . . how did . . .

SADE: [*tough*] What a fine question *that* was! Are you a bank robber?

VIC: Huh?

SADE: [*no comment*]

VIC: [*puzzled*] Am I a *bank* robber?

SADE: That's the kind of a mean blunt question you asked *me*. [*quotes angrily*] "Did you relay that information to Helen Guller?" [*bitter giggle*] Boy, you must think I'm a *wonderful* person.

VIC: I didn't intend any *insult*. I was just tryin' to track down . . .

SADE: Never mind. Don't do any good *talkin'* about it. Harm's all been *done now*. Rush, trot out in the kitchen an' get the grocery pad. How many times must a person *speak*?

RUSH: [*coldly dignified*] The grocery pad is in your lap.

SADE: [*without interest*] Oh.

RUSH: [*coldly dignified*] Perhaps in the future when a common ordinary American citizen attempts to . . .

SADE: [*to Vic*] Yes sir, I really shinnied up the wrong tree when I thought Helen *Guller* was such a fine person. I backed the sick horse *that* trip.

VIC: [*little chuckle*] Kiddo, as long as you seem disposed to *continue* this discussion won't you put me right about . . .

SADE: [*irritably*] *I* explained. Mis' Husher's *mad* at me. Her *secret* got back to her. *Naturally* she don't like everybody in creation to know her husband sends his shirts to Wisconsin for his mother to wash an' iron.

VIC: [*little chuckle*] Well, before you hit me over the head with a baseball bat may I inquire how Helen *Guller* found out Brother Husher sends his shirts to Wisconsin?

SADE: [*dully*] Every week. Parcel post. *You've* seen the box, Rush.

RUSH: *Thousands* of times. In fact, on one occasion I *mailed* that box. Mis' Husher paid me a dime an' give me a handful of salted peanuts. I took that dime an' bought . . .

SADE: Here . . . take this pad an' write down salt.

RUSH: Um.

SADE: [*after a pause, to Vic*] What ya lookin' at me funny for?

VIC: I'm *thinking* is all. I'm wondering how Helen Guller got the information about . . .

SADE: Insist on sayin' *I* told her, huh?

VIC: *No.*

SADE: *I* can keep a secret. [*ironically*] I expect that's big astonishing news to *you.* But it's a *fact.* It really *is.* I can keep a secret.

VIC: Ah . . . were you the only person Mis' Husher confided in?

SADE: [*briefly*] *I* said I was.

VIC: What did Helen Guller say to Mis' Husher that made her mad at you?

SADE: [*quoting*] "Mis' Husher, I understand your mother-in-law is a wonderful hand at washing an' ironing. I understand Mr. Husher sends his shirts to her home in Wisconsin every week to be laundered."

VIC: [*thoughtfully*] Um.

SADE: [*bitterly*] Yeah, just *wait* till she comes honeyin' around me with her sweet smiles an' wishy-washy axle-grease.

VIC: [*after a pause*] Ah . . . did Helen Guller dream *up* her little speech?

SADE: Write down cabbage, Rush. [*to Vic, briefly*] What little speech?

VIC: "Mis' Husher, I understand your mother-in-law is a wonderful hand at washing an' ironing. I understand Mr. Husher sends his shirts to her home in Wisconsin every week to be laundered."

SADE: Dream it up?

VIC: If you're the only person Mis' Husher confided in an' you didn't pass along the dope to Helen . . .

SADE: [*heatedly*] *Now* we got *this* again, huh? [*the martyr*] *All* right. Suit yourself. *I* give away a secret. *I* told Helen Guller.

VIC: Well—*did* ya?

SADE: [*tough*] *No.* No, no, *no.* How many times do I hafta *tell* ya no?

VIC: If you'll answer one question I'll leave ya alone an' go sit out in the alley till it gets dark: where'd Helen Guller get the information Friend Husher sends his shirts to Wisconsin?

SADE: [*as though this were something perfectly understood all along*] *Ruthie* told her.

VIC: [*enlightened*] *Oh.*

SADE: [*after a pause, tough*] *Now* I s'pose you're gonna jump on *Ruthie.*

VIC: Not at *all.* I only . . .

SADE: Ruthie Stembottom is my best friend, ya know, Vic. *I* don't keep trash from *Ruthie.*

VIC: Um.

SADE: [*as though Vic were guilty of something*] *You* appreciate I don't keep trash from *Ruthie.*

VIC: Um.

SADE: An' *she* made the same mistake about Helen Guller *I* did. *She* didn't know but what Helen could keep a secret. Poor little timid-as-a-rabbit *Ruthie* didn't know. *She* was innocent. At our last Thimble Club meeting Ruthie an' Helen sat next to each other. More to make conversation than anything else she mentioned this business about Mr. Husher an' his shirts. *That* was all.

VIC: Um.

RUSH: [*cheerily*] To sum the matter *up,* folks, Mis' Husher told Mom, Mom told Mis' Stembottom, Mis' Stembottom told Mis' Guller, an' Mis' Guller told . . .

SADE: [*tough*] Why don't you write down salt like I told ya to?

RUSH: [*very gently*] I *did* write down salt. An' also cabbage.

SADE: [*tough*] All *right* then.

VIC: [*after a pause*] Ah . . . kiddo, I was wondering if you . . .

SADE: [*tough*] Wanta talk some *more,* huh?

VIC: I just thought I'd ask if . . .

SADE: [*tough*] Talk, talk, talk! That's all I hear! I'm going upstairs!

Which concludes another brief interlude at the small house half-way up in the next block.

First broadcast 1941.

10

Vic Is Elected
to the Congress
of Distinguished Americans

It's a few minutes past twelve o'clock noon as we enter the small house half-way up in the next block now, and here in the kitchen we find Mrs. Victor Gook and her young son Rush. This latter individual has just arrived home from work, and is saying to his mother:

RUSH: I got a ride with Homer Croyman. That's how come I'm here so early.

SADE: Why didn't Homer Croyman give your dad a lift too?

RUSH: He *offered* to, but Gov was walkin' along with Mr. Kneesuffer an' there wasn't room for all of us in the car so he declined.

SADE: Uh-huh. *Lands,* I been busy this morning. Haven't even got my table set yet. Wanta help?

RUSH: Sure.

SADE: I pitched into *your* clothes closet this morning. An' what a job it *was.* How one boy can get his things in such a mess is beyond *me.* I bet I picked up enough junk in that closet to . . . Golly, son, I guess you got to go to the store. Not a smidgin of salt in the house.

RUSH: Maybe there's some in the salt-cellar in the buffet.

SADE: No, I emptied that the other day. Trot, will ya? Gov'll be home in half a minute.

RUSH: I'll go over to Mis' Fisher's an' *borrow* enough salt to . . .

SADE: [*negative*] Uh-uh. Go on to the store. Got any money in your pocket?

RUSH: No.

SADE: In the top right-hand buffet drawer—fetch my purse.

RUSH: [*moving off*] I never keep any cash in my overall pocket. It has a tendency to fall out. Overall pockets are so roomy, nickels an' dimes slosh around an' . . .

VIC: [*opening screen door*] Hi-de-hi. Ho-de-ho.

SADE: *Well*, mister.

VIC: The day is bright; the sun is warm; my wife is cute.

SADE: [*as screen door slams*] Your wife's been awful *busy* this morning.

VIC: [*closer*] That's nice.

RUSH: [*off*] Hello, Gov.

VIC: [*calls*] What?

RUSH: [*off*] Hello.

VIC: [*calls*] O. K. [*to Sade*] Mrs. Gook, I am gratified to be able to tell you your husband has been signally honored.

SADE: That so? Has Mr. Ruebush decided to . . .

RUSH: [*calls*] Mom, there's a dime on top of the buffet. Shall I take that?

SADE: [*to Vic*] What's he say?

VIC: There's a dime on top of the buffet. Shall he take that?

SADE: [*calls*] All right. [*to Vic*] He's got to go to the store for salt. We'll wait till he gets back before we sit down to the table.

VIC: Uh-huh.

SADE: What'd you say happened?

VIC: Your husband has been picked out of the common herd an' honored by . . .

RUSH: [*coming up*] Anything else, Mom?

SADE: No, just salt. Kinda *step* on it. We can't eat till you get back.

RUSH: [*up*] O. K. Pretty *hot* walkin' up the alley, wasn't it, Gov?

VIC: Yeah.

RUSH: [*moving off*] You oughta have high-class friends like *I* got. Whip you around in their automobile.

VIC: I wouldn't ride in that tractor *you* come home in for five dollars.

RUSH: [*opening screen door*] No? Allow me to tell you that the motor in that job is a six-cylinder . . .

SADE: Rush, *go*.

RUSH: Just salt, huh?

SADE: Just salt. [*screen door slam*] [*to Vic*] That boy will stand around an' talk your arm off an' kill time at his own funeral.

VIC: I expect he will.

SADE: You get a raise in your pay?

VIC: No. Why?

SADE: You said somethin' had happened, an' I thought maybe . . .

VIC: Oh. No, *here's* what I was talkin' about. Permit me to read you a letter that arrived in this morning's mail.

SADE: Wish they'd get *busy* on that raise in your pay. They promise a person a thing an' then forget all about it.

VIC: Yeah. Listen to this: [*reads*] "Dear Mr. Gook. The Board of Advisers of the Congress of Distinguished Americans has elected you to membership. Please accept our hearty congratulations and those of President Lester M. Cuff, our honorary supervisor and worthy patron. Henceforth you will be privileged to wear the badge of our order and append to your name the letters P. C.—Public Commander. Your engraved certificate will follow shortly. New York, Chicago, and Los Angeles newspapers have been notified. Yours very truly. Hamilton T. Looperman, Royal Chieftain."

SADE: What *is* it?

VIC: What is *what*?

SADE: All that.

VIC: Perhaps I didn't *read* clearly.

SADE: Do you *belong* to something?

VIC: I thought the letter was couched in understandable English. Of *course* I belong to something. I belong to the Congress of Distinguished Americans. I'm a "P. C."

SADE: P. C.?

VIC: Public Commander.

SADE: You *get* anything out of it?

VIC: Whatcha *mean* "get anything out of it"?

SADE: Money?

VIC: Aw, shucks. If you were elected President of the United States would you ask if you *got* anything out of it?

SADE: Sure.

VIC: I can't *understand* some people.

SADE: Well, *I* don't know what that business is about.

VIC: Sade, the Congress of Distinguished Americans is an organization that selects outstanding men.

SADE: I never heard of it.

VIC: Neither did I till I got this letter, but apparently it's a darn important thing.

SADE: They select outstanding men, huh?

VIC: Yeah.

SADE: *Then* what do they do?

VIC: Who?

SADE: The ones that . . . I mean what do you do after you *belong?*

VIC: [*exasperated*] What does a soldier do after he gets a *medal?*

SADE: Kisses the general, I guess. [*laughs at her own waggishness*]

VIC: [*tough*] Oh, thunder.

SADE: Well, *I* don't know what kind of a business it is ya joined.

VIC: I didn't *join* any business. I have been voted a member of an honorary society. Just like Henry Ford the other day got made a college professor or somethin'.

SADE: Oh.

VIC: He gets to put degrees behind his name. So do *I*. I'm a P. C. [*tastes the sound of it*] Victor Gook, P. C.

SADE: Public what . . . was it?

VIC: Public Commander.

SADE: Um. Victor Gook, P. C., huh?

VIC: Right.

SADE: Am I *Mrs.* Victor Gook, P. C.?

VIC: *No.*

SADE: Thought maybe I was. [*laughs at her humor*]

VIC: [*tough*] Pretty doggone funny, ain't it?

SADE: Well, lands.

VIC: I expect if the Czar of Russia give me the Royal *Garter* you'd laugh.

SADE: Goodness, a person'd think . . .

VIC: Look, Sade, I've been honored by a group of illustrious men. Is *that* comical?

SADE: No, but . . .

VIC: How ya s'pose I feel? Come home with a wreath of triumph to lay in my wife's lap an' what do I get but a lot of dumb kiddin'.

SADE: If I *understood* more about . . .

VIC: Here, let me read you the names of some of the *other* Public Commanders.

SADE: All right.

VIC: [*reads*] "Jason B. Slopklinker, President of the Wilson Welding Works; H. Y. Flubby, President of the Treason Tire Company; I. Clayton Smart, Secretary-Treasurer of the Oglesby National Bank, Oglesby Arizona; Piping N. Toothler, Mayor of Indian Tree, North Dakota; O. N. Price, Professor of Astronomy, Eldorado University; Orbit U. Hunk, Chief of Staff, Happy Roller Hospital."

SADE: Um.

VIC: Pretty impressive-soundin' lay-out, wouldn't you say?

SADE: Yeah.

VIC: [*with relish*] Victor Gook, P. C.

SADE: Um.

VIC: Know what I think I'll have done?

SADE: What?

VIC: Think I'll have some *cards* made with that on.

SADE: P. C.?

VIC: Yeah. Not to hand *around* to everybody, of course. That'd look silly. But just to kinda carry in my card-case, ya know.

SADE: Uh-huh. Say, does this business *cost* you anything?

VIC: Well, yes, a *small* amount.

SADE: How much?

VIC: I'll read you the post-script. [*reads*] "Public Commanders are assessed a small fee of seventy-five cents which is used to maintain the records. The engraved membership certificate is one dollar and is sent to you C. O. D. Another charge of one dollar is made to cover cost of having member's name printed on the Royal Roster in the Garfield Room of our National Capitol in Washington, D. C." [*to Sade*] Think of *that*, kiddo.

SADE: Um. Any other money to pay?

VIC: "The badge of our order, which is simply a small fleur-de-lis to be worn in the lapel, will be sent to you for fifty cents."

SADE: How much does that make altogether?

VIC: Ah . . . [*adds*] . . . three dollars an' a quarter.

SADE: Goodness.

VIC: You don't call that much, do ya?

SADE: I call it a lot for what ya *get.*

VIC: Great *guns,* how some people figure.

SADE: You said you never even *heard* of this club till you . . .

VIC: Don't call it "club."

SADE: You said you never even *heard* of it till ya got that letter.

VIC: I *didn't.*

SADE: How ya know it ain't a *fake?*

VIC: Oh—*fake.*

SADE: Well, *you* don't know. There's plenty of people in this world that do *any* ol' thing to cheat . . .

VIC: [*mad*] Look at this letterhead. Here's the address an' everything. "888 West Logansport Avenue, New York City." An' here's the . . .

SADE: What's that little business up in the *corner?*

VIC: That's a representation of the pin you wear in your lapel.

SADE: Fred *Stembottom's* got one like that.

VIC: Aw, get out.

SADE: He *has.* Little flower. *Exactly* like that.

VIC: [*tolerant laugh*]

SADE: *I'm* not foolin', Vic.

VIC: Fred *Stembottom* a Public Commander?

SADE: [*firmly*] Must be.

VIC: [*laughs*] Shucks.

SADE: [*a little annoyed*] I s'pose Fred can join a thing same as the next person.

VIC: Listen kiddo, I don't wanta run down Fred Stembottom. Fred's O. K. I *like* Fred. But he's hardly a fella the Board of Advisers of the Congress of Distinguished Americans would be likely to select. . . . Where ya goin'?

SADE: [*moving off a little*] Call up Ruthie an' *ask.*

VIC: [*enjoys a laugh*]

SADE: [*off a little*] An' I bet you five *cents* I'm right.

VIC: [*laughs louder*]

SADE: Be still so I can talk. [*to phone*] 2572-J, please. Yes. [*to Vic*] Wanta *take* that bet?

VIC: [*a good laugh*]

SADE: Laugh all ya want but just the same . . . [*to phone*] Hello, Ruthie. Say, I'm sorry if I dragged you away from the table, but Vic and me was just havin' a little argument an' I wanted to ask you a question. Yes. Well, ya know that little blue button of Fred's you give little Charlie to play with last week? Yes, a button you wear in your coat.

VIC: [*laughingly*] Ask her if the Queen of Spain give Fred a . . .

SADE: Be quiet. [*to phone*] Yeah, that's the one, Ruthie. What? Oh. Oh, uh-huh. Public Commander? *Yeah.* [*aside*] Vic, she says . . . [*to phone*] What, Ruthie? Yes. [*giggles*] Yes. Uh-huh. [*laughs*] Whatcha know. All right, Ruthie. Sorry I bothered you. All right. Good-bye. [*hangs up*] [*to Vic*] Now what do you say?

VIC: If she said Fred Stembottom was . . .

SADE: She said Fred Stembottom was a Public Commander an' furthermore she said it only cost him twenty-five cents. A bunch of the fellas from the machine shops . . .

VIC: Aw, there must be some mistake. Heck, I know good an' well . . .

SADE: Wait, let me tell you the *funny* part. Ruthie joshes Fred because he belongs to the same thing Mr. Gumpox does. *He's* a Public Commander.

VIC: The garbage man?

SADE: The garbage man. He's got a little pin like Fred's an' . . .

RUSH: [*opening screen door*] Sorry I was so long, Mom. Couldn't get anybody to wait on me. [*door slam*]

SADE: Hello, Mr. Gook, P. C. [*laughs*]

RUSH: [*up*] What's the joke, Mom?

SADE: Got an *awful* good one on your father. [*laughs*]

RUSH: Here's the doggone salt. Darn them clerks in the grocery store. They let a guy stand around an' . . . What's this?

SADE: [*slyly*] A letter Gov got this morning.

RUSH: Public *Commander*, huh?

SADE: *You* know anything about that?

RUSH: Sure. *I'm* a Public Commander.

VIC: *You* are?

RUSH: Have been for over a *year*. *I* got a pin like this one.

VIC: Where'd ya get it?
RUSH: Saved up chewin' gum wrappers. Only *takes twenty.*

Which concludes a brief interlude at the small house half-way up in the next block.

First broadcast 1935.

II

Caramels on a Hot Day

Well sir, it's the latter part of a soft, lazy, summer afternoon as we approach the small house half-way up in the next block now, and here on the bottom-most step of the front porch sits Mr. Rush Gook. He seems to have a pile of what appear to be caramels beside him, and he . . . . But here's somebody else coming up the sidewalk. It's Mr. Victor Gook . . . who greets his young hopeful with a cheery:

VIC: Hi.
RUSH: Hi.
VIC: Warm day.
RUSH: Yeah.
VIC: Whatcha doin'?
RUSH: Just drummin' up a little excitement for myself.
VIC: That *candy* ya got there?
RUSH: Carmels. Want one?
VIC: No thanks. They look soiled.
RUSH: They *are* soiled. I'm lettin' the sun shine on 'em.
VIC: With what object in view?
RUSH: The sun melts 'em, get the angle, an' then I take 'em between my hands an' roll 'em into balls.
VIC: Why?
RUSH: Furnishes me mild excitement.
VIC: Soon as I get a dollar an' a quarter ahead I'm gonna have the doctor examine your skull.
RUSH: I fail to get the idea you're attempting to put across.
VIC: Don't it strike you peculiar a man fourteen years old can amuse himself playin' with little sticky hunks of candy?

RUSH: [*good-natured chuckle*] Oh, I see. Well, after all, this is a hot day. An individual's got to take his fun where he finds it.

VIC: Guess I'll sit down then.

RUSH: Help yourself.

VIC: Ya don't happen to have a carmel that ain't been *fooled* with, do ya?

RUSH: *Here's* a square one.

VIC: Thanks.

RUSH: It *was* rolled into a ball.

VIC: This one was?

RUSH: Yeah. I rolled it in a ball an' then made it square again with a couple bricks.

VIC: Very interesting. Here, you may have it back again.

RUSH: Don't ya want it?

VIC: I've had a change of heart.

RUSH: Thought you *liked* carmels.

VIC: I *do*—now an' again. However, I'm a somewhat fickle carmel-eater. Catch me one day I dote on 'em, catch me the next day ya couldn't give me one for five dollars.

RUSH: Smelly Clark's the same way with weenies.

VIC: Yeah?

RUSH: Catch him one day he dotes on 'em, catch him the next day ya couldn't give him one for five dollars.

VIC: Quite a coincidence. Say, *here's* a pretty respectable lookin' carmel. Has *it* been rolled in a ball?

RUSH: No.

VIC: I might consider eatin' this carmel.

RUSH: Help yourself.

VIC: Thanks.

RUSH: These is a pretty good grade of carmels. Three for a cent.

VIC: [*with his mouth full*] Uh-huh.

RUSH: Good?

VIC: Uh-huh.

RUSH: Funny thing about that carmel.

VIC: [*mouth full*] Which carmel? *This* carmel?

RUSH: Yeah. Ya see I . . . It's all right, Gov. You don't hafta take it outa your mouth.

VIC: Before I put it back *in* my mouth, please tell me what's so humorous about this carmel.

RUSH: *Nothin'.*

VIC: You said funny thing about this carmel.

RUSH: I was gonna say that that one wouldn't *melt. That's* all.

VIC: *Why* wouldn't it melt?

RUSH: I dunno. It just got soft on one side. I stuck it up against the side of the house for a long time but it stayed hard as a rock. I guess . . . hey, what's the idea throwin' it away?

VIC: I've lost interest in it.

RUSH: That was a darn good carmel.

VIC: It may have been. But carmels that have been stuck up against the side of the house lose their charm for me.

RUSH: Stickin' it on the house didn't hurt it.

VIC: Perhaps not.

RUSH: *Here's* one, Gov. It's got a rock stuck in the middle of it but if ya kinda eat around . . .

VIC: No. Thanks just the same. My appetite for carmels has vanished like a bird on the wing. Just like I said before, catch me one day an' I'm a *fiend* for carmels; catch me the next . . . Aha!

RUSH: [*looking up*] Huh?

VIC: A friend of ours is coming up the sidewalk.

RUSH: Where? Oh. [*calls*] Hi, Mom.

SADE: [*off*] Hello there.

VIC: [*calls*] What's the name, please?

SADE: [*smartly*] Puddin' Tame. Ask me again I'll tell you the same.

RUSH: [*to Vic*] I just about forgot that joke. Usta pull it on guys a lot when I was in the third grade.

VIC: [*to Sade*] We enjoy warm weather.

SADE: [*up*] Lands, yes. Let me sit down a minute. Never *felt* the sun so hot. What's going on here?

RUSH: I'm rollin' carmels into little balls.

SADE: What for?

RUSH: Oh—just for the excitement of it.

SADE: Looks to me like you're ruining good candy. Gimme one.

RUSH: Want a square one or one that's been rolled in a ball?

SADE: Square one. I certainly wouldn't eat the ones you've rolled around . . . what's the matter, Vic?

VIC: Matter?

SADE: You winked?

VIC: Did I? Perhaps I was trying to imply in the most delicate manner possible, without hurting anybody's feelings, that I strongly advise against the eating of them carmels.

SADE: What's the matter with 'em?

VIC: Why . . . a . . .

RUSH: Nothin's the matter with 'em, Mom. Heck, Gov, whatcha wanta run down a guy's carmels for?

VIC: My suspicions may be unjustified. Before Mom eats that carmel, though, I'd like to inquire if at any time in the past it has been shaped into a *ball?*

RUSH: No.

VIC: Has it been stuck up against the side of the house?

RUSH: No.

VIC: Has it got a rock in it?

RUSH: [*indignantly*] No.

VIC: Has it got *any* foreign matter in it?

RUSH: Heck, no. *I'd* tell Mom if I stuck somethin' inside.

VIC: You certify then that that carmel in Mom's hand has not been molested since it was purchased?

RUSH: Sure.

VIC: Sade.

SADE: Yes?

VIC: Eat.

RUSH: Well, of course I *did* . . .

VIC: One second, Sade. Yes, Rush? You were saying . . . ?

RUSH: It didn't hurt the *carmel* none, but we *did* kinda play a couple minutes *catch* with it.

VIC: By "we" you mean . . . ?

RUSH: Guy down at the livery stable an' me.

VIC: I submit my case, Sade.

SADE: [*reproachfully*] Rush.

RUSH: [*defensively*] What?

SADE: Givin' your Mom old thrown-around candy to eat.

RUSH: *That* candy's all right. Heck, it don't hurt carmels to . . . Aw, ya threw it away.

SADE: Sure I did.

RUSH: I coulda made a ball out of it. I coulda . . .

SADE: Great big enormous boy fiddlin' around with such silliness *anyway*. I bet they don't teach you in *high* school to sit on your front porch an' mess with lick-dab like a baby.

RUSH: [*tough*] Everybody throws my carmels away.

SADE: Look out somebody don't throw *you* away.

VIC: [*guffaws at this*]

SADE: [*laughs because she's pleased with her wit*]

RUSH: Darn carmels *cost* three for a cent. Hate to have everybody act like they grow on trees an' throw 'em in the street.

SADE: Might as well throw 'em in the street as ruin 'em the way you're doin'.

RUSH: It don't hurt carmels to roll 'em around. Science tells us . . .

SADE: [*impatiently*] Take my hat.

RUSH: O. K. [*moving off*]

SADE: Hang it *behind* the hall-tree so things don't brush against it.

VIC: [*to Sade*] Been callin' on Ma Corkle this afternoon?

SADE: Yes. Almost ashamed to show my face over there I've let it go so long. Curtis off his feed an' all, an' none of us callin' up or inquirin' how he feels or anything.

VIC: How's he feel?

SADE: Better. He can lay down in bed now.

VIC: He can?

SADE: Uh-huh. Laid down for a while when *I* was there.

VIC: What's he *been* doin' all this time? Standin' up?

SADE: Sittin' up. It's his *back*, ya know. The doctor didn't let him lay down for weeks.

VIC: Oozy-woozy-squoozy.

SADE: Huh?

VIC: Whee.

SADE: Does sound kinda funny . . . person well enough to lay down in bed. Ya generally hear of a person well enough to *sit up* in bed.

VIC: Yeah.

SADE: Mis' Corkle passed a remark on that this afternoon. She called up the newspaper to tell 'em Curtis was healthy enough to lay down in bed an' they thought she was givin' 'em the blueberry an' . . . [*lower tones*] Hey, there goes Mr. Vogel.

VIC: [*to Sade*] Go sit on a tack, Vogel.

SADE: Bet *he's* warm . . . so stout.

VIC: He looks all soft an' runny like Sam's carmels.

SADE: Must be a real trial to a fat person in weather like this. I know Mis' Ropeholder there on West Monroe Street that boards with the Wilsons suffers just terrible when . . . [*to Rush*] Hang it up nice?

RUSH: Sure.

SADE: I wanta be real careful with that hat. If I treat it nice it'll do me next summer too. Lands, it's warm.

VIC: Pretty soon the sun'll go down an' it'll cool off.

RUSH: [*accusingly*] Who kicked this carmel off on the ground?

VIC: *I* didn't.

SADE: We haven't moved from right here.

RUSH: Found it right in the dirt.

SADE: You musta knocked it off yourself.

RUSH: [*finds the world full of grief*] Shucks.

SADE: Listen, Mister Funny-face, get over that peevishness. Somebody's liable to give you something to be peevish *about*. Vic.

VIC: Uh-huh?

SADE: Know what I'd like to do?

VIC: No.

SADE: Take supper at the cafeteria.

VIC: O. K.

SADE: Be all right?

VIC: Sure.

SADE: I never ordered any groceries today, an' besides I think it does a person *good* to eat other peoples' vittles now an' then.

VIC: Be nice to stroll down towards town later on.

SADE: Might go to the show afterwards too, huh?

VIC: Sure.

SADE: I feel like I *need* a little spree. [*raises voice*] Rush?

RUSH: [*off a little*] Yeah?

SADE: How'd ya like to eat supper at the cafeteria?

RUSH: [*coming up*] Fine.

SADE: Go to the picture show afterwards.

RUSH: Fine.

SADE: Trot up in the swing an' get the newspaper. We'll see what they got on.

RUSH: I *know* what they got on. Rex Radley in . . .

SADE: I like to see for myself. [*to Vic*] That's one of the things Curtis missed the most while he's been sick. Picture shows. He used to go every single evening. Sometimes he even . . . There goes Mis' Eaglefrump.

VIC: Got her hair fixed different, ain't she?

SADE: Yeah. That's called the Stream-line Tuck. Her daughter brings all them fancy hair-fixin' tricks from Decatur. I think that's too young for a woman Mis' Eaglefrump's age, don't you?

VIC: Looks a trifle racy.

RUSH: [*coming up*] Here's what they got at the show, Mom. "Rex Radley in *The Burning Stars of Love*—a symphony of two hearts torn in the great conflict of . . ."

SADE: Give it here so I can see.

RUSH: Picture of a guy with a revolver shootin' a lady in the head. The guy is Rex Radley . . .

SADE: Let *loose*, will ya. Lands. [*to Vic*] Here's what they got, Vic. [*reads*] "Rex Radley in *The Burning Stars of Love*—a symphony of two hearts torn in the great conflict of career or riches."

VIC: Rootle-tootle.

SADE: [*reads*] "Burn to the kisses of Rex Radley. Thrill to the tears of Irma Illington."

VIC: Habble-strabble.

SADE: See the picture? Fella shootin' a lady in the head.

VIC: Uh-huh.

SADE: Sounds like it oughta be pretty good.

RUSH: Rex Radley always takes the part of a guy . . .

SADE: [*reads*] "Also Happy Hyena Comedy, News Events, an' travelogue"—how ya say that—travelogue?

VIC: Yeah.

SADE: An' travelogue, "With Bill an' Bernice through the Red Hills of Rooglie, East Africa."

RUSH: That's one of them darn things where ya see guys climbin' trees an' ladies dancin' around an' funny birds an' . . .

SADE: [*reads*] "Extra added attraction: two full reels of world-famous boxing match between Cannon-cracker Clark an' Buffalo Barnes." [*approvingly*] Uh-huh.

VIC: *That* oughta be pretty good.

RUSH: Couple guys havin' a fist-fight.

SADE: It don't state who the leading lady in the main picture is. Irma Illington always takes the part of the *mother*, so she can't be . . .

RUSH: There goes Four-eyes Johnson.

SADE: Huh?

RUSH: I say there goes Four-eyes Johnson.

SADE: Who's he?

RUSH: Just a kid. Resides on East Jefferson. Left-handed.

SADE: What?

RUSH: He's a left-handed kid.

SADE: Oh. [*to Vic*] Say, listen, it's going on five o'clock, ain't it?

VIC: Must be. I'll find out. [*fishes for watch*]

SADE: Rush, you better throw that junk away an' get started. Get started gettin' ready. You're gonna hafta take a bath an' everything.

RUSH: I took such an intense bath just last *night* I . . .

SADE: You played baseball an' helped me this morning.

RUSH: Yeah, but just the same . . .

SADE: We don't need to talk about it. What time was it when you looked, Vic?

VIC: It was . . . Doggone, I forgot. [*fishes again*] It's . . . a . . . ten minutes to five.

SADE: That late? We better *all* go in the house. You better change your shirt, Vic. Real nice people take meals at that cafeteria.

VIC: O. K.

SADE: C'mon, son.

RUSH: Mm, O. K.

And so we've spent a while sitting on the front steps. Don't you feel a little uncomfortable from those hard boards?

First broadcast 1936.

12

⸱•⸱⸱•⸱

Vic Confides in Rush
about Mothers

Well, sir, it's late afternoon as we enter the small house half-way up in the next block now, and here in the living room we find Mr. Victor Gook and his son Mr. Rush Gook. The gentlemen are seated on opposite sides of the library table, marking another step in their long, long rummy tournament, which has been in progress now for a good many years. Listen:

RUSH: I *know* you're waiting for me to discard a *jack.*
VIC: You appear to know quite a bit for one so handicapped in the upper storey.
RUSH: That's all right about the insulting slurs. I'm gonna hold *onto* this jack.
VIC: In the meantime it'd be nice if you *played.*
RUSH: Here's the six of hearts.
VIC: Can't use it. I'll draw from the pack.
RUSH: If I take this game it'll make me three outa five.
VIC: If *I* take this game it'll make *me* three outa five.
RUSH: I wouldn't bet a nickel against the court-house on your chances of takin' this game. Discardin' the ace of spades, huh?
VIC: So it would seem.
RUSH: I'll just snag onto that.
VIC: Your privilege. Like I used to say to Buffalo Bill there in Cody, Wyoming—"Bill," I'd say, "Why doncha go wipe off your chin an' quit all the time . . ."

RUSH: [*triumphantly*] Have a look.

VIC: [*mildly*] You card-sharpin' scoundrel.

RUSH: Three deuces, three nines, an' the jack, queen, king, an' ace of spades.

VIC: There must of been a misdeal.

RUSH: Misdeal *nothin'*. This game makes me three outa five. Guy that wins the most outa ten is champion of the Sahara Desert, the Pennsylvania Railroad, an' the roundhouse. Your turn to crank out the tickets.

VIC: Let's take time out for a second.

RUSH: I got you on the run, huh?

VIC: Far from it. I just want to arrange a piece of strategy in my mind so I squash you into a sick oyster during the next encounter.

RUSH: [*chuckles*] Go ahead. *Arrange* your strategy. Take all the time ya want.

VIC: [*after a brief pause*] Randolph, old peanut-roaster.

RUSH: Uh-huh?

VIC: This might be a good opportunity for us to have a private confab.

RUSH: [*chuckles*] O. K. I expect you want my secret on how to be a champion rummy player.

VIC: Yeah, that'd be nice to have. However, what I had in mind talkin' about was somethin' else.

RUSH: Shoot.

VIC: It's not anything of any great importance I don't s'pose, but as long as your mother's away I thought I might solicit an opinion or two from ya.

RUSH: Somethin' about Mom?

VIC: Yeah. Where is she, by the way?

RUSH: I heard her telephone Mis' Stembottom just before I left for school this noon. I expect they're downtown shoppin' or callin' on some lady or something.

VIC: Uh-huh.

RUSH: What *about* Mom?

VIC: This verges a little on the *delicate*, Heinie. I'm somewhat at a loss as to the best way to begin.

RUSH: Go ahead. You're among friends.

VIC: Well—to bull right in roughshod, I'll start off by askin' a question.

RUSH: O. K.

VIC: Do you think you've been givin' your mother all the breaks she's entitled to?

RUSH: [*instantly serious*] How ya mean?

VIC: Maybe I don't mean anything; maybe I don't even know what I'm talkin' about; but . . . look, George, *I've* never given you the old heavy-father run-around, have I?

RUSH: [*waiting for more*] No.

VIC: At least not for a long time. 'Course when you were a *little* punk I may of slapped on the goose-grease some, but since you've got *big* I've taken a hands-off policy. That right?

RUSH: [*waiting for more*]

VIC: That's because I figure a guy going on fifteen years old is more of a man than a boy an' preachin' from the old man is just so much time wasted.

RUSH: What you gettin' at, Gov?

VIC: Do you really think you've been givin' your mother all the breaks she's got comin'?

RUSH: I haven't thought anything *about* it.

VIC: Well, *think* about it once. [*after a pause, chuckles*] Don't get scared, Water-bucket, *I'm* not gonna bawl ya out. This is just a sociable chat.

RUSH: I'm all in the *dark*.

VIC: I'll put ya straight about what I'm talkin' about.

RUSH: O. K.

VIC: Seems to me, Sam, I've noticed you're beginning to take your mother kinda *cool*. By that I mean . . . well, you're apt to be a little careless in what you *say* to her . . . in the way you *treat* her. Don't get me wrong now, but . . .

RUSH: [*tough*] Gov, if you're accusin' me of bein' *mean* to Mom, I'd like to . . .

VIC: Keep your shirt on. I'm not accusin' you of *anything*.

RUSH: Well, I wish you'd come right out with whatever ya got up your sleeve an' not beat around the bush an' . . .

VIC: O. K., I will.

RUSH: [*tough*] Whatcha *mean* "the way I treat" Mom?

VIC: Bullfrog, little kids stick pretty close to their mother's apron-strings till they're your age. When they get around thirteen or fourteen they're liable to let *go* some. That's *natural*. A lad gets to be a dozen years old or so an' he finds new interests away from home an' makes a lotta friends an' gets to be a pretty busy guy. That keeps up the older he grows. After he's twenty he's apt to get married any time an' then he's almost *completely* cut off from his parents. That's good, that's fine, that's the way things *are*.

RUSH: I don't see what . . .

VIC: Let me say some more here. The upshot of what I'm tryin' to say is, as a boy grows older his mother is gradually going out of business. *You* can see how that is. A woman's business is her family an' she works at it an' enjoys it an' sometimes makes it pay an' sometimes doesn't. But the time finally comes along when the kids get big an' move down the road an' Mama finds herself without a job. You check on that?

RUSH: Um.

VIC: *Now* . . . don't you think a guy oughta play *ball* around home . . . for his mother's sake?

RUSH: *I* thought I was playin' ball O. K.

VIC: You *are*. You're doin' *fine*. I just wanted to see if ya didn't *agree* with me on these little angles.

RUSH: Um.

VIC: Yessir, you're doin' fine. However, a fella *is* liable to get *careless* now an' then.

RUSH: Have I been careless?

VIC: Oh, *some* maybe.

RUSH: You're tellin' me in a round-about way I been *mean* to Mom.

VIC: Not at all.

RUSH: How have I been careless in the way I treat her?

VIC: You want a specific example?

RUSH: Yeah.

VIC: Well . . . 'course you *are* a great *big* hulk an' I s'pose you got a *right* to stay out late at night.

RUSH: [*indignant*] Late at *night*. I'm *always* in at *ten*.

VIC: It was eleven last night, wasn't it?

RUSH: A guy can't *help* slipping *once* in a while.

VIC: That's true too.

RUSH: An' I don't consider even *eleven* o'clock late.

VIC: *Some* people do. I believe your *mother* considers eleven o'clock late. Now look, Walter, I don't care what you do at night. That is I might *care*, but I don't figure I could *do* much about it because if you feel like playin' pool an' smokin' cigars you're gonna play pool an' smoke cigars regardless.

RUSH: *I* don't play pool an' smoke cigars.

VIC: That's fine. I hope you don't start either one for a while yet. But it *would* be kinda nice if you could manage to stick around a little more evenings.

RUSH: I *got* to stick around evenings now. School's on an' I hafta *study*.

VIC: That's what you say *every* year, but it generally turns out you handle most of your work during study periods at school. Well, no matter: the point *is* you know an' I know you really don't amount to much, but I think you'll agree with me that it'd be smart to encourage your mother in the belief that you're hot stuff. See, she's got that mistaken idea an' it won't hurt to let her keep it.

RUSH: Uh-huh.

VIC: You're at that "smart age," but I think you're smart enough so you won't *be* smart. If you get what I mean.

RUSH: I guess I do.

VIC: An' in that connection there's *another* little item I'd like to bring up.

RUSH: O. K.

VIC: I've noticed a tendency on your part lately to kinda *belittle* your mother.

RUSH: [*tough*] Aw now, *listen*, Gov. You can . . .

VIC: You don't do it *purposely*. You're not *mean* about it. But she'll say a thing that sounds a little . . . *foolish* maybe . . . an' you'll *rib* her about it.

RUSH: When'd I do that?

VIC: It's happened quite a *few* times.

RUSH: When?

VIC: Well . . . the other day Mom said something about New York City bein' on the shore of the Pacific Ocean. You rode over her pretty rough-shod. *Laughed* kinda nasty.

RUSH: I was only . . .

VIC: Those things *cut.* An' you got pretty high an' mighty last week over at *Stembottom's* when your mother made some crack or other. What *was* that?

RUSH: Don't know.

VIC: [*remembering*] Oh . . . Mom said George Washington was in the Civil War an' . . . what *was* that she said?

RUSH: Don't know.

VIC: Well, whatever it was you more or less held her up to ridicule in front of her friends. [*pauses, then chuckles*] *Don't* get sore, Sam. Like I say, this is just a sociable chat.

RUSH: I never held her up to *ridicule.*

VIC: It *amounted* to that. You corrected her like you were a college professor an' she was in the first grade.

RUSH: Never *meant* anything by it.

VIC: *I* know ya never. But I know darn good an' well it *hurt.*

RUSH: Mom mention it to *you?*

VIC: No.

RUSH: Um.

VIC: 'Course up till *recent* years I would advocate takin' a *razor* strap to a boy that'd pull a thing like that, but *thunder . . . you're a man.*

RUSH: Um.

VIC: An' I think you oughta be *consulted* like a man. Boys can be whipped up till the time they're eighteen, but I'm not much in *favor* with that. Whipping is all right for *dumb*-heads, but a guy that can bring home fair grades from high school shows he's got some *sense.*

RUSH: Um.

VIC: Your mother never finished school, ya know, so there's a good many things she's pretty much in the dark about. But the *slant* is to straighten her *out* . . . not make *fun* of her.

RUSH: I never made fun of Mom in my life.

VIC: Perhaps not *consciously.* But a man's apt to say some pretty rotten things if he don't keep an eye on himself.

RUSH: Um.

VIC: Am I right or wrong?

RUSH: Um.

VIC: Well?

RUSH: Right, I s'pose. Anything else?

VIC: I've noticed a couple times that you're liable to put up some pretty heavy arguments when your mother asks you to do something. Your arguments may be *sound* arguments, but after all ya wanta realize your mother is still the boss an' what she says goes. Now an' again maybe you *are* asked to do something that seems foolish an' unnecessary, but so *what? You* got plenty of time.

RUSH: Um.

VIC: *I* usta get a clout upside the *head* at home if *I* got outa line.

RUSH: Um.

VIC: The whole thing in a nut-shell, Box-top, is that a lad oughta rally around his mother an' do the big thing every chance he gets. Excuse the wishy-washy phrase, but a lad don't *have* a mother *forever* . . . an' when she's gone he's apt to start kickin' himself all over the place.

RUSH: Uh-huh.

VIC: *That's* all I got to say, I guess.

RUSH: Um.

VIC: Whose deal here?

RUSH: Ah . . . yours.

VIC: Slam over the paste-boards then. How do we stand?

RUSH: I've won two; you've won two.

VIC: I see I'm bein' crowded to the wall. However, this next game will be a different story. I'm gonna unloose great surges of uncanny skill.

RUSH: Oh, sure.

VIC: I *am.* I'm gonna play with the cool brain of a duelist. I'm gonna concentrate my medulla-oblongata, my cerebrum, an' my cerebellum to the . . .

RUSH: Gov.

VIC: Uh-huh?

RUSH: I'm not gonna make any *speech* or anything.

VIC: No, *don't.* For *gosh* sakes.

RUSH: I'll say just one thing.
VIC: O. K., what is it?
RUSH: Thanks for the tip.

Which concludes another brief interlude at the small house half-way up in the next block.

First broadcast 1937.

13

Uncle Fletcher and Sade
Will Have Lunch Together

Well sir, it's about eleven-thirty o'clock as we approach the small house half-way up in the next block now, and here on the front porch we discern a familiar figure. Mrs. Victor Gook is seated on the top step but one, reading a postcard and enjoying fine warm sunshine. And say, here's another friend. Uncle Fletcher appears around the corner of the house. Listen:

FLETCHER: [*off a little*] Good morning, Sadie.
SADE: [*pleased*] Well—good *morning.*
FLETCHER: [*coming up*] Glorious day?
SADE: *Isn't* it, though?
FLETCHER: [*up*] Best we've had so far this year.
SADE: Sit down. On your way home to dinner?
FLETCHER: [*somewhat importantly*] No, I'm not. My landlady's outa town.
SADE: Really?
FLETCHER: Run up to Dixon for the day.
SADE: [*interested*] Oh?
FLETCHER: Left at five o'clock this morning; gets back ten o'clock tonight.
SADE: Little visit, I suppose?
FLETCHER: Little visit. See, she hasn't been to Dixon since she *moved* from Dixon.
SADE: Uh-huh.
FLETCHER: Got a little visit to Dixon *comin'.*

SADE: Sure. I bet she's been *homesick* for Dixon.

FLETCHER: Yes, more or less. *Women,* ya know. *They* get homesick.

SADE: Uh-huh. Well, *look:* eat with *me* this noon.

FLETCHER: I've *got* my dinner.

SADE: You've *had* your dinner?

FLETCHER: No, I've *got* my dinner. In this *box.*

SADE: [*glances at the box he's carrying*] Oh.

FLETCHER: Mis' Keller put it up before her train left this morning.

SADE: [*approvingly*] Well, *that* was thoughtful of her.

FLETCHER: Uh-huh. Oh, she's A-number-one when it comes to landladies, Mis' Keller is. You take *lots* of landladies, they'd hike on up to Dixon an' leave their boarders to paddle their own *canoe.* An' *I* wouldn't care. *I* enjoy restaurant meals. But Mis' Keller *insisted.* "*No* now, Mr. Rush," she says, "I'm going to pack you your *lunch.*" An' she *done* it. Right here in this box. Cold chicken, bread-and-butter sandwiches, watermelon pickles, cabbage cole slaw, an' coffee in a thermos bottle.

SADE: How *nice.*

FLETCHER: Uh-huh. [*impressively*] An' at *home,* Sadie.

SADE: Yes?

FLETCHER: I got *another* box like this.

SADE: With your *supper* in it, I bet.

FLETCHER: [*chuckles*] With my *supper* in it, by George.

SADE: You've got a *dream* of a landlady.

FLETCHER: Mis' Keller's all right, Mis' Keller's all right.

SADE: I've known *some* landladies that wouldn't move their little *finger* to . . .

FLETCHER: Stuff I got at home in my *supper*-box, Sadie, is *different* than what's here in my *dinner*-box.

SADE: Oh, she's a jewel.

FLETCHER: Uh-huh. One *other* time—years ago when we lived in Dixon—Mis' Keller went to pay her *daughter* a visit an' left me alone for the day. That time she set out my dinner on the kitchen table an' my supper on the dining room table. At noon I ate in the kitchen; at night I ate in the dining room, see?

SADE: Uh-huh.

FLETCHER: But it didn't work *out* satisfactory. I'm pretty much all thumbs when it comes to warming up potatoes an' stuff. I spilled gravy an' broke dishes an' tipped over the coffee pot an' everything else.

SADE: Um.

FLETCHER: *This* trip she decided to pack me my meals in *boxes*.

SADE: Um.

FLETCHER: *I* agreed. No rubbish to clean up an' I can eat any place I please.

SADE: [*cordially*] Well, *hey*—eat with *me*.

FLETCHER: Oh, you got your family an' . . .

SADE: No, I *haven't*. Got no more family than a rabbit.

FLETCHER: Where's Vic and Rush?

SADE: Vic's takin' luncheon with Mr. Buller the Chicago man down in the Butler House Hotel an' Rush is eatin' at the high school cafeteria this noon. I'm all by *myself*.

FLETCHER: [*pleased*] *Well.*

SADE: I'd *love* to have company.

FLETCHER: Fine.

SADE: [*giggles*] *My* dinner's gonna be little pick-up odds an' ends *too*. We can have a *picnic*.

FLETCHER: *Sure.* I'll dibby up my cold *chicken* with ya. Mis' Keller packed this box with enough cold chicken for half a *dozen* fellas.

SADE: [*giggles*] All right. An' maybe I can find something in the pantry *you* like. Hungry *now?* Wanta go inside?

FLETCHER: Whenever you say, Sadie.

SADE: Well, it's early yet, I think. Can't be much more'n eleven-thirty. An' there's nothing to cook. Shouldn't we soak up a little more of this lovely sunshine?

FLETCHER: Fine.

SADE: *Such* a lovely day.

FLETCHER: I been up since four o'clock this morning.

SADE: Really?

FLETCHER: Mis' Keller's train left at five.

SADE: Oh, sure.

FLETCHER: She'll be back at ten o'clock this evening. Maybe you an' Vic and Rush would like to go down to the depot an' *meet* her.

SADE: [*skeptically*] Ah—maybe. [*brightly*] Say, *here*—postal card from *Bessie.*

FLETCHER: Got a postal card from Bessie *myself* day before yesterday.

SADE: Really?

FLETCHER: Forgot what I *done* with that postal card. I'm a *crime* when it comes to postal cards. Can't trust me with a postal card five minutes. *I'll* mislay postal cards. Mislay 'em every time.

SADE: Oh well, they're not important after you've *read* 'em. I throw away postal cards *myself* after I know what they *say.*

FLETCHER: Fine. No, *I'll* mislay 'em. [*chuckles*] Never bet your money on *me*, Sadie, when it comes to *postal* cards. I'll mislay a postal card quicker'n you can say Glenn Webster.

SADE: Uh-huh. Well, here's what Bessie says in this one.

FLETCHER: [*chuckles*] I oughta be shot at sunrise the way I mislay postal cards.

SADE: Bessie says, "Dear sister an' all, thought I would . . .

FLETCHER: Who's this?

SADE: Bessie.

FLETCHER: Oh, uh-huh. Mentions Walter likely.

SADE: Yes. She says, "Dear sister an' all, thought I would . . .

FLETCHER: *Walter's* a good boy.

SADE: Yes.

FLETCHER: Walter's all right. Always *liked* Walter. Bessie got a good man in Walter. Walter works hard.

SADE: Yes. Say, Uncle Fletcher, I bet you're hungry. Shall we go inside an' . . .

FLETCHER: Go ahead an' read Bessie's postal card.

SADE: All right.

FLETCHER: [*chuckles*] Don't trust any postal cards to *me* though. I'm strictly a *wash*-out when it comes to postal cards. Mislay 'em!—Ladies, please remove your *hats!*

SADE: [*laughs moderately with Uncle Fletcher at this conceit*]

FLETCHER: [*milking the jest*] Ladies—please—remove—your—hats!

SADE: [*very brief giggle, then*] "Dear sister an' all, thought I would write an' see how you are feeling. We are all well an' Walter's kneecap seems to have let up definitely on the twinges. He hasn't complained since 'way last February. Hasn't the weather been grand? This is just a rotten little line to say I received the nightie an' it was so pretty an' thanks sixteen bushels. I'll write a long letter soon. Tell Uncle Fletcher hello when you see him. Love to Vic and Rush. Your sister Bess."

FLETCHER: Mailman bring *me* that postal card an' two minutes later I wouldn't know what'd *become* of it.

SADE: So glad Walter's kneecap is better.

FLETCHER: *Walter* works hard.

SADE: *They've* been having this elegant weather *too*.

FLETCHER: Walter works hard. [*chuckles*] No, Sadie, don't trust *me* with your postal cards.

SADE: Um.

FLETCHER: [*chuckles*] Be the biggest mistake you ever made in your life.

SADE: Um.

FLETCHER: [*his pet joke again*] Ladies—please—remove—your —hats!

SADE: [*brief giggle and then brightly*] Well, how about it? Shall we go in the house an' eat our picnic dinner?

FLETCHER: Fine.

SADE: All right, I'll investigate my pantry an' . . .

FLETCHER: *Could* go some place *else*.

SADE: Where?

FLETCHER: Long as Vic an' Rush won't be home.

SADE: How ya mean, Uncle Fletcher . . . "some place else"?

FLETCHER: [*rather importantly*] Well, *here* was *my* thought when I stopped past.

SADE: Yes?

FLETCHER: Thought I'd either take my lunch-box over to Ed Kennedy's gas-station on Morris Avenue or stroll downtown to the court-house square.

SADE: Ah . . . an' *eat* at one of those places?

FLETCHER: Yes. See, Ed Kennedy's gas-station's right there on Route Sixty-six. Good many automobiles come in around noon-time. Fella'll see license plates from *everywhere*. An' Ed's got a big roomy wooden bench sittin' there on the drive. We could sit on that bench in the shade an' eat an' watch the travelers.

SADE: [*doesn't fancy this proposal*] Uncle Fletcher, I think *I'd* rather just eat in my kitchen an' . . .

FLETCHER: Fine.

SADE: . . . if *you'd* rather go to . . .

FLETCHER: Fine. [*rather importantly*] Or . . . there's the court-house *square*.

SADE: [*somewhat startled*] Ah . . . spread out your lunch on the *grass?*

FLETCHER: Fellas *do* it. I've seen *dozens* of fellas . . . [*little chuckle*] What's the matter?

SADE: [*giggling*] I was wondering what Vic and his stylish Chicago friend Mr. Buller'd say if they stepped out of the Purple Room of the Butler House Hotel an' saw me sittin' in the court-house yard eatin' my lunch out of a shoe-box.

FLETCHER: Fellas *do* it, Sadie. An' there's a lot going *on* downtown during the noon-hour.

SADE: Yes, I expect there is. [*giggles*] But I'm afraid you'll hafta count me *out* this time.

FLETCHER: [*disappointed*] Fine.

SADE: *You* run along though. I bet you'd *rather.*

FLETCHER: [*stoutly*] No now, not at *all. I'll* eat in the kitchen.

SADE: Don't eat in the kitchen on *my* account. Goodness, don't make the slightest difference . . .

FLETCHER: [*stoutly*] *I'll* eat in the kitchen, Sadie. *Forget* it. Anyway I want you to taste Mis' Keller's cold chicken.

SADE: I'd *like* to.

FLETCHER: Best half-wit cold chicken you ever put in your mouth.

SADE: Yes, I've heard you say so. I understand she's a *wonderful* . . .

FLETCHER: An' watermelon pickles, cabbage cole slaw, bread-and-butter sandwiches, coffee, an' cookies. Never *mentioned* the *cookies,* I guess. Made fresh yesterday afternoon. *Molasses.*

SADE: Molasses cookies is delicious.

FLETCHER: No, *I* just thought you might like the idea is all. Ed Kennedy's got this big comfortable wooden bench right there in front of the gas-station by the pumps. Highway Sixty-six, ya know.

Chicago to Saint Louis. Lots of machines going past this time of the year. Fella'll see licenses from *every* place.

SADE: Uncle Fletcher, I think you'd prefer to take your dinner-box an' . . .

FLETCHER: *Acquainted* with Ed, are ya?

SADE: I don't *believe* so.

FLETCHER: Lives right next door to his gas-station there.

SADE: [*negative*] Uh-uh.

FLETCHER: *Rush* knows him.

SADE: Um.

FLETCHER: Rush knows him well.

SADE: [*giggles*] Rush knows everybody.

FLETCHER: Uh-huh. No, *I* just thought you might like the idea. Long as your family's not home an' . . .

SADE: Uncle Fletcher, *you* go. Tell ya the honest truth I'm not very hungry to *begin* with.

FLETCHER: Fine.

SADE: I thought I'd hardly bother with dinner at *all.* Throw myself a couple jelly sandwiches together an' maybe a glass of milk an' . . .

FLETCHER: [*rather bluntly*] Who's *that* fella 'cross the street?

SADE: [*after glancing*] Man that boards around the corner on Kelsey Street somewhere. I see him almost every day walkin' past. Never *heard* his *name. Pleasant* man. Always nods polite an' smiles.

FLETCHER: Puts me in mind of Steve Yowper I usta know in Belvidere.

SADE: Uh-huh.

FLETCHER: Ever make the *acquaintance* of Steve Yowper?

SADE: I don't think I ever made the acquaintance of *any* Belvidere people.

FLETCHER: Fine. Steve passed away in nineteen-aught-ten. Got in a rassling match with a fella when the thermometer was at a hundred an' two in the shade, got overheated, asked for a glass of cold lemonade, climbed on his bicycle, waved to the girl he was gonna marry, keeled over, an' kicked the bucket.

SADE: [*sympathetically*] Oh, my.

FLETCHER: Would of been forty-seven years old his next birthday.

SADE: [*sympathetically*] Um.

FLETCHER: [*thoughtfully*] Stuff happens, don't it?

SADE: Yes, indeed.

FLETCHER: Stuff happens.

SADE: [*after a pause*] Uncle Fletcher, it's almost noon an' I know you're hungry an' I bet you'd like to take your lovely box of dinner to your friend's gas-station an' . . .

FLETCHER: [*stoutly*] No sir, now—not at *all*. I'm eatin' with *you*. Right out there in the *kitchen*.

SADE: Ah—all right.

FLETCHER: [*stoutly*] Sure.

SADE: Well . . . shall we go inside?

FLETCHER: Fine.

SADE: [*giggles*] I think we'll have a real nice time.

FLETCHER: [*stoutly*] *Glorious* time.

SADE: Um.

FLETCHER: Wait, here's your postal card from Bessie.

SADE: Oh, sure, my postal card.

FLETCHER: [*chuckles*] Better get it out of *my* sight. *I'm a crime* when it comes to postal cards. *Mislay* 'em! By *George*, how I mislay 'em. I'll mislay postal cards every *trip!*

SADE: Uh-huh.

FLETCHER: [*chuckles*] Ladies—please—remove—your—*hats!*

Which concludes another brief interlude at the small house half-way up in the next block.

First broadcast 1941.

14

---·•·---

The Stillness of an Afternoon
Is Broken

Well sir, it's early afternoon as we enter the small house
half-way up in the next block now, and here in the living room we
find Mrs. Victor Gook all by herself. Mrs. Gook is at the telephone
conversing with her close friend and confidante Mrs. Frederick
Stembottom. Listen:

SADE: [*to phone*] I didn't take you away from anything, did I, lady?
Well, ish, I haven't really got anything to say now that I've *called*
you. [*giggles*] Yes . . . well, what happened I went like a house
a-fire all morning long and done nine million jobs around the house
and then got dinner and pitched in on my upstairs the minute the
boys left for the office an' school, and finally *did* quit and wash and
put on a clean apron and then discovered I'd been on the go so
much I couldn't settle *down*. [*laughs*] *You* know how that is, lady.
Person gets theirself all keyed up and they hafta slow down gradual
or the boiler explodes. [*laughs*] Yes . . . so I telephoned *you*. Hey,
maybe that's not very *complimentary*. [*loud lady laugh*] No, but you
appreciate how I mean, Ruthie. Sure. Yes, *isn't* it a quiet afternoon.
One of them hushedy-hushedy afternoons where a person sits and
listens to pins dropping. Little bit ago I was out on the back porch
shaking my mop and 'way off in the distance somewhere I heard
some fella say giddap to his horse and I bet twenty-five cents he was
clear away over on Chestnut Street and that's eight hundred miles
from here if it's an inch. Yeah . . . you run inta *real* still afternoons
every so often. Like *Sunday* kinda. I was sayin' to . . . say, lady,

hang on a second, I think I heard my kitchen door open. [*calls*] Hello? Groceries? You, Irving?

RUSH: [*off*] Hi, Mom.

FLETCHER: [*off*] Afternoon, Sadie honey.

SADE: [*calls, in some surprise*] Well—hello. [*to phone*] Uncle Fletcher and Rush just walked in, Ruthie. I can't imagine what Rush's doing home from school. [*crash in the kitchen*] Oh, my goodness. [*calls*] What happened?

FLETCHER: [*cheerfully, off*] Fell down.

SADE: [*calls sharply*] Who fell down?

RUSH: [*off, cheerfully*] We both fell down.

SADE: [*not loud*] Oh, for mercy's sake. [*to phone*] What, Ruthie? No, we don't need to hang up. There's no reason why *we* hafta cut our conversation short just because . . . huh?

RUSH: [*approaching*] Uncle Fletcher tripped on his shoelace, Mom.

FLETCHER: [*approaching, cheerfully*] No broken bones, Sadie honey, no broken bones.

SADE: [*to phone*] Well, whatever you say, lady. Seems like a shame though. I take you away from whatever you're doing and just because my family busts in we hafta cut short our . . . [*giggles*] . . . well, ish.

RUSH: [*coming up*] Principal called a special teachers' meeting, Mom.

FLETCHER: [*coming up*] Using the telephone, are you, Sadie?

SADE: [*to phone*] No, *you* needn't bother to call back, Ruthie.

FLETCHER: [*gently*] Mama's using the telephone, Rush. I'd stop my titters, whimpers, and guffaws.

RUSH: [*amused*] O. K.

FLETCHER: [*sententiously*] When the older folks is using the telephone it's always best to let up on the titters, whimpers, and guffaws.

RUSH: [*chuckling*] I'm letting up on 'em.

FLETCHER: You're a good boy.

SADE: [*to phone*] Well, all righty, Ruthie, whatever you say. Dandy. Fine.

FLETCHER: [*to Rush, sententiously*] There was a little boy in Detroit Michigan neglected to let up on his titters, whimpers and guffaws while Mama was using the telephone and he disappeared and all they ever found was one of his tiny patent leather booties, the tassel singed at the bottom.

RUSH: [*chuckles*] I'll *remember* that.

FLETCHER: [*gently*] Yes—it teaches us a lesson.

SADE: [*to phone*] All righty then, Ruthie lady, we'll leave it like that. You bet. All righty, Ruthie. You betty, lady. Good-bye. [*hangs up*]

FLETCHER: [*softly*] The tassel singed at the bottom.

SADE: [*brightly*] What *is* all this now?

FLETCHER: Afternoon, Sadie honey. I was just telling Rush here . . .

SADE: [*to Rush*] Why ain't you in school, Mister?

RUSH: Principal called a special teachers' meeting.

SADE: [*rather sharply*] *Another* one?

RUSH: Why, we haven't had a special teachers' meeting since 'way last . . .

SADE: Seems like he calls a special teachers' meeting every five seconds. When *I* was little and went to school, I had to go to *school.*

RUSH: Um.

SADE: Ish, kids any more. I don't see how they soak up any education at all, they get excused so much.

FLETCHER: I once knew a railroad section foreman in Cedar Rapids Iowa that could . . .

SADE: [*briefly*] Who fell down out in the kitchen just now?

RUSH: *We* did.

SADE: [*rather sharply*] You and Uncle Fletcher *both?*

RUSH: Yeah.

SADE: How could *that* be?

FLETCHER: [*gently*] I tripped over my shoestring, Sadie honey.

SADE: [*to Rush*] What did *you* trip over?

RUSH: [*rather sheepishly*] I just . . . fell down.

FLETCHER: [*offhand*] He was keeping me company.

SADE: [*sharply, incredulous*] No.

FLETCHER: [*offhand*] Just keeping me company. Rush is a good boy.

SADE: [*sharply, to Rush*] You fell down just because somebody else fell down?

RUSH: [*low tones*] Um.

SADE: By gollies, that's the horse that choked Billy Robinson. Here you are a boy fourteen years old and a monstrous big important high school student and pulling off babyish monkeyshines an *infant* would refuse to . . .

RUSH: [*rather sulky*] Somebody in the kitchen.

SADE: [*rather sharply*] What?

RUSH: [*rather sulky*] I heard the kitchen door open.

SADE: [*briefly*] That's my groceries, that's Irving. [*calls*] Hello, groceries? That you, Irving?

VIC: [*in the kitchen*] Hi-de-hi, ho-de-ho.

SADE: [*to Fletcher and Rush, in surprise*] Well goodness.

VIC: [*in kitchen*] I got an uncle and his name is Joe.

SADE: [*to Fletcher and Rush, in surprise*] Everybody home in the middle of the afternoon. [*calls briefly*] Hi.

FLETCHER: [*polite interest*] Grocery boy, Sadie honey?

SADE: No, it's Vic home from the office.

FLETCHER: Fine.

RUSH: [*raises voice*] Hi, Gov.

VIC: [*coming up*] Why, my darling little son *Rush*. Climb up on my *knee*. Well, and Uncle Fletcher too. Climb up on my *other* knee, Uncle Fletcher. Sadie-de-wadie, how are *you?*

SADE: All right.

VIC: [*up*] Did a beautiful woman heavily veiled and greatly agitated come to the door and demand the kisses of old Vic Gook?

SADE: No.

VIC: I am astonished. What's everybody doing home?

SADE: I'm wondering myself. Nine seconds ago I was talking over the phone with Ruthie and chattering away about what a quiet afternoon it was and here four minutes later I got seven million relatives under my feet.

VIC: [*to Rush*] What you doing home from school, Pete?

RUSH: Principal called a special teachers' meeting.

VIC: He is a scoundrel and a wretch.

FLETCHER: Tell you why *I* stopped past, Vic honey.

VIC: [*genially*] Wish you *would*, wish you *would*.

FLETCHER: I thought you people might be interested in a romance which has developed between my landlady Mis' Keller and Mr. Rishigan Fishigan from Sishigan Michigan.

VIC: [*mock incredulity*] What you're saying cannot be *true*.

FLETCHER: [*stoutly*] A romance has developed between my landlady Mis' Keller and Mr. Rishigan Fishigan from Sishigan Michigan.

VIC: I must know all the details.

FLETCHER: Rush, perhaps you had better go down cellar.

VIC: Naw.

FLETCHER: [*gently*] This is not a matter to be discussed before the tiny children. It concerns love and romance and such junk.

RUSH: That's O. K.

SADE: [*bluntly to Vic*] What *you* doing home?

VIC: I'm only home for a brief moment. Any second you'll hear an automobile horn honk out in front and it'll be the boss. We're driving down to the Chicago and Alton railroad yards to inspect a shipment of lumber that arrived this afternoon.

SADE: Why did you come home at *all* so early?

VIC: I took care of some errands downtown and got through with 'em earlier than I expected to.

SADE: Did you buy a hat?

VIC: I did.

SADE: Where is it?

VIC: Kitchen table.

SADE: Um.

VIC: A beautiful *thing* happened in the hat store.

SADE: What was that?

VIC: The gentleman who waited on me turned out to be . . .

FLETCHER: [*rather pompously*] There'll be another automobile horn honk directly, Vic, and it'll be for me. Gumpox the garbage man is stopping past to pick me up.

VIC: Has he got an auto horn on his wagon?

FLETCHER: [*proudly*] He has. Old-*fashioned* auto horn.

VIC: Um.

RUSH: Smelly *Clark* is stopping past for *me*. We're going to play ball in Tatman's vacant lot.

VIC: Smelly got an auto horn?

RUSH: He's going to beat on a dishpan with a club.

FLETCHER: Smelly is a good boy.

VIC: Smelly is the sweetest flower on the face of the earth.

FLETCHER: That's right.

VIC: I love Smelly.

FLETCHER: [*soberly*] Fine.

SADE: [*giggles*] Oh ish. [*to Vic*] What was so remarkable happened in the hat store?

VIC: My faith in human nature was revitalized. I walked out of that hat store with renewed warmth in my heart for my fellow men.

SADE: [*briefly*] Uh-huh.

VIC: Here's what happened: the gentleman that waited on me . . .

FLETCHER: "You are beautiful tonight, Helene."

SADE AND VIC: [*rather startled*] What?

FLETCHER: [*soberly*] That's what Rishigan Fishigan of Sishigan Michigan said to my landlady Mis' Keller.

VIC: Heck he did.

SADE: [*curiously*] What'd he say?

FLETCHER: "You are beautiful tonight, Helene."

RUSH: He said that in connection with romance, hey, Uncle Fletcher?

FLETCHER: [*gently*] Go down cellar, Rush honey.

RUSH: [*chuckles protestingly*] *Naw.*

FLETCHER: Love, romance and such junk is not for tiny children.

RUSH: [*contemptuous*] "Tiny children."

FLETCHER: [*with gentle dramatic warmth*] "You are beautiful tonight, Helene."

SADE: [*rather sharply*] Since when did Mis' Keller's name get to be Helene?

FLETCHER: It's not. It's Helen. "Helene" is the *fashionable* way of saying Helen.

SADE: Um.

FLETCHER: It's the way your bang-up blue-blooded dead-game *sport* says Helen.

SADE: Um.

FLETCHER: Rishigan Fishigan from Sishigan Michigan stood on the cistern lid there in the backyard last night oiling up his shoes. He had a toothpick in the corner of his mouth, he was wearing his leather necktie, his sleeve-garters, and his corduroy cap. He removed his toothpick from his mouth, he scratched his ankle, and he looked my landlady Mis' Keller right in the eye. And then, his voice quivering with romance, he said, "You are beautiful tonight, Helene."

SADE: Um.

VIC: What'd Mis' Keller do?

FLETCHER: She done what *any* woman would of done under the circumstances. She whimpered, tittered, and guffawed.

RUSH: Smelly Clark tells about a lady friend of his that . . .

FLETCHER: [*sternly*] Rush, I ordered you down cellar.

RUSH: [*chuckles*] Oh heck, I'm not . . .

FLETCHER: She done what *any* woman would of done under the circumstances. She whimpered, tittered, and guffawed. [*gently*] You can understand that, can't you, Sadie?

SADE: [*giggles*] I guess so.

FLETCHER: [*sharply*] You'd whimper, titter and guffaw *yourself* if some half-wit sauntered up to ya and said I love you Helene.

SADE: Yes, I expect I would.

FLETCHER: No doubt about it.

SADE: [*brief pause*] Now tell about the hat store, Vic.

VIC: I had bought the hat, paid for it, and received my change. I suddenly *thought* of something. "I'd like my *initials* put in this hat," I said. The clerk looked at me and smiled a little smile. "*Look* in the hat once," he murmured softly. I looked in the hat. There were the initials . . . *my* initials, "V. R. G." I was *astonished*. "How did *you* know my initials were V. R. G.?" I demanded. Once again a slow sweet enigmatic smile crossed his face. "You told me yourself in the course of our conversation," he said. And then I *remembered*. He had cleverly wormed the information out of me by means of shrewd questioning.

SADE: [*some distaste*] Seems to me you make an awful lot out of just . . .

VIC: [*eagerly*] No—listen. He said to me, "*My* name is Willis. What's yours?"

SADE: Oh, ish.

RUSH: Smelly Clark's Uncle Strap dearly loves to . . .

SADE: [*contempt*] "My name is Willis. What's yours?"

VIC: [*eagerly*] No, now—listen.

FLETCHER: This friend of mine that's a section foreman there in Boone Iowa told me one time . . .

VIC: [*to Sade*] He said, "My name is Willis. *Arthur* Willis. What's *your* name?" "Victor Gook," I told him. "Haven't you got any *middle* name?" he teased.

SADE: [*finds this childish*] Oh my.

VIC: "Sure I got a middle name," I said. "My middle name is Rodney."

SADE: These is grown-up men talking.

VIC: [*ignores this*] He'd learned my name was Victor Rodney Gook, so he was able to put two and two together and figure out my initials were V. R. G.

SADE: [*dryly*] Boy, he's one brainy fella and no mistake.

VIC: [*defensively*] Just the same it made me feel good that a fellow creature out of the generous warmth of his heart went to the bother of . . . [*pounding on dishpan in distance*]

RUSH: [*promptly*] There's Smelly Clark pounding on his dishpan. I got to go.

SADE: Where you going?

RUSH: Tatman's vacant lot.

[*auto horn*]

VIC: [*promptly*] There's the boss; there's Mr. Ruebush.

SADE: Be home for supper?

VIC: Right on the dot.

[*different auto horn*]

FLETCHER: [*promptly*] There's Gumpox honking the horn on his garbage wagon. I'll be sauntering on outdoors, Sadie honey.

SADE: [*cheerfully*] *Everybody* leaving me.

[*telephone rings*]

VIC AND RUSH: Telephone is ringing, telephone is ringing.

SADE: I'll get it.

FLETCHER: [*off a ways*] Good-bye.

SADE: Good-bye, Uncle Fletcher. So long, fellas.

VIC: [*moving off*] So long, kiddo.

RUSH: [*moving off*] So long, Mom.

SADE: [*to phone*] Hello? [*warmly*] Oh *yes*, lady. Why, bless your old sweet heart, you *did* call back. [*giggles affectionately*] Gee, lady, I *still* haven't got anything to *say*. It was just such a still quiet lonesome afternoon I felt like I had to *talk* to somebody. *Isn't* it quiet though. Person runs into quiet afternoons like this every so

often. Yes. [*giggles*] Well . . . quietness is *nice* sometimes. Gollies
. . . I don't think I've spoken to a soul all day. No. [*and then
briskly*] *Who* had an operation, Ruthie? Mis' McFreemer? Which
Mis' McFreemer? The one on South Morris Avenue or the one on
West Monroe Street?

*Which concludes another interlude at the small house half-way up
in the next block.*

15

Books

Well sir, it's early evening as we enter the small house half-way up in the next blook now, and here in the living room we find all our friends assembled. Mr. Victor Gook occupies his easy chair beneath the floor lamp; Mrs. Victor Gook quietly darns socks on the davenport; and young Mr. Rush Gook, established at the library table, reads a volume of feverish fiction. And at length remarks:

RUSH: By gosh, Gov, Third-Lieutenant Clinton Stanley makes two touch-downs at one an' the same time.
VIC: Amazing.
RUSH: I'll say.
VIC: How's he work it?
RUSH: Well, he's a student at Yale College an' also a student at Harvard College. Both Harvard an' Yale are playin' football games on the same Saturday. Harvard's playin' the University of Europe an' Yale's playin' the University of South America.
VIC: I bet Third-Lieutenant Stanley plays for Yale an' Harvard both.
RUSH: [*chuckles*] Yeah. An' they line up the two gridirons in a row. Third-Lieutenant Stanley gets the ball an' runs the length of one gridiron an' then keeps right on going an' runs the length of the *other* gridiron. Two touch-downs at one an' the same time.
VIC: Um.
SADE: Is that a *new* Third-Lieutenant Stanley book, Rush?
RUSH: Yeah. "Third-Lieutenant Clinton Stanley on the Campus," or "Winning Laurels for Old Alma Mater."

114

SADE: What become of the *other* one that was around here?

RUSH: "Third-Lieutenant Clinton Stanley's Big Love Affair"?

SADE: Where he give the Arabian Princess the gunny-sack full of diamonds.

RUSH: Yeah, "Third-Lieutenant Clinton Stanley's Big Love Affair." I give it back to Blue-tooth Johnson.

SADE: *I* was readin' that.

RUSH: Yeah?

SADE: Off an' *on,* I was.

RUSH: I'll get it *back* from Blue-Tooth.

SADE: Oh, don't make any difference. Prob'ly wouldn't of finished it anyway. How'd it turn out? Did Third-Lieutenant Stanley escape from that sheik fella that was gonna jab him with the knife?

RUSH: Sure. In fact he *assassinated* that sheik fella. Hit him with a camel.

VIC: A camel?

RUSH: Uh-huh. Third-Lieutenant Stanley picked up a camel by the hind feet an' used him like a club an' give that sheik such a bash in the head he expired on the spot.

VIC: Um.

SADE: I don't know as books like that is *good* for boys. [*to Vic*] Say, speakin' of books, *we're* gonna get a book.

VIC: Yeah?

SADE: [*giggles*] From our brick-mush man.

VIC: How so?

SADE: Premium. After you've bought so much brick-mush you're entitled to a free book.

VIC: What's the name of the book?

SADE: Ya got to choose from a long list. Rush, out on top the buffet there's a little leaflet. Go bring it, will ya?

RUSH: Okay.

SADE: We'll select our book.

VIC: Who's *giving* these premiums? The brick-mush man himself?

SADE: Yeah. His own idea.

VIC: He must be kind of an enterprising chap.

SADE: He is. Full of push an' go. I bet he gets rich. Why, he told me this morning as soon as one of his customers buys enough brick-mush to add up to a ton he's gonna give 'em a free bass-viol.

VIC: Bass-viol?

SADE: One of those monstrous big *fiddles,* ya know. Hafta stand it on the floor to play it.

VIC: Isn't that kind of an odd premium?

SADE: [*giggles*] Yeah. But that's what he's gonna give to whoever buys a ton of his brick-mush first.

VIC: Quite an incentive to buy brick-mush. I need a bass-viol so bad I can't hardly stand it.

SADE: I expect he knows where he can buy bass-viols *cheap* or something. He's a business man through an' through. [*to Rush*] Thanks.

RUSH: This what ya mean?

SADE: Uh-huh. [*to Vic*] I think books is kinda odd premiums too, to give.

VIC: How much brick-mush did we *buy* to be entitled to the book?

SADE: I don't know. He told me but I never paid much attention. He keeps track on a piece of paper, see? When we buy brick-mush he marks it down.

VIC: Um.

RUSH: By gosh, Gov, Third-Lieutenant Clinton Stanley hazes fifteen college freshmen singlehanded.

VIC: Sometimes I hope somebody pastes Third-Lieutenant Clinton Stanley on the snoot.

RUSH: [*reads*] " 'You better watch out,' said one big lubberly freshman. But Third-Lieutenant Stanley only smiled. His hand darted out with the speed of lightning an' a moment later his victim lay writhing on the campus with a broken leg."

VIC: Pretty rough hazing.

RUSH: Yes, indeed.

SADE: These books don't sound like they'd be very *interesting*.

VIC: What *are* some of 'em?

SADE: "Dorothy an' Her Daddy or Romping Among the Buttercups."

VIC: These books for kids?

SADE: *This* one evidently is.

VIC: How'd ya like to be all by yourself in a big old house with a storm raging outside an' have nothin' to read but "Dorothy an' Her Daddy or Romping Among the Buttercups"? Wouldn't ya be scared?

SADE: Yeah. Here's "A Brief Biography of the Father-in-law of Tyson R. Poppell."

VIC: Who's Tyson R. Poppell?

SADE: Don't say. "Tricks a One-legged Man Can Perform with a Dead Gorilla!"

VIC: [*chuckles*] Aw.

SADE: [*laughs*] Yeah. *That's* here. "Tricks a One-legged Man Can Perform with a Dead Gorilla."

VIC: If ya knew a one-legged man with a dead gorilla, that'd be the ideal Christmas present for him, wouldn't it?

SADE: Uh-huh. "A Report of the Work of the Sub-committee on the Boundary-changing Issues of South-Central Indiana." *That* certainly sounds interesting.

VIC: Yeah. Once ya pick it up ya couldn't lay it down till ya finished it.

SADE: Know what I bet?

VIC: What do you bet?

SADE: I bet these are second-*hand* books. I bet our brick-mush man's got a whole basement full of old books an' that's why he's givin' 'em away as premiums.

VIC: You're probably right.

SADE: Sure.

VIC: Well, which one shall we select? The one about the guy's father-in-law or the one about . . .

SADE: There's lots more here. "The Life of U. S. McGraw" . . . "The Romance of the Hinge" . . . "Twinkling Tunes for Tiny Tots" . . . here's a familiar name, "Sightseeing In Sunny Kansas." We got that in the bookcase right now.

VIC: Ever read it?

SADE: [*giggles*] No.

VIC: Where'd we get it?

SADE: [*giggles*] Rush found it layin' on the streetcar tracks.

RUSH: [*looking up*] What's that?

SADE: The book "Sightseeing In Sunny Kansas." You found it on the streetcar tracks.

RUSH: Oh, uh-huh.

SADE: It's in the bookcase.

RUSH: Not any more.

SADE: What become of it?

RUSH: I give it to Elton Keefer. He traded me a skate key.

SADE: Elton *Keefer?*

RUSH: Yeah. His father's our brick-mush man.

VIC: *That* certainly throws a light on this premium business.

SADE: Sure does. Well, if *he* ain't the tricky somebody.

VIC: He's a shrewd operator.

RUSH: Elton's just like him. Elton Keefer'll swap ya outa your shoes.

SADE: As I remember that book it was all *frayed.*

RUSH: Yeah, an' somebody'd drew mustaches on the pictures of the people.

SADE: Some premium.

VIC: Yeah.

SADE: [*inspects the list again*] How'd ya like to read *this?* "Fun and Excitement You Can Have While Polishing Silverware."

VIC: [*chuckles*]

SADE: [*giggles*] Goodness.

RUSH: Gov, Third-Lieutenant Clinton Stanley lands his . . .

VIC: I'm gettin' just a little *tired* of Third-Lieutenant Clinton Stanley.

RUSH: No, but he lands his airplane right on the baseball diamond an' jumps out just in time to catch a high fly an' win the game for dear ol' Yale.

VIC: What the heck is *that* one doin' in *college?* Up on the window-sill in the bathroom the other day I saw a book called "Third-Lieutenant Clinton Stanley as President of a South Sea Island Republic." He must be at least sixty years old.

RUSH: Yeah, that *is* kinda peculiar. There's *one* volume in the series entitled "Third-Lieutenant Clinton Stanley in the Tropics or Twenty Years among Savage Cannibals."

VIC: An' *now* he's in *college.*

RUSH: Yeah. [*reads*] "Hastily he cut his motor an' swooped down on the baseball diamond for a perfect three-point landing. The pretty girls in the stands screamed with joy an' Third-Lieutenant Stanley gallantly doffed his cap. His old mother proudly . . ."

VIC: His old *mother?*

RUSH: [*chuckles*] Uh-huh.

VIC: Last I heard of *her* she was walkin' a tightrope across Niagara Falls.

RUSH: [*chuckles*] Maybe *she's* attending college too. [*reads*] "His old mother . . ."

SADE: Rush, is our copy of "The Soul of Bernie Gummerman" in the bookcase?

RUSH: Don't know.

SADE: Look an' see once, will ya?

RUSH: Okay.

SADE: [*to Vic*] *That's* down on this list.

VIC: "The Soul of Bernie Gummerman"?

SADE: Yes.

VIC: Where'd we ever get a-hold of that?

SADE: Mis' Grink lent it to me one time. I never thought to return it when they moved to Tennessee.

RUSH: [*off a little*] No.

SADE: [*raises voice*] Not there?

RUSH: No.

SADE: Did you give it to the Keefer boy?

RUSH: By gosh, I believe I did that.

SADE: Just like I thought.

RUSH: It wasn't much of a book, Mom. It'd been left out in the rain an' was all fat and puffy, remember?

SADE: [*no comment*]

RUSH: I expect I could get it *back* if ya want it.

SADE: [*giggles*] I can get it back *myself.* I've bought so much brick-mush I'm entitled to it as a premium.

RUSH: Um.

VIC: How about callin' Fred and Ruthie an' stirring up a little Five Hundred?

SADE: They got company tonight. Edna Warbel an' her man.

How'd ya like to read "Famous Indian Fights of South Dakota"?

VIC: Fine. Wonder if Ike Kneesuffer's home.

SADE: He's home but he's workin'.

VIC: Yeah?

SADE: She told me this *afternoon* that's what he was gonna do.

VIC: Um.

SADE: "The Great Warm Heart of My Uncle, Oscar Y. Slump."

VIC: How about the Bijou?

SADE: I don't care.

VIC: What's on?

SADE: What's on at the Bijou, Rush?

RUSH: Gloria Golden in Foreign Legion something.

SADE: "Foreign Legion, Farewell" it is. Mis' Donahue saw it. Here's a book called "How to Handle Ill-tempered Horses."

VIC: Um.

SADE: Uncle *Fletcher* could of used *this*. He had an ill-tempered horse back in Dixon years ago. Kicked him in the shin.

VIC: Who kicked who?

SADE: Uncle Fletcher.

VIC: Kicked the horse?

SADE: No, the other way around. Hurt something fierce. Boy, did he growl at the supper table. "Drat that horse," he said. I remember it so well . . . Bess an' I were visitin'.

VIC: Um.

SADE: [*reads*] "I Hate Money."

VIC: Huh?

SADE: [*giggles*] 'Nother one of the free books you can get if ya buy enough brick-mush.

VIC: How about the Bijou?

SADE: All right. "Little Princess Peggy an' Her Punkin-headed Pig."

RUSH: Gov, Third-Lieutenant Clinton Stanley hurls the body of a . . .

VIC: Oh, to heck with Third-Lieutenant Clinton Stanley!

RUSH: [*chuckles*] Okay.

SADE: Last book on the list is "East Duckworth, Oklahoma, Land of Sunset Dreams."

VIC: Um.
SADE: Well . . . [*yawns*] . . . picture show?

Which concludes another brief interlude at the small house half-way up in the next block.

First broadcast 1938.

16

How Neighbor Ladies Greet Each Other When on the Outs

Well sir, it's about seven-thirty o'clock in the evening as we enter the small house half-way up in the next block now, and here in the living room we find our friends abiding quietly at home. The male members of the family face each other across the library table playing rummy. Wife and mother Sade occupies a corner of the davenport, glancing listlessly through the newspaper. Young Rush is speaking at the moment and we hear him say:

RUSH: If I had saved queens instead of nines an' aces instead of fours I'd of beat you all hollow.
VIC: Those statistics can hardly be expected to interest me.
RUSH: Why?
VIC: I won the game fair an' square. A detailed recital of how *you* might of won I find very dull.
RUSH: No, but *look;* you discarded the queen of diamonds, didn't ya?
VIC: I forget. Whose deal?
RUSH: Mine.
VIC: Pick up the tickets then.
RUSH: [*persistent*] You discarded the queen of diamonds an' I could of had it. But instead I drew from the pack an' got the four of clubs. Well, if I had *taken* that queen of diamonds I . . .
VIC: Pish, pash, push, an' posh.
RUSH: Huh?

VIC: Your fascinating data leaves me cold. I s'pose if we run a foot race an' I come in six miles ahead of you, instead of slappin' me on the back an' sayin' "Congratulations, old man" you'd slop out a long speech about how your supper disagreed with you an' a slight limp contributed to . . .

RUSH: *No.* I'm only explaining how . . .

VIC: Yip, yap, yep, an' yup. *Deal.* Like to be dealt in this hand, Doctor Sleetch?

SADE: [*listless*] Play cards?

VIC: Sure.

SADE: All right.

VIC: [*chuckles*] Don't do us any big *favors.*

SADE: A few rummies might cheer me up.

VIC: Are you dismal, sad, mournful an' blue?

SADE: No . . . just kinda half-way thoughtful an' stodgy is all.

VIC: "Bemused" is the word. [*to Rush*] Milk-bottle, old egg-crate, step to the dining room an' bring Mama in a chair.

RUSH: Um.

VIC: [*to Sade*] What's hot in the newspaper tonight?

SADE: Nothin'.

VIC: Why are you dismal, sad, mournful an' blue?

SADE: [*giggles*] I'm not dismal, sad, mournful an' blue.

VIC: Why are you bemused?

SADE: Oh . . . person gets that way sometimes.

VIC: Uh-huh.

SADE: Last five ten minutes I been thinkin' about this darn *neighborhood.*

VIC: Yeah?

SADE: It's such a *jumble.*

VIC: Jungle?

SADE: *Jumble.*

VIC: Why?

SADE: Well, what started me *off* was thinkin' about Mis' *Husher* bein' mad.

VIC: I s'pose it *is* depressing to have enemies.

SADE: Oh, she's no *enemy.* We speak. But, of course, there's *chilliness.* An' a person is uncomfortable when . . . [*to Rush*] Thanks, Willie.

RUSH: Not at all.

SADE: [*rather vaguely*] Rummies, huh?

VIC: Like to play some *other* three-handed game?

SADE: *Rummies* is all right. A few rummies might cheer me up.

RUSH: [*jovially and archly yet with teeth in his speech*] Gov, we oughta extract a promise from Mom to pay *attention* this trip.

VIC: Yeah.

RUSH: She always begins talkin' an' forgets she's *in* a card game.

VIC: Uh-huh.

RUSH: [*archly chuckling*] Isn't that *right*, Mom?

SADE: [*listlessly*] Something on your chin.

RUSH: Where?

SADE: [*folds her upper lip over her lower in order to designate the spot, thereby seriously impeding her diction*] Right here.

RUSH: [*brief pause*] Hunk of coconut.

VIC: [*to Rush*] As soon as you've removed trash, debris, an' other impedimenta from your countenance please deal out the pasteboards. Seven apiece, ya know, in a three-handed game.

RUSH: [*somewhat irritated*] I know.

SADE: [*to Vic*] No . . . sittin' on the davenport glancing through the newspaper an' thinkin' about Mis' Husher bein' starchy with me put me in mind of *other* chillinesses in the neighborhood.

VIC: Um?

SADE: [*little giggle*] It's *such* a mixed-up jumble.

VIC: Why?

SADE: Well, Mis' Husher's mad at *me*.

VIC: Uh-huh.

SADE: Mis' Donahue's mad at Mis' Scott.

VIC: Um.

SADE: Mis' Scott is mad at Mis' Razorscum.

VIC: Um.

SADE: Mis' Razorscum an' Mis' Harris barely nod. Also there's coolness between me an' Mis' Scott. Coolness between me an' Mis' Harris *too*. On account of that Christmas card defugalty, ya know.

VIC: Uh-huh.

SADE: Workin' it the other way around now, Mis' Scott is mad at Mis' Donahue.

VIC: Uh-huh.

RUSH: [*briskly*] *All* right, people.
SADE: [*to Vic*] Mis' Razorscum is mad at Mis' Scott.
VIC: Um.
RUSH: [*briskly*] Here we go.
SADE: [*to Vic*] Mis' Harris an' Mis' Razorscum are on the outs. Mis' Harris, Mis' Scott, an' Mis' Husher are all frosty with *me*.
VIC: Um.
RUSH: [*briskly*] O. K. friends, a good old jolly dog-eat-dog game of cards.
SADE: [*to Vic, giggling wryly*] So it's a funny, funny business.
VIC: Yeah. Believe it's your first play.
RUSH: Yep. Your first play, Mom. I turned up the seven of clubs for ya.
SADE: [*thoughtfully*] I don't *care* about Mis' *Scott* bein' chilly with me. Tell the actual truth that's the way I'd rather *have* it. Otherwise it's arms-around-the-neck dear-old-chum run-back-and-forth-to-each-other's-*kitchen* nineteen times a day. An' that's a great big bother an' nuisance.
RUSH: [*briskly*] Yes sir, Mom, you're entitled to the seven of clubs.
SADE: [*vaguely*] What?
RUSH: [*gaily*] Tut tut now. Watch your step. Remember what we *agreed.*
SADE: Agreed?
RUSH: [*jovially*] We extracted a promise you'd pay attention to the game.
SADE: Is it my rummies?
RUSH: [*brightly*] Yep. I dealt an' it's your first play.
SADE: I better investigate what I got in my hand here.
RUSH: [*brightly*] Sure thing.
SADE: [*without particular interest*] Kings, queens, an' jacks by the bushel. Never *seen* so many face-cards.
RUSH: [*chidingly*] Well, don't *tell* us.
SADE: They couldn't of been *shuffled* very thorough. I got all face cards here except one. Ten of hearts.
RUSH: Don't *tell* us what you're holdin'. You'll give your *hand* away.
SADE: Um.
RUSH: [*to Vic*] Reminds me of Blue-tooth Johnson.

VIC: Does it?

RUSH: Blue-tooth attempts to pull off a stunt in algebra class where he asks Mis' Monroe a question where if she gives him the correct answer he'll get a free hint about stuff in a written examination. I've never seen it work though. She just gives him a cold level glance an' says, "If you'll stop by my desk after class I'll . . .

SADE: [*idly*] It's funny how the *friends* line up.

VIC: Beg pardon?

SADE: It's funny how the *friends* line up here in the neighborhood.

VIC: Is it?

RUSH: [*politely*] I don't believe you *played,* Mom, did you?

SADE: [*negative*] Uh-uh. [*to Vic*] I'm friends with Mis' Donahue an' Mis' Razorscum. Mis' Husher's friends with Mis' Harris, Mis' Donahue, an' Mis' Scott. Mis' Scott is friends with Mis' Husher an' nobody else.

VIC: Um.

SADE: 'Course nobody's tooth-and-nail hot fightin' jumpin' up an' *down* mad at anybody. It's just the *chilliness.* [*quotes an embattled lady, courteous though distant*] "*Good* morning, Mis' Husher. *Such* a grand day, *isn't* it?"

VIC: Um.

SADE: [*quotes*] "*Afternoon,* Mis' Razorscum. Your clothes look *so* white on the line."

VIC: Um.

SADE: Ladies lean over backwards, don't ya know, bein' polite to the neighbors they're mad at.

VIC: [*little chuckle*]

RUSH: [*somewhat frosty*] Have you decided to *take* the seven of clubs, Mom?

SADE: [*negative*] Uh-uh.

RUSH: You prefer to draw from the pack?

SADE: [*to Vic*] Mis' *Scott* is the worst in the *politeness* department.

VIC: Is she?

SADE: [*giggles*] I hope to pass *away* she is.

VIC: Um.

SADE: Oughta hear her when she bumps into Mis' Donahue along the alley or in Croucher's grocery or some place. See, they just had their squabble a little over a week ago. It's still fresh an' boiling.

Calls for extra *special* axle-grease an' peach-butter. That is it calls for extra special axle-grease an' peach-butter as far as Mis' *Scott* is concerned. Mis' *Donahue* don't *bother*. She nods an' says good morning but she don't *gush*. It's Mis' *Scott* that *gushes*.

VIC: Um.

RUSH: [*coldly*] Mom, if we're gonna play rummy I suggest . . .

SADE: [*gently*] I wonder if I could be allowed to tell what I'm telling, Rush? [*to Vic*] I was in Croucher's grocery just *yesterday* when they were. Mis' Donahue was siftin' through a box of strawberries an' Mis' Scott waltzed in from the butcher shop part of the store. Why, you'd of thought she'd spotted her long-lost uncle.

VIC: Um.

SADE: [*quoting*] "Why, Mis' *Donahue*," she says, "looks like *somebody* is gonna have *strawberries* for supper. They're *so* red an' juicy this season, *aren't* they?" [*frivolous gay laughter*] "Ha, ha, ha, ha. Ha, ha, ha, ha." An' then she turned to the grocery clerk all smiles an' sweetness an' give her order.

VIC: Um.

SADE: [*giggles*] It was the limit.

VIC: [*after a pause*] Shall we proceed with the rummy game?

SADE: All right. No, there's ladies an' ladies. You take Mis' *Harris* now. No slather an' slush in *her* make-up. With her it's strickly a nose-in-the-air I'm-mad-and-I-don't-care-who-knows-it proposition.

VIC: Um.

RUSH: [*coldly*] I realize perfectly well that any remark or suggestion from me will be greeted with contemptuous . . .

SADE: [*briefly*] You *still* got stuff on your face.

RUSH: Where?

SADE: [*folds her upper lip over her lower, impeding her diction*] Same place. Right here. You never wiped it off.

RUSH: Ump.

VIC: Sadie, I see you have the choice of picking up that seven of clubs or drawing from the pack. Which is your . . .

SADE: [*giggles*] Ruthie *Stembottom's* the *funny*-actin' guy when she bumps into somebody she's on the outs with.

VIC: Um.

SADE: Gets that pitiful little timid *rabbit* expression on her face.

VIC: Um.

SADE: Makes me so *mad* sometimes. I could just *shake* her. "Ruthie," I tell her, "*you* don't hafta behave like you been horsewhipped." "*I* know," she says, "but I can't *help* it. I feel so embarrassed an' terrible when I meet people I've had squabbles with."
VIC: [*polite chuckle*]
SADE: [*giggles*] Ain't that Ruthie for ya though?
VIC: Yeah.
SADE: Got as much gumption an' backbone as anybody else but can't come out in the *open* with it.
VIC: Um.
SADE: [*shaking her head sadly*] Ruthie, Ruthie, Ruthie.
VIC: Um.
SADE: [*cheerfully*] Whose turn here in the rummies?
RUSH: [*almost explosive*] *Yours.*
SADE: [*after a pregnant pause, gently*] Why, Rush Gook.
RUSH: [*uneasy*] I . . . never meant to speak so loud.
SADE: [*gently*] Is this what comes of card-playing, Vic?
VIC: [*little chuckle*] We haven't *played* any cards *yet*. We've been sittin' here a quarter of an hour an' it's your first play an' you still haven't . . .
SADE: [*sadly*] So this is what comes of card-playin', is it? *Well.*
RUSH: [*uneasy*] I never meant to speak so loud, Mom.
SADE: [*gently*] It's *my* turn in the rummies?
RUSH: Yeah.
SADE: [*gently*] All right. Let's see, I can either take that seven or draw from the pile, can't I?
RUSH: Yes.
SADE: [*gently*] I better investigate the rummies I'm *holdin'*.
RUSH: Um.
SADE: [*after a pause, to Vic*] Ya know who's just the *opposite* from Ruthie, don't ya?
VIC: No.
SADE: When she bumps into somebody she's on the outs with, I mean.
VIC: No.
SADE: Mis' *Brighton.*
VIC: Yeah?

SADE: [*giggles*] Oh *boy*.

VIC: Um.

SADE: [*giggles*] It's no pitiful little timid rabbit stuff with *her*. It's mutterin' an' shoulder-shruggin' an' scornful titterin' an' all *kinds* of wild actions.

VIC: Um.

SADE: I was in the Underwear there at Yamilton's one time. I was *shoppin'* with Mis' Brighton. Well sir, who should stroll up but Mis' Keeney. Mis' Brighton an' Mis' Keeney had had a squabble. Mis' Keeney come up to the counter an' told the clerk what she wanted. Mis' Brighton commenced to titter an' grunt an' mutter an' snicker an' choke till I was actually embarrassed.

VIC: Um.

SADE: [*giggles*] Boy.

VIC: Um.

SADE: Oh, there's ladies an' ladies an' no mistake.

VIC: Um.

SADE: Ladies an' ladies an' no mistake.

VIC: Um.

SADE: [*after a pause*] Still my turn in the rummies?

RUSH: [*just a shade on the brief side*] Yeah.

SADE: [*gently*] What?

RUSH: [*like a lamb*] It's still your turn.

SADE: Uh-huh. [*thoughtfully*] Let's see, what'd I better *do* here . . . .

Which concludes another brief interlude at the small house half-way up in the next block.

First broadcast 1941.

17

Manual for Wives of Sky-Brothers in the Sacred Stars of the Milky Way

Well sir, Mr. and Mrs. Victor Gook are in the living room as we join them at the small house half-way up in the next block now. It's late afternoon, and the master of the ménage has just arrived home from the office. And his wife is saying:

SADE: [*dryly*] I received a peachy letter from lodge headquarters this afternoon.
VIC: [*surprised*] *You* did?
SADE: They wanta sell me a book.
VIC: Was the letter *addressed* to you?
SADE: Sure.
VIC: What kind of a book?
SADE: [*little giggle*] A fine elegant book I'm s'posed to *study*.
VIC: What's the name of it?
SADE: I don't know. "A Manual for Wives of Sky-Brothers in the Sacred Stars of the Milky Way" or something.
VIC: Where's the letter?
SADE: Believe I left it on the kitchen sink. Rush still out there?
VIC: Yeah. Studyin' algebra.
SADE: [*calls*] Willie, bring in that yella envelope an' trash on the sink.
RUSH: [*off*] O. K.
SADE: [*to Vic*] Them Chicago fellas sure got their nerve.
VIC: Why?

130

SADE: [*giggles*] They tell me I oughta wash my face nice an' clean so my husband won't be ashamed of me.

VIC: [*incredulous*] Aw.

SADE: Truth. One of the rules to be followed by wives of lodge members. [*quotes*] "Keep the face an' hands clean at all times."

VIC: Um.

SADE: [*with some heat*] Who are *they* to insinuate I go around with a dirty face?

RUSH: [*coming up*] That stuff cookin' on the gas-stove O. K., Mom?

SADE: Why?

RUSH: [*up*] Makin' a gurgling sound like it needed water.

SADE: It's all right. You through studyin' algebra?

RUSH: For the time being. I may get in a few more licks after supper. Hello, Gov.

VIC: I believe I greeted you in the *kitchen* a moment ago.

RUSH: Yeah, ya did.

VIC: Then I won't waste my breath with further hellos.

RUSH: [*chuckles*] O. K. Here's your letter, Mom.

SADE: Thanks.

RUSH: [*to Vic*] Be interested in a hand or two of rummy?

VIC: [*negative*] Uh-uh.

RUSH: Smelly Clark passed an astonishing remark this afternoon. He was sittin' on a bench in the gymnasium takin' his shoes off an' he noticed a hole in his sock an' says, "Fellas, let me call your attention to . . ."

SADE: [*to Vic*] Your chum Homer U. *McDancy* wrote this elegant book lodge headquarters wants to sell me. [*reads*] "A Manual for Wives of Sky-Brothers in the Sacred Stars of the Milky Way," by Homer U. McDancy.

VIC: [*interested*] Well.

RUSH: He's on your all-star marching team, isn't he, Gov?

VIC: Yeah. [*to Sade*] They didn't send you the book *itself*, did they, kiddo?

SADE: No. Just samples an' selections from the different chapters. Here's a list of rules. The one about keeping my face clean is right up on top. [*reads*] "To be a true an' loyal wife of a Sky-Brother in the Sacred Stars of the Milky Way, madame will take pains with the neatness of her person. She will never appear in her husband's presence with soiled hands or dirty face."

VIC: Um.

SADE: [*strong distaste*] Now I *ask* you!

VIC: [*little chuckle*] Well, it's good *advice*.

SADE: Homer U. McDancy must be in the same class with *those other* idiots.

VIC: What other idiots?

SADE: H. K. Fleeber, Y. Y. Flirch, Robert an' Slobert Hink.

VIC: [*prefers not to resent this*] Read me your letter.

SADE: I dropped it on the floor. Pick it up, will ya, sonny?

RUSH: [*O. K.*] Um.

SADE: Here's *another* beautiful rule I'm s'posed to follow.

VIC: Um.

SADE: [*reads*] "To be a true an' loyal wife of a Sky-Brother in The Sacred Stars of the Milky Way, madame will refrain from stealing property belonging to others, using coarse language, and engaging in rough street brawls."

VIC: [*some distaste*] That *is* pretty *stupid*.

SADE: [*airily*] No, it's fine advice. I'm so used to stealing property belonging to others, though, an' using coarse language, an' engaging in rough street brawls I don't know whether I could quit now or *not*.

VIC: [*to Rush*] Read that letter, George.

RUSH: [*O. K.*] Um.

SADE: [*to Vic*] Three dollars an' seventy-five cents they want for this dandy book.

VIC: Um.

SADE: Believe I'll send for a *dozen*.

RUSH: [*reads*] "Mrs. Victor R. Gook. Madame: We take pleasure in announcing a new volume just off the press. "A Manual for Wives of Sky-Brothers in the Sacred Stars of the Milky Way," by Homer U. McDancy. Mr. McDancy is a distinguished author residing in East Brain, Oregon, and his latest work promises to set high standards for books in the practical field. You will find enclosed a leaflet containing excerpts from the Manual. We hope, Mrs. Gook, that you will . . ."

SADE: [*dryly*] . . . cough up three seventy-five.

RUSH: [*looking up*] Huh?

SADE: [*dryly*] "We hope, Mrs. Gook, that you will cough up three dollars an' seventy-five cents."

RUSH: [*chuckles*] Yeah . . . that's what it's leading *up* to.

VIC: Give me the letter, Tomato juice.

RUSH: Um.

SADE: Latin also I'm s'posed to learn it says here.

RUSH: [*chuckles*] Yeah?

SADE: [*reads*] "To be a true an' loyal wife of a Sky-Brother in the Sacred Stars of the Milky Way, madame will acquaint herself with a treasury of Latin phrases to be committed to memory an' recited at mealtimes. Here are a few typical examples."

RUSH: [*little chuckle*] Read 'em.

SADE: [*reads*] "In hoc spittle dum cluck yeep. Ad agricola spinach est fobo raymond beerman itch. Ickle yamp libertas cum cornucopia feesh." [*giggles*] Goodness.

RUSH: [*chuckles*] Read some more.

SADE: [*giggles*] No.

RUSH: [*chuckles*] Go ahead.

SADE: [*giggles*] At mealtimes I sit down to the table but instead of sayin' "Please pass the potatoes," I say . . . [*consults leaflet*] . . . "Yammer fump ad Gallia divisa tres partes hunk."

RUSH AND SADE: [*laugh*]

VIC: [*soberly*] It's a *handsome* enough book.

SADE: Is it?

VIC: [*reads*] "Mr. McDancy's volume is bound in fine red leather, inscribed with gold. It is printed on Bible paper and furnishes a very attractive adornment for the bookcase or library table."

SADE: It *should* . . . for all *that* money.

VIC: "Copies personally autographed by Mr. McDancy, four dollars an' a quarter."

SADE: Charges fifty cents for just writing his name, huh?

VIC: Um.

SADE: Ink must be *expensive* in Oregon.

VIC: [*reads*] "Copies with a photograph of Mr. McDancy in full lodge regalia serving as a frontispiece, five dollars an' ten cents."

SADE: Um.

VIC: [*reads*] "Copies with photograph an' autograph *both,* six dollars an' a half."

SADE: *Those* are the copies *I* want. A whole gunny-sack full of 'em.

VIC: Um.

RUSH: Another nice rule for ya to follow, Mom.

SADE: What's that?

RUSH: [*reads*] "To be a true an' loyal wife of a Sky-Brother in the Sacred Stars of the Milky Way, madame will see that the home is kept swept and dusted at all times. It is suggested that madame purchase a broom and use it regularly."

SADE: [*dryly*] Good old Homer U. McDancy. He's right up to snuff. Rush, wanta go to the store an' buy me a broom? I've always wondered what a broom looks like.

VIC: [*seriously enough*] *I'm* surprised at this nonsense *myself,* Sade. A bunch of *nit*-wits must of filtered into Lodge Headquarters. I can't understand why they'd go to the expense of publishing any such dumb book as they describe on that leaflet.

SADE: Homer U. McDancy is about as big a nit-wit as *anybody.*

VIC: [*thoughtfully*] He's s'posed to be smart. H. K. Fleeber wrote me one time and said McDancy was one of the brainiest men he'd ever met. Taught school as a young fella.

SADE: Um.

RUSH: [*chuckling*] Were you listening, Gov, when Mom read the Latin?

VIC: No.

RUSH: Slop him out some Latin, Mom.

SADE: [*giggles, negative*] Uh-uh.

RUSH: Go ahead.

VIC: Is there some Latin in the leaflet?

RUSH: [*chuckles*] Sure.

SADE: [*giggles*] It's trash I'm s'posed to memorize an' then recite to my husband at suppertime.

VIC: Um.

SADE: I sit down to the table an' instead of saying, "Would you mind passing the butter, please, Victor?" I say . . . [*consults leaflet*] . . . "Yop voomer in pluribus hunk. In hoc signo veni vidi webster stockdale horse. Ip extra-curricular feep."

RUSH AND SADE: [*laugh*]

VIC: [seriously] I'm surprised at this nonsense. Homer U. McDancy is a member of the lodge all-star marching team too. I can't understand headquarters giving an honor like that to a lame-brain.

SADE: There's plenty other lame-brains on that marching team.

VIC: [coldly] Are there?

SADE: Well—H. K. Fleeber.

VIC: [coldly] You're not even acquainted with H. K. Fleeber.

SADE: No, I'm not. But he sent me a pair of men's easy-slippers at Christmastime addressed to "Charlie, Gus, Walter, an' Margaret." What'd he send you, Willie?"

RUSH: [chuckles] A pipe without any stem on it addressed to "Hazel, Eddie, Herman, and Fat."

SADE: [to Vic] H. K. Fleeber for ya.

VIC: Name over some more lame-brains on the all-star marching team.

SADE: Everybody knows Y. Y. Flirch isn't bright.

VIC: [coldly] Really?

SADE: Wears his shoes on the wrong feet.

VIC: [coldly] Does that conclude the list of lame-brains?

SADE: Are Robert an' Slobert Hink on your marching team?

VIC: Yes.

SADE: [dryly] If they're in their right minds I'll send my undershirt to Detroit Michigan parcel post.

VIC: [coldly] Do Robert an' Slobert wind up your list of lame-brains?

SADE: Who else is in the outfit?

VIC: O. X. Bellyman.

SADE: Don't know anything about him.

VIC: J. J. J. J. Stunbolt.

SADE: Don't know anything about him either.

VIC: I. Edison Box an' Harry Fie.

SADE: [negative] Uh-uh.

RUSH: Another nice rule for ya to follow, Mom.

SADE: Um.

RUSH: "To be a true an' loyal wife of a Sky-Brother in the Sacred Stars of the Milky Way, madame will at all times be cheerful, truthful, and obedient. She will be on the alert to anticipate her husband's slightest wish."

SADE: [*airily*] Trust *me*, Homer.

RUSH: [*chuckles*] Shucks.

SADE: [*to Vic*] Going someplace?

VIC: [*not ill-humored*] Ike Kneesuffer's home. I told him I might drop around for a game or two of indoor horseshoes before supper.

SADE: Um.

VIC: [*moving off*] What time we eatin'?

SADE: I *think* my things'll be ready by six.

VIC: [*moving off*] O. K.

SADE: [*raises voice*] Better be back a little before then to be on the safe side though.

VIC: [*moving off*] O. K.

SADE: [*after a pause, to Rush*] Movie show might be nice this evening.

RUSH: Yeah.

SADE: What's on?

RUSH: Gloria Golden an' Four-fisted Frank Fuddleman.

SADE: Name of the picture?

RUSH: "Gazing into Your Eyes Like This Is Heaven, Minor-league Assistant Umpire Drake."

SADE: S'posed to be good?

RUSH: According to the *paper*.

SADE: [*little yawn*] Well, we'll see what your father says.

RUSH: Um.

SADE: Here . . . take this letter an' leaflet.

RUSH: Don't want 'em?

SADE: No.

RUSH: Garbage bucket?

SADE: [*yawns*] Garbage bucket.

Which concludes another brief interlude at the small house half-way up in the next block.

First broadcast 1941.

18

---·-◆◆◆-·---

Cleaning the Attic

Well *sir, it's a few minutes past nine o'clock in the morning as we enter the small house half-way up in the next block now, and we find Mrs. Victor Gook and her son, Mr. Rush Gook, not in the kitchen, not on the porch, not in the living room or dining room, not upstairs, but high aloft in the attic. The light is inadequate, and we're barely able to discern our friends. Young Rush is saying discontentedly:*

RUSH: Gosh, but it's *dark* and *stuffy* and *miserable* and *hot* and *dusty* up here.
SADE: Yes, hurry up and open the window.
RUSH: Aw, I'll peel off my shirt.
SADE: Open the winda first. We have to have light and air before we *choke.*
RUSH: Atmosphere like this makes an individual feel *mean.* Keep a person up here eight minutes, and they're liable to get the impulse to paste their grandmother one upside the snoot. I was readin' in the newspaper where four guys were cooped up in a boxcar, and they got ta stickin' pins in each other's flesh . . .
SADE: Slide that winda up, will ya?
RUSH: [*struggling with the window*] I'm tryin' to. It works stiff as a *horse.*
SADE: Ya want some *help?*
RUSH: Naw, *I'll* get it. [*loud, squeaky noise*]
SADE: Ish, what a nasty noise. It gives ya the willies.
RUSH: Fresh air feels *good.*
SADE: Yes, move to one side so a little blows on me.

RUSH: Ahhh . . .

SADE: What's the *matter?*

RUSH: So *that's* what's become of Rooster Davis' taped-up tennis ball.

SADE: Is it on the porch roof?

RUSH: Yeah. Wonder if I'm still *little* enough to climb out of this window.

SADE: *Look,* sonny, we're up here for *work.* We've put this attic off, and *put* this attic off. Now that we're here, let's make every minute count. I know it's not pleasant on a nice summer morning to have to breathe this awful stale old air . . .

RUSH: [*calling out the window*] Hey, Blue-tooth! [*to Sade*] Blue-tooth Johnson's strollin' up the street.

SADE: Well, leave him stroll. Now, the *first* thing that . . .

RUSH: [*out the window*] Blue-tooth, hey!

SADE: [*is impatient*] All right, all right.

RUSH: [*to Sade*] *Look,* he can't locate me. He's starin' at the house, but the tree hides me from view. C'mere and see the bewildered expression he's got on his *face.* [*calling out the window*] Look up over your *head,* Blue-tooth! I'm on top of the telegraph pole! [*chuckles*] [*to Sade*] He's lookin' *up.* [*calling out the window*] No, the *other* telegraph pole, Blue-tooth!

SADE: [*sharply*] Rush, we're not gonna have any shenanigans, and that's all there is about it. Come away from that winda.

RUSH: Aw.

SADE: Let's pitch in and use some elbow grease and get through. Shouldn't take us more than an hour and a half if we hustle.

RUSH: [*horrified*] An hour and a half? Mom, are you calmly tellin' me we have to skulk around in this horrible . . . ?

SADE: You can cut out the complainin' and bellyachin' right here and now, Mister.

RUSH: No, but holy smoke! Flesh and blood can't endure . . .

SADE: Just forget about flesh and blood. We planned to get after this attic way early this *summer* when school first let out. Goodness, your vacation's almost over, and we're only just *tacklin'* the job. You've *stalled* me off and *stalled* me off. I've got ya up here at *last,* and I don't wanta hear any grousin' an' sobbin' an' . . . You sittin' down?

RUSH: I might as well sit down while you're tellin' me . . .

SADE: [*warningly*] Get up from there this *second!* When was it, just last Thursday, we're all set to clean the attic, and I let you traipse off to Towanda or someplace? You said then you'd work like a beaver straightin' around up here . . . [*loud bangs and a thud*] Oh, for mercy's sake!

RUSH: Oh, doggone it!

SADE: Can't ya stand on your feet?

RUSH: [*tough*] That's a *fine* lot of sympathy to give a guy that falls down and almost murders theirself.

SADE: *Hurt* yourself?

RUSH: *Sure.*

SADE: I imagine you'll live. What'd you *trip* over?

RUSH: Half-wit popcorn popper.

SADE: Pick it up and lay it on the trunk.

RUSH: [*savagely*] I oughta sling it out the winda and *smash* it in eight million fragments.

SADE: It's strictly your *own* fault. *You're* the party that tosses that popcorn popper up here on the floor. When *I* put it away, I lay it carefully on the steps.

RUSH: [*still tough*] I like ta broke my leg.

SADE: Rub it a little. I've got everything pretty well organized in my head how we're goin' about this job. You do exactly what I tell ya to do and report promptly the minute you finish each little assignment, and that way, working together, we'll be down . . .

RUSH: *Listen!*

SADE: Huh?

RUSH: I *heard* somebody.

SADE: *I* don't hear anybody.

RUSH: Yeah, probably Blue-tooth Johnson prowlin' around huntin' for me. He couldn't locate my voice an' I bet forty dollars he's out in the yard lookin' all over . . .

SADE: [*crisply*] Let's put Blue-tooth Johnson and everything else out of our minds for the next couple hours or so.

RUSH: [*horrified*] Next couple *hours* or so? You said an hour an' a *half.*

SADE: [*crisply*] I don't know how long it'll take us. I know this much, though—we're gonna stay 'till we get done.

RUSH: My *leg* hurts.

SADE: Most likely you're on the point of *death*. Now let's get movin'. First thing I want you to do is pick up all the junk that's scattered . . .

RUSH: Listen!

SADE: And don't tell me listen anymore, either.

RUSH: No, but . . . Ya hear that?

SADE: Hear what?

RUSH: Listen once.

FLETCHER: [*calls from long way off*] *Say*-dee!

RUSH: Uncle Fletcher, by *George*.

SADE: [*groans*] Oh . . . my.

RUSH: [*shouting*] We're in the attic, Uncle Fletch . . . !

SADE: [*urgently*] No, no, you don't. Be *still*. *Quiet!*

RUSH: You're going to ignore him?

SADE: Well, I certainly *am*.

RUSH: [*with righteousness*] It is hardly *like* you, Mom, to ignore visitors that call at your home . . .

SADE: Oh, ish, he just *wandered* in, he'll wander *out* again in a minute.

FLETCHER: [*in the distance*] Sadie!

RUSH: *Listen* to 'im.

SADE: First thing I want you to do, Willie, is pick up this accumulation of stuff litterin' the floor. And while you're busy with that . . .

RUSH: [*pleadingly*] *Listen* to 'im.

SADE: What?

RUSH: *Poor* old Uncle Fletcher.

FLETCHER: [*coming closer*] Sadie!

SADE: *He'll* go away directly. Now *please*, Rush, hop in an' buckle down. What are you doin'?

RUSH: Peelin' off my lame-brain shirt. I like ta choke from the heat.

SADE: [*exasperated*] *Anything* to make a diversion. *Anything* to kill time. And after all those . . .

FLETCHER: [*downstairs shouting*] Sadie!

RUSH: Uncle Fletcher's comin' upstairs.

SADE: [*almost whispering*] Let's lower our voices.

RUSH: [*in his normal tones*] It isn't *like* you, Mom, to treat flesh and blood relations like they were some . . .

SADE: [*softly*] Oh, flesh and blood relations, my eye! Be fine if he joined us, wouldn't it? We'd get plenty accomplished, wouldn't we?

RUSH: [*normal tones*] He knows we're around somewhere. He . . .

SADE: *Lower* your voice!

RUSH: [*softly*] He knows we're around somewhere.

SADE: How does he?

RUSH: Because all the doors are open. He appreciates we wouldn't go off and leave the house wide open.

FLETCHER: [*coming closer*] Upstairs, are ya, Sadie?

SADE: [*resigned to this interruption*] Aw, *darn it.*

RUSH: He'll track us down.

FLETCHER: [*shouting*] Not taking a *bath*, are ya, Sadie?

RUSH: Might as well give up the ghost, Mom.

SADE: Yes, we'd feel awful foolish gettin' caught up here all guilty like we were hidin'.

RUSH: Shall I holler to 'im?

FLETCHER: [*shouting*] Sadie!

RUSH: [*eagerly*] Mom, shall I holler to 'im?

SADE: All right.

RUSH: [*calls*] Hello, Uncle Fletcher! *Hey* down there, Uncle Fletcher!

FLETCHER: [*shouting*] Is that you, Rush?

RUSH: [*calls*] Yeah, I'm in the attic.

FLETCHER: [*shouting*] Why? Attic, huh?

RUSH: [*calls*] Yeah, Mom's with me.

FLETCHER: [*still shouting*] *Fine.*

RUSH: [*calls*] Come on up!

SADE: [*hurried hushed voice*] Oh, you needn't have told him that. He might have decided to trot on along about . . .

FLETCHER: [*shouting up to them*] Glorious morning!

RUSH: Yeah!

SADE: [*with warmth, of course*] How *are* you, Uncle Fletcher?

FLETCHER: [*still shouting*] Like ta scream myself to *death!*

SADE: [*calls down the steps*] Watch out for your *head* comin' up those stairs!

FLETCHER: [*climbing the stairs*] Who's this?

SADE: [*urgently in hushed voice to Rush*] Now look, *Mister*, maybe we can still get something accomplished. I'll sit Uncle Fletcher down on the trunk out of our road. He won't want to stay in this hot, sticky, dusty place more than five minutes, and then we can go ahead . . .

FLETCHER: [*up to microphone*] Bumped into your sidekick, Blue-tooth Johnson, outside, Rush.

RUSH: Oh, did ya?

FLETCHER: Yes, I did. He's standin' out in the yard, and I . . . by *George*, it's *dark!*

SADE: Yes, Uncle Fletcher. I just imagine you won't want ta stay. We're straightin' around up here, and we're anxious to get done.

FLETCHER: Fella gets kind of a *sticky* sensation.

SADE: That's because it's so close and airless.

FLETCHER: *Fine.* Sadie, I saw Ted Stembottom a while ago also.

SADE: [*correcting her uncle*] Fred. [*to Rush*] Willie . . . you needn't stand there. Have you picked up *one* single thing yet?

RUSH: No, I'm still peelin' off my shirt.

SADE: [*little groans*]

RUSH: [*struggling with his shirt*] Oh, shucks!

FLETCHER: Yes, I saw old Ted Stembottom.

SADE: *Fred* Stembottom.

FLETCHER: That's what I say. I jollied him. Ted and I jolly back and forth all the time. "Ted," I said, "you ought ta be arrested for orderin' this weather." Ted laughed. "The weatherman's a scoundrel," he says—"I believe the next time I see 'im I'll punch 'im in the nose." I give old Ted back as good as he said. "Ted," I said, lookin' serious, "they say there's gonna be a law passed forbiddin' everybody to wear their overshoes . . ."

SADE: "Uncle Fletcher, why don't you . . ."

FLETCHER: ". . . unless the temperature is forty below zero. Furthermore, Ted," I said, "I noticed that . . ."

SADE: [*more insistent*] Uncle *Fletcher.*

FLETCHER: You *heard* this joke, have ya, Sadie?

SADE: No. I was just gonna suggest that maybe you'd like to sit down on the *trunk* there.

FLETCHER: *Glorious!*

SADE: That way Rush and I can go *ahead* with our work.

FLETCHER: Yes.

SADE: [*to Rush in lowered voice*] Now stop the stallin', you. We've been here almost half an hour and what have we done? Absolutely nothing. I've stood for about all the nonsense I'm gonna stand for . . . [*loud thumping crash*]

RUSH: Oh . . . oh . . .

SADE: *Goodness*, Uncle Fletcher!

FLETCHER: I fell *down*.

SADE: You didn't *hurt* yourself?

FLETCHER: *Sure*, I hurt myself. Think I fall down for *fun*?

RUSH: What'd ya trip over?

FLETCHER: Numbskull *popcorn* popper.

SADE: [*to Rush*] You didn't pick up that popcorn popper?

RUSH: I *started* to, but you attracted my attention by givin' a speech about all the stuff you wanted me to do an' in order to listen . . .

SADE: [*to Rush*] Well, pick it up now. Uncle Fletcher might have *killed* himself.

FLETCHER: *Yes.*

RUSH: [*muttering almost to himself*] . . . come any closer to killin' himself than I did.

SADE: [*sharply, in low tones*] Pick up that popcorn popper—not another word!

FLETCHER: Sadie, do you remember Irma Flo Kessy there in Belvidere?

SADE: No.

FLETCHER: Moved to Dubuque, Missouri, married a man thirty-six years old and later died?

SADE: No. [*in lower tones*] Rush, I *warned* you.

RUSH: I'm pickin' up stuff. I got my arms *full* of stuff I picked up.

SADE: Well, keep right *on*. No more dawdlin'.

FLETCHER: Rush, this Irma Flo Kessy, who was such a great friend of your mother's in Belvidere, used to have a little habit of slappin' her husband's face in public. She was a *peevish* woman, see. Least little thing make her mad. [*chuckles*]

SADE: [*low tones*] Goin', Rush?

RUSH: Uncle Fletcher's *talkin'* to me.

SADE: You can listen an' *work*.

FLETCHER: How's that?

SADE: Nothing.

FLETCHER: Uh-huh. Well sir, Rush, Irma Flo Kessy's husband would say: "Believe it's gonna rain, Irma Flo." Irma Flo'd turn an' hit him upside the *jaw*. Her husband's statement it was gonna rain rubbed her the wrong way, ya understand? Or maybe at the dinner table he'd say: "Please pass the *pepper*, Irma Flo." Irma Flo'd smack 'im for *that*. Half-wit husband got so every time he opened his *mouth*, he'd hide his face in his arms so his wife . . . [*loud crash*]

SADE: Oh *my* . . . *gracious* . . . *sakes* . . . *alive!*

RUSH: He slipped off the *trunk*.

SADE: *Hurt* yourself, Uncle Fletcher?

FLETCHER: *Sure*.

SADE: Well, how'd ya *happen* to fall off the trunk?

FLETCHER: It's slippery. I *slid* off.

SADE: [*to Rush in low tones*] I give up, Rush.

RUSH: Huh?

SADE: I give up.

RUSH: You mean . . . ?

SADE: We're goin' downstairs.

RUSH: Oh?

SADE: Come on, Uncle Fletcher. We're *all* goin' downstairs.

FLETCHER: Fine.

SADE: Step along . . . everybody.

FLETCHER: Attic looks much better now that you've cleaned it up.

SADE: [*dryly*] *Yes*, doesn't it?

FLETCHER: Rush makes a nice helper for ya.

SADE: [*dryly*] He makes a *glorious* helper.

RUSH: Which way ya *headed*, Uncle Fletcher?

FLETCHER: Oh, up the alley, I guess.

RUSH: Over to Tatman's vacant lot?

FLETCHER: [*affirmative*] Uh-huh.

RUSH: I'll go *with* ya.

Which concludes another brief interlude at the small house half-way up in the next block.

19

---•◦•---

Sade and Ruthie Each Mail the Other a Five-Dollar Bill

Well, sir, Mr. and Mrs. Victor Gook are home alone as we enter the small house half-way up in the next block now. It's early evening, and our friends are in the living room, occupied with sections of the newspaper. Young Rush is absent, having departed a few minutes ago for the Y. M. C. A. to watch the fat men play handball. And at the moment his mother is saying to his father:

SADE: [*almost blurting*] Vic, I told you no mail come this morning but some *did* come.
VIC: [*inquiringly*] Hey, hey?
SADE: [*some embarrassment*] I received a letter.
VIC: A *secret* letter?
SADE: [*giggles*] No, not a secret letter.
VIC: Have you been corresponding with some rich and handsome New York broker behind my back?
SADE: *Ruthie* wrote.
VIC: Ruthie Stembottom?
SADE: [*giggles*] Uh-huh.
VIC: [*chuckles*] *Well.* What's new with *Ruthie?*
SADE: She sent a little note with a five-dollar bill pinned to it.
VIC: [*sternly*] *Unravel* this mystery.
SADE: [*after a pause, little giggle*] It's all so kinda half-way foolish I didn't think I'd *tell* ya about it. Afraid you'd laugh an' make fun.
VIC: Um.
SADE: [*brief pause*] *More* money mix-up stuff.

145

VIC: Um?

SADE: Appreciate what I'm talking about?

VIC: No.

SADE: [*reminding him*] Ruthie an' me always going shopping an' gettin' confused an' not havin' any idea where we stand or who owes who what an' tryin' to straighten out . . .

VIC: [*remembers and chuckles*] Oh, uh-huh. Has *that* happened again?

SADE: Yes.

VIC: You weren't downtown *today*, were you?

SADE: Yesterday.

VIC: [*seriously*] Kiddo, if you'd only take my advice you wouldn't have any trouble. Keep your money *separate*. Don't either one of ya make a single purchase without takin' the dough out of your own personal pocketbooks an'.........

SADE: I know, I know. An' that's what we decided to do. But yesterday was different.

VIC: How so?

SADE: Mis' *Trogel* went shopping with us.

VIC: Oh.

SADE: *Her* being along put a different *complexion* on stuff. Three instead of two, don't ya know. Otherwise prob'ly we'd of been all right. Seemed like we got off on the wrong foot right off the bat, though, an' the confusion got worse as the afternoon went on.

VIC: Mis' Trogel got weighed an' Ruthie paid. You bought a nickel's worth of gum-drops an' Mis' Trogel paid. Ruthie an' Mis' Trogel went in cahoots on a spool of thread an' *you* paid. Mis' Donahue showed up in Yamilton's store an' Mis' Trogel owed her fifty cents an' you paid a dime of it an' Ruthie paid . . .

SADE: [*giggles*] No, not quite *that* bad. But *almost*. It turned out to be a *horrible* mixed-up muddle.

VIC: You say Ruthie mailed you five bucks?

SADE: It come this morning.

VIC: Adjusting, I presume, the deplorable state of . . .

SADE: Yes. Let me tell ya.

VIC: All right.

SADE: Mis' Trogel left us at the corner of Main an' Monroe streets yesterday an' Ruthie an' I walked home together. We both felt silly an' sheepish about money matters.

VIC: Um?

SADE: See, we'd made such good resolutions.

VIC: Um.

SADE: An' there we were in a worse botch than ever.

VIC: Uh-huh.

SADE: Ruthie said like this: she said, "We got to get straightened out an' *stay* straightened out." I agreed.

VIC: Uh-huh.

SADE: But there were so many twists an' *angles* involved. I've owed Ruthie a dollar an' eighty cents since 'way week before last. Ruthie has owed me two separate items of seventy-five cents an' a quarter for even longer than that. Then there's a two dollar an' fifteen cent debt neither one of us has been able to figure out who owes to who. An' *other* trash.

VIC: Um.

SADE: Other trash on top of going shopping with Mis' Trogel yesterday where we *really* got up to our ears in confusion.

VIC: [*chuckles*] Uh-huh.

SADE: [*brief pause*] So I received a note this morning with a five-dollar bill pinned to it.

VIC: Um.

SADE: [*little giggle*] An' been afraid to tell ya about it all day for fear you'd laugh an' make fun.

VIC: Not at *all*. Is that the note you have there in your lap?

SADE: Yes. Wanta read it?

VIC: *You* read it.

SADE: [*little giggle*] All right.

VIC: Um.

SADE: [*reads*] "Dearest Sadie." [*aside, giggling*] That silly girl.

VIC: What's the matter?

SADE: Known me all these many many years an' still don't know how to spell my name.

VIC: How's she spell it?

SADE: S - A - *I* - D - I - E.

VIC: Slops in an extra eye, huh?

SADE: [*giggles*] Yeah. Well maybe she's got an excuse at that . . . far as I know this is the first time she's ever *wrote* to me. When it comes to Christmas cards an' trash like that, of course, mail is always addressed to "Mrs. Victor Gook."

VIC: Uh-huh.

SADE: [*thoughtfully*] *Wait*, though. She's wrote me letters different times when I've visited in Carberry.

VIC: Misspell your name on those occasions?

SADE: [*brief thoughtful pause*] I don't remember. [*more briskly*] Well, anyway, . . . [*reads*] . . . "Dearest Sadie. Fred an' I sat down with paper an' lead-pencil an' figured everything out from Aye to Zee. I owe you five dollars an' here it is. Now we can start fresh. Ha, ha. Love. Ruthie."

VIC: [*approvingly*] A brief and incisive epistle, direct and to the point.

SADE: Yes, but don't you see the defugalty?

VIC: No.

SADE: It's just a cute little stunt to wipe the slate clean an' begin over.

VIC: Um.

SADE: Her an' Fred couldn't any more sit down an' figure everything out from Aye to Zee than the man in the moon. There's too many twists an' angles. *We've* never been able to sit down with paper an' lead-pencil an' figure everything out from Aye to Zee, have we?

VIC: [*chuckles*] No.

SADE: Raymond Belcher Bierman, the bright one from Buffalo, couldn't do it.

VIC: Um.

SADE: *No* sir, it's just a cute little stunt of Ruthie's to wipe the slate clean an' start fresh like she says. [*quotes*] "I owe you five dollars an' here it is. Now we can start fresh. Ha, ha. Love. Ruthie."

VIC: Well . . . *fine.*

SADE: [*brief pause, slowly and thoughtfully*] No—*not* fine.

VIC: It solves the *problem* in a convenient way, don't it?

SADE: No.

VIC: *Sure.*

SADE: [*slowly*] Vic, I'm gonna tell you something now where you *will* laugh an' make fun.

VIC: [*brief pause*] O. K.

SADE: [*slowly*] I pulled off the same cute little stunt as *Ruthie.*

VIC: [*not quite sure he understands*] Yeah?

SADE: [*slowly*] Last night after supper I had Rush drop a letter in the mailbox.

VIC: [*catching on and laughing incredulously*] No.

SADE: I sent Ruthie Stembottom a note with a five-dollar bill pinned to it.

VIC: [*laughs in genuine amusement*]

SADE: [*giggles wryly*] I'm a dunce. No mistake.

VIC: [*chuckling*] I'm not laughing in any way derogatory to you, kiddo. The co-*incidence* is funny. Both you girls . . .

SADE: [*a little sadly*] I know . . . don't apologize.

VIC: [*chuckles*]

SADE: We each sent each other five-dollar bills last night. We each received the other one's this morning. An' the *notes* were almost identical.

VIC: [*chuckling*] Really?

SADE: Let's see; what did I say in mine? [*brief pause, quotes*] "Dearest Ruthie. Vic and I went to work on our little money mix up an' got everything ironed out. It figures five dollars in your favor. Enclosed pleased find the five dollars. Now that we're even we can be careful after this to watch our pees an' cues. Love. Sadie."

VIC: [*chuckling*] That's the *darndest* co-incidence, kiddo.

SADE: Yes.

VIC: Ah—did you do any actual *figuring* before you sent the money?

SADE: No. An' I know good an' well Ruthie didn't either. We both thought of the same cute stunt: pay the other one five dollars, wipe the slate clean, an' be careful in the future.

VIC: I'd like to of seen Ruthie's face when she opened your note this morning.

SADE: [*dryly*] You should of seen *my* face when I opened *her* note this morning.

VIC: Ah—have you *talked* to her today?

SADE: [*negative*] Uh-uh.

VIC: No telephone conversations, huh?

SADE: [*negative*] Uh-uh. I feel like a nit-wit an' I expect she does too. I *thought* of calling her but couldn't quite make myself do it. An' chances are she was the same way.

VIC: [*chuckling*] This is a very interesting thing.

SADE: I don't s'pose you'll *tell* your wife's silliness around?

VIC: Oh, 'course not.

SADE: Um.

VIC: [*brief pause*] Ah . . . you mentioned shopping involvements yesterday. What were they?

SADE: Oh, same old stuff—complicated by Mis' Trogel bein' along.

VIC: Well, *tell* a fella.

SADE: So a fella can *laugh*?

VIC: *No. I'm* interested.

SADE: [*with some weariness*] Well, we all got ice-cream sodas in at the Greek's an' Ruthie an' I both paid.

VIC: *Both* paid?

SADE: *I* paid the *Greek* an' *Ruthie* paid the *clerk.*

VIC: For the same merchandise?

SADE: Yes. Ruthie didn't know I was payin' the Greek; I didn't know she was payin' the clerk. All three ice-cream sodas got paid for twice.

VIC: Um.

SADE: [*wearily*] Then in Yamilton's there was a beautiful remnant of white silk. I couldn't use it all an' Mis' Trogel couldn't use it all, but we both wanted part. So we decided to buy it an' divide it. Ruthie paid the money. I lost the package.

VIC: *Lost* the package?

SADE: Somewhere on Washington Street. We went back to hunt but never found it. Made me *mad. I'm* not careless with packages. Never lost a package in my life.

VIC: Um.

SADE: [*wearily*] Then in the ten-cent store we all three got weighed. Mis' Trogel's penny was bent or something. It didn't go down the slot proper an' the machine wouldn't register anything. I put in two more pennies an' they got stuck too.

VIC: Um.

SADE: Ruthie bought socks for Fred in at Kleeberger's; Kleeberger's didn't have any small change on hand; an' it got finagled around where I handed over thirty-five cents.

VIC: Um.

SADE: That's the way it went all afternoon.

VIC: Um.

SADE: All afternoon.

VIC: [*chuckles*] Say, you really had a time.

SADE: Yes.

VIC: Well . . . what you gonna *do* about the Ruthie situation?

SADE: [*rather hopelessly*] I don't know.

VIC: *Somebody'll* hafta telephone *somebody*.

SADE: I s'pose.

VIC: After all, no *harm's* been done.

SADE: Except it's such a wild *ridiculous* business.

VIC: I think both you girls acted with generous, unselfish, praiseworthy motives.

SADE: Maybe. Also we acted like lame-brains.

VIC: I don't agree. In fact I consider you both smart. Each decided to pay the other five dollars an' put an end to a disturbing nuisance. Five dollars, of course, is a substantial sum but it won't break either family. An' since nobody in the world could ever figure out your indebtedness to Ruthie or Ruthie's indebtedness to *you* I think we can let the matter rest an' . . .

SADE: [*on an impulse*] All right, *call* her.

VIC: Call Ruthie?

SADE: Yeah.

VIC: *Me* call her?

SADE: Don't ya want to?

VIC: [*hesitant*] Well—I *will.*

SADE: Go ahead.

VIC: Ah—suggest Five Hundred?

SADE: [*hesitant*] We've played awful *recent.*

VIC: I wouldn't know what else to *talk* about. I can't just phone out of a clear sky without a *reason.*

SADE: All right. Five Hundred then.

VIC: O. K.

SADE: Invite 'em here.

VIC: O. K.

SADE: Ah . . . I wouldn't mention the *notes*.
VIC: O. K.
SADE: I mean make jokes about 'em or anything.
VIC: O. K. [*to phone*] 2572-X, please. Correct. [*to Sade*] I didn't laugh at your mix-up, kiddo.
SADE: Um.
VIC: *Did* I?
SADE: Guess not.
VIC: No foolin', I considered it a smart operation. For the sum of five dollars you planned to rid yourself of an irksome . . . [*to phone*] *Hello* there. Is this the Fire Department? [*chuckles*] How are ya, Doctor Sleetch? Uh-huh. Say, here's a fella with long black whiskers wants to talk to ya, Ruthie.
SADE: [*sharply*] *No.*
VIC: [*tendering the telephone*] Here.
SADE: *You're* gonna talk.
VIC: Take this telephone.
SADE: *I* don't wanta talk.
VIC: Take this *telephone.*
SADE: [*distressed*] Oh, *lands.*
VIC: I'll step to one side so you'll have elbow-room.
SADE: [*after a pause, speaks into the telephone in excited, flustered, but affectionate tones*] Oh, darn it, Ruthie.

Which concludes another brief interlude at the small house half-way up in the next block and here we leave Vic and Sade until the next time.

First broadcast 1941.

20

Harold ("Rotten") Davis
Takes Up the Tobacco Habit

Well sir, it's early evening as we enter the small house half-way up in the next block now—about seven o'clock—and here in the living room we find Mr. and Mrs. Victor Gook comfortably settled on the davenport with sections of the newspaper. And now a somewhat prolonged silence is broken as the husband says to the wife:

VIC: Read this about Mis' Slimer?

SADE: No. Paper state something about her?

VIC: Yeah. She almost got killed.

SADE: Really?

VIC: [reads] "Mrs. L. W. Slimer, 718 West Market Street, narrowly escaped serious injury late last evening when her automobile stalled on the Chicago and Alton tracks at Morris Avenue directly in the path of a freight train. Fortunately E. E. Rogers, who was in charge of the locomotive, was able to come to a stop."

SADE: *My!*

VIC: That's woman drivers for ya. I bet she got scared when she saw the train an' put on the brake.

SADE: She's s'posed to be a very *good* driver.

VIC: Women are too high-strung to operate automobiles. I read the other day where some college professor worked out some statistics that showed . . .

RUSH: [off] Hey.

SADE: [calls] Yes?

RUSH: [closer] Rooster an' Harold get here yet?

SADE: Who?

RUSH: [*closer*] Rooster an' Harold Davis. Said they'd be right over.

SADE: We haven't seen anything of 'em.

RUSH: [*closer*] They'll be here any minute then.

SADE: Did you go 'way over to Williams' an' back in just this little time?

RUSH: [*up*] I took a streetcar home.

SADE: What was the idea?

RUSH: I wanted to be here when Rooster an' Harold come. Hello, Gov.

VIC: Hello.

RUSH: [*to Sade*] Is it O. K. me havin' a little company tonight?

SADE: I guess so. Harold's comin' too, huh?

RUSH: Yeah. I'm surprised they haven't showed up. See, I met 'em on my way over to Williams' an' they said they'd . . . That them?

SADE: Where?

RUSH: I heard somebody run up on the porch.

SADE: Oh, that's the kids from up in the next block. They been doin' that all evening. It's a game of Run Sheep Run.

RUSH: Oh.

SADE: How's it happen *Harold*'s comin'? He's a lot older'n you an' Rooster, ain't he?

RUSH: Yeah.

VIC: Who's Harold?

RUSH: Rooster's big brother.

VIC: Oh, the gawky guy with the hair all gummed down slick with stickum?

RUSH: Yeah. The *reason* he's comin', Mom, is to show off his tobacco habit.

SADE: His what?

RUSH: His tobacco habit. It's a brand new habit. Beginning this evening he's startin' to smoke an' chew. I invited him an' Rooster over so he could enjoy a cigar with Gov.

VIC: Who's gonna furnish the cigar?

RUSH: *He* is. He's got cigars by the thousand. All his pockets are crammed with 'em.

SADE: How *old* is Harold?

RUSH: Twenty. Be twenty-one the third of November. See, he promised his mother he wouldn't smoke 'till he got to be of age, but he's been puttin' the pressure on her an' today she finally give in an' let him have permission to cultivate the tobacco habit.

SADE: My.

RUSH: He's so happy an' excited he don't know what to do. Wait'll ya *see* him. Just *bulges* with cans of tobacco an' cigars an' stuff. Rooster says he's spent over ten dollars.

SADE: He buy ten dollars worth of tobacco?

RUSH: He bought a box of cigars, a fancy cigarette lighter that works by machinery, a leather pouch, a cigar-cutter, an' a silver case with his name on it.

SADE: Um.

RUSH: We still got that cuspidor around any place?

SADE: Haven't seen it in ages. What ever become of that, Vic?

VIC: Didn't Laurastine Price's youngest kid break it last time they visited?

SADE: Oh, sure. He was lookin' for it in the dark an' knocked a chair over on it.

RUSH: I wish we *had* a cuspidor or somethin' for Harold. He'll be smokin' so much he'll prob'ly enjoy an occasional spit.

VIC: I've seen that guy around the barber shop quite a bit. Always struck *me* as a little *simple*.

RUSH: *Harold's* a fairly bright fella. Got a memory like a horse. He can rattle off the batting averages of every player in the big leagues.

VIC: What's he do for a living?

RUSH: He's *out* of a job right *now*. Up until a month ago he carried water for the extra gang down in the Chicago an' Alton yards but somebody in Washington D. C. pulled a boner an' he got let out.

VIC: Somebody in Washington D. C. pulled a boner, huh?

RUSH: Yeah. It was a political mix-up of some kind. I don't know all the ins an' outs of it but Harold says if it wasn't for the trouble they're havin' in Europe he'd still have his job.

VIC: I think I'll *ask* Harold about it when he arrives.

RUSH: Yeah. You can enjoy a pleasant manly chat over your cigars.

VIC: I'm interested in finding out how a waterboy on a railroad section gang can lose his job on account of a war threat in Europe.

RUSH: Oh, *you* know how things are in Washington D. C. A senator forgets to sign a bill or something an' there's the dickens to pay.

VIC: Uh-huh.

RUSH: Maybe you'd like to chat with Harold too, Mom, while he puffs away on his cigar.

SADE: [*giggles*] All right.

RUSH: Funny they don't *get* here. Said they'd be right over.

SADE: Maybe Harold stopped to enjoy a smoke with some *other* people.

RUSH: Maybe he did. Boy, he sure feels swell about his tobacco habit. See, he's been battlin' with his mother a long time. Months an' months. "Mama, *please* let me cultivate the tobacco habit. *I'm* gonna be twenty-one in a few months." Today she finally give in.

VIC: How are *you* gettin' along with the tobacco habit?

RUSH: Me? Oh, I haven't indulged for years.

SADE: Did you usta indulge?

RUSH: When I was a kid, sure.

SADE: What'd ya smoke?

RUSH: Oh, Indian cigars from that Indian cigar tree behind Call's house; Cubebs, cornsilk, buggy-whip handles . . . *all* the junk young kids smoke. I expect you done the same thing, Gov.

VIC: Yeah.

SADE: Ever smoke any tobacco?

RUSH: Couple times I did.

SADE: *I* better not catch ya.

RUSH: Like I say, I haven't indulged for years. Bein' one hundred percent *frank* with ya I really don't *care* much for the tobacco habit.

SADE: No, an' ya better not.

RUSH: When I'm twenty-*one*, I'll prob'ly be around draggin' down a few snappy lungfuls of high-class smoke.

SADE: Ump.

RUSH: Wait'll ya see how hepped up *Harold* is. By gosh, bein' a victim of the tobacco habit's been one of his principal ambitions. Why ever since his fifteenth birthday he's been puttin' coffee on his fingers every day.

SADE: Coffee?

RUSH: Sure.

SADE: Why?

RUSH: To give a *stain*. Sometimes he uses *walnut* hulls. To look at his thumb an' forefinger an innocent passerby'd get the impression he used tobacco by the peck.

SADE: Oh, my.

RUSH: An' when he meets a stranger he always trembles an' acts nervous.

SADE: What for?

RUSH: He desires to put across the idea he's shot to pieces from havin' his system so full of nicotine.

SADE: Lands.

VIC: An' that's the guy I'm gonna have a pleasant manly chat with, huh?

RUSH: *You'll* enjoy chattin' with Harold. He can converse on any subject ya care to mention.

VIC: I bet.

RUSH: That's no joke.

SADE: Did he finish high school?

RUSH: Harold? No, he never. Somebody in Washington D. C. pulled a boner an' he got expelled.

VIC: Certainly are a lot of boners pulled in Washington D. C.

RUSH: Yeah.

SADE: What'd he get expelled for?

RUSH: For cribbin' in three final examinations, the Board of *Education* claimed.

VIC: What's *Harold* claim?

RUSH: The way *Harold* tells the story an Illinois Congressman in Washington D. C. got jealous of him an' pulled some *political* wires.

VIC: Hotsy-totsy.

RUSH: He's had some hard luck in his career, Harold has.

VIC: I can see that.

RUSH: Why, just last week his *girl* jilted him.

SADE: He got a girl?

RUSH: Not any more, he hasn't. She give him the gate.

SADE: Anybody I know?

RUSH: [*negative*] Uh-uh. She's a moving picture actress out in California. Goes under the name of Quenteena Quarles.

SADE: Quenteena *Quarles!* Why, she's the great big enormous *star.*

RUSH: Yeah.

SADE: Tonight's paper says Wilbert Willison, America's honey-boy, is *her* beau.

RUSH: *Harold* was her beau up until last *week.*

SADE: Aw, I don't believe it.

RUSH: *Ask* him when he gets here.

SADE: How *could* he be her beau?

RUSH: Harold usta write her a letter every day of the week.

SADE: Did she write *him?*

RUSH: I *s'pose* so. Anyway, it's all off *now.*

VIC: I bet I know what broke *up* the romance.

RUSH: What?

VIC: Somebody in Washington D. C. pulled a boner.

RUSH: [*surprised*] How'd *you* know?

VIC: Is that right?

RUSH: Sure. Harold was tellin' me about it just the other evening. Seems like the Chinese ambassador to France was in Washington D. C. an' got acquainted with a senator from California an' between 'em they cooked up some big *lie* about Harold.

VIC: Sometime somebody in Washington D. C.'s gonna pull a boner an' your friend Harold'll wind up in the insane asylum.

RUSH: Be just his luck. Well, he's got his tobacco habit to cheer him up. Mom, you might make things pleasant for him by handin' out a few *compliments.*

SADE: How ya mean?

RUSH: Oh . . . "Gosh, Harold, you sure hold that cigar like an old timer." "Harold, that smoke sure smells peachy." "Here, Harold, dump your ashes in *this* ashtray for a change."

SADE: [*giggles*] All right.

RUSH: Wonder why the heck they don't *get* here.

VIC: Somebody in Washington D. C. prob'ly pulled a boner.

SADE: [*giggling*] I was gonna say that too.

RUSH: Hey, you people ain't gonna make *fun* of Harold, are ya?

VIC: No.

RUSH: I advise ya *not* to. When it comes to witty come-backs he's the world's champion. Anybody that pokes josh at Harold Davis gets josh poked right back . . . with plenty of steam on the ball.

VIC: I'll be very careful.

RUSH: A guy got funny down at the barber shop the other day an' did *he* wish he'd kept still.

VIC: Harold burn him down?

RUSH: I'll say. This guy says, "Hey, is that thing you got your hat on a head or is it an egg?" Harold looked at him a minute in silent contempt. Then he says, "If you think it's an egg, try puttin' a little salt on it."

VIC AND SADE: [*laugh*]

RUSH: [*laughing*] Oh, when it comes to comical wise-cracks Harold takes the cake. Know what he said to Mis' Stormer that works there in the library?

VIC: No, what'd he say?

RUSH: Well, I'll hafta tell ya the *first* part.

VIC: O. K.

RUSH: Mis' Stormer caught him markin' up books with a pencil. She says, "Oh, so *you're* the one that's been drawin' mustaches on people. If you do it again I'll have you arrested." Harold says, "They're not *your* books." She says, "They're property of the public library an' I'm in charge of 'em." "All right," says Harold, "if you're the one that's in charge, how much'll ya charge me for a shave an' haircut?"

SADE: [*somewhat disgusted*] Oh my.

RUSH: Wasn't that comin' back at her like a ton of bricks?

SADE: Kid like that oughta be given a dose of the razor strap, twenty years old or *no* twenty years old.

RUSH: You just don't appreciate the humorous slant, Mom.

SADE: I guess I don't.

RUSH: Hey, I'm gonna call *up* them guys.

SADE: From what I've heard of this Harold I don't know whether I want him around my house or *not*.

RUSH: Oh, you'll like him fine.

SADE: I'll probably just *love* him.

RUSH: There's plenty of girls that *do*. [*to phone*] 2860-J, please. Yes. [*to his folks*] They're prob'ly on their way *here* but I might as well check up. Mom, we better have every ashtray in the house

around handy. Harold'll prob'ly . . . [*to phone*] Hello . . . Mis'
Davis? . . . *Rush*, Mis' Davis . . . say, I saw Roost . . . Alvin an'
Harold a little while ago an' they said they'd . . . huh? Yeah?
Really? Well . . . ah . . . I hope . . . oh, I see. Yes. Uh-huh. Well
. . . ah . . . thank you, Mis' Davis. No, needn't bother askin' Alvin
to come to the phone. No. All right, Mis' Davis . . . good-bye.
[*hangs up*]
VIC: What's the verdict?
RUSH: Harold has give up the tobacco habit.
VIC: So soon?
RUSH: He was downtown across from the courthouse. He whipped
out a cigar an' lit up. He took three puffs . . . only three puffs . . .
turned white as a sheet . . . an' fell down in a dead faint right there
on the public street. They brought him home in an ambulance.

*Which concludes another brief interlude in the small house
half-way up in the next block.*

First broadcast 1937.

21

---·•·---

Vic Is "Arch" to
an Old Friend

Well sir, it's a few minutes past twelve o'clock noon as we enter
the small house half-way up in the next block now and here in the
kitchen we find Mrs. Victor Gook and her son Mr. Rush Gook. It's
time to eat, but we are persuaded, by certain signs, that the meat's
not done. However, let's listen to Rush, who is saying:

RUSH: When *will* the meat be done?
SADE: Oh, it'll be quite a little bit, I'm afraid.
RUSH: Have I got time to run over an' see Heinie Call?
SADE: Oh, you don't wanta bust in on people at *noon*. They're at
the dinner table.
RUSH: Heinie assures me I'm welcome at his house at any hour of
the day or night.
SADE: Better stick around. See Heinie this afternoon.
RUSH: O. K. My business ain't a matter of life or death anyway.
SADE: Hungry?
RUSH: *Ravishing.*
SADE: We're gonna have nice eats—if they ever get themselves
cooked.
RUSH: Wonder why Gov don't come home.
SADE: He is home.
RUSH: Yeah?
SADE: He's in the other room lookin' at his mail.
RUSH: Whatcha know about that. I was under the impression he
was still at the office.

SADE: Um.

RUSH: Gives an individual a strange sensation to find out somebody's in the next room when all the time ya thought ya were alone.

SADE: Uh-huh.

RUSH: *I* get any mail?

SADE: No. Just Gov.

RUSH: I *never* get any mail. [*chuckles*] Ain't it funny how the United States of America with a hundred million people in it leaves me out in the cold? Nobody ever drops me a line.

SADE: I don't get many letters myself. Except for Bess an' a note now and then from . . .

VIC: [*off*] Sade.

SADE: [*calls*] Yes?

VIC: [*off*] This letter's from Ed Staker.

SADE: [*to Rush*] Who?

RUSH: Don't know.

SADE: [*calls*] Who?

VIC: [*closer*] Ed Staker.

RUSH: [*to Sade*] Ed Staker.

SADE: [*to Rush*] Who's that?

RUSH: Don't know.

VIC: Darndest letter ya ever saw.

SADE: Who's Ed Staker?

VIC: [*almost up*] *You've* heard me speak of Ed. We used to buddy around together as young fellas years ago. [*notices his son*] Hello, Sam. Didn't know you were on the premises.

RUSH: I didn't know you were on the premises either. I passed the remark to Mom . . .

VIC: Uh-huh. Kiddo, I mentioned Ed Staker just the other day. Doncha remember I come across his name in the Lodge Magazine where it said he was recently elected Exalted Little Dipper of the Sleepy Saturn Chapter?

SADE: No.

VIC: Ed's located in Saint Paul Minnesota now.

SADE: What's he writin' to you about?

VIC: [*chuckling*] Doggondest thing ya ever heard of.

SADE: Money?

VIC: Huh?

SADE: Want money?

VIC: What give ya *that* idea?

SADE: That's what most of your friends *do* want when they write.

VIC: [*coldly*] If you'd thought *over* that remark a second, Sade, I don't believe you'd of given it *utterance*.

SADE: [*composedly*] What's eatin' *this* fella?

VIC: This "fella"—as you choose to call him—in this letter pays me about as fine a compliment as one man can give to another.

SADE: Um?

VIC: [*impressively*] Ed Staker—writes—to ask me—to be his—best man.

SADE: [*not excited*] Gonna get married?

VIC: [*sarcasm*] I would *presume* so.

SADE: [*giggles*] That *was* a foolish question, wasn't it? I do that all the time. More absentmindedness than anything else, though. This morning Mis' Donahue says, "They took Ol' Mister Ginwhelp to the hospital." I says, "Is he sick?" [*laughs*]

VIC: Um.

RUSH: S'pose that meat's done now, Mom?

SADE: No, we got quite a little wait yet.

VIC: Kiddo, if I go to Saint Paul Minnesota over Saturday an' Sunday do you people suppose you could get along all right?

SADE: Saint Paul *Minnesota?*

VIC: That's where Ed Staker's located.

SADE: Well, what on *earth?*

VIC: I think I'll run up there an' *be* Ed's best man.

SADE: [*dismissing the whole ridiculous business*] Oh, for mercy's sake.

VIC: A request to stand up with a friend while he gets married is not to be handled lightly.

RUSH: I got a standing *invitation* to be best man. Smelly Clark said I could have the job every time he gets married an' he plans to marry *several* different ladies during his lifetime as he . . .

VIC: Let me talk, will ya, Dry-rot?

RUSH: Sure.

VIC: *You* guys can make out by yourselves O. K. while I'm gone, can't ya, kiddo?

SADE: Oh, you're not gonna do any such silly thing.

VIC: Silly *thing?* So you think bein' best man to a dear ol' chum is a silly thing, huh?

SADE: "Dear ol' chum." When was the last time ya *saw* this man?

VIC: Last time I saw Ed was in . . . nineteen-seventeen.

SADE: Nineteen-seventeen, nineteen-twenty-seven, nineteen-thirty-seven. Twenty years ago.

VIC: Yeah.

SADE: Sick snake.

VIC: You lead me to believe you consider the passage of time dulls friendship's holy bonds.

RUSH: There's a little *poem* I know with that thought in it, Gov. [*recites*] "The hours are weary, pal o' mine. The night is black an' . . ."

VIC: *Will* you pipe down?

RUSH: Sure, but I'd love to point out . . .

VIC: Sade, I could grab the four-forty-five to Chicago an' . . .

SADE: Saint Paul Minnesota is a million miles away.

VIC: Naw.

SADE: It's 'way up there by Canada, isn't it?

VIC: Naw, it's only about five hundred miles northwest of Chicago.

SADE: You'd travel five hundred miles on such a crazy business, huh?

VIC: You're not very particular about the *phrases* you use. When we got married an' Harley Eggsocket was *my* best man ya didn't think of it as a crazy business.

SADE: Harley Eggsocket never had to come clear from *China* to be best man.

VIC: Listen, I can grab the four-forty-five for Chicago this afternoon. There's a *dozen* night trains that go to the twin cities. Ioll be in Saint Paul tomorrow morning.

SADE: [*disgusted*] Heavens.

VIC: Lemme read ya Ed's letter.

RUSH: Mom, how about the meat?

SADE: *I'll* tell ya when it's done.

VIC: Listen, kiddo.

SADE: Ump.

VIC: [*reads*] "Thursday, January 21, 1937. 2724 29th Avenue South, Saint Paul Minn. Dear Arch."

SADE: Who?

VIC: Arch.

SADE: Who's Arch?

VIC: I am. [*chuckles*] All *through* the letter he calls me Arch.

SADE: What's he do that for?

VIC: He's got me mixed up with a *cousin* of mine that was in our gang of young fellas. *Archie* Gook his name was. Archie's been dead now for a good many years.

SADE: Maybe he *means* the letter for your cousin.

VIC: [*negative*] Uh-uh. He means me all right. See, he sent this to the correct address, an' also he refers to us both bein' in the same lodge. That's *another* reason why I oughta come through an' go to Saint Paul. My dear ol' buddy I usta chum around with is gettin' married, an' he's a dear ol' buddy that holds an office in the Sacred Stars of the Milky Way.

SADE: He's sure some dear ol' buddy. He don't even know your name.

VIC: Ed's an absentminded cuss. Got me mixed up with ol' Archie.

RUSH: This Archie was your cousin, huh, Gov?

VIC: Second cousin.

RUSH: What relation would that make him to me?

VIC: Uncle or somethin'.

RUSH: *Naw.* Make him my third cousin. By gosh, that makes an interesting little *item* to tell my various friends. I got a third cousin named Archie that dies an' . . .

VIC: I'm tryin' to read your mother this letter, doggone it.

RUSH: O. K.

VIC: [*reads*] "Thursday, January 21, 1937. 2724 29th Avenue South. Saint Paul Minn. Dear Arch. This is the first time I've ever written to you, but better late than never, I guess. Ha-ha."

SADE: Ha-ha?

VIC: Ha, ha. Laugh. Ha, ha.

SADE: Oh.

VIC: "But better late than never, I guess. Ha-ha. Well, Arch, here's . . ."

SADE: [*intense deprecation*] Arch.

VIC: May I read, please?

SADE: [*low tones*] Arch.

VIC: May I read, please?

SADE: Go ahead.

VIC: [*reads*] "Well, Arch, here's . . ."

SADE: [*low tones*] Arch.

VIC: Please.

SADE: Ump.

VIC: [*reads*] "Well, Arch, here's the dope. After all these years I'm about to take the leap. Saturday, January 23, at three o'clock in the afternoon I am marrying Miss Dorothy Upjohn of Minneapolis. So the ol' bachelor got hooked at last, Arch, ha-ha."

SADE: [*low tones*] Arch.

VIC: [*reads*] "Arch, I haven't forgotten the old days we had together. In fact they stand out as the happiest of my life. Also I'm remembering that we're both Sky-Brothers in the Sacred Stars of the Milky Way. That's why I'm asking you to come to Saint Paul an' be my best man. Yes, Arch, that's what I'm asking you to do—come to Saint Paul an' be my best man. Will you write me at once? I'm counting on you. Regards to Irene an' Little Gus. Your friend. Ed Staker."

SADE AND RUSH: Who's Irene an' little Gus?

VIC: Huh?

SADE: Who's Irene an' little Gus?

VIC: I don't know. Ed must have me confused with somebody else.

SADE: What a hot ol' chum *he* is. Got ya mixed up with two other fellas.

VIC: Ed's a little absentminded. [*affectionate chuckle*] One of his most lovable characteristics.

SADE: Ed's a little soft in the *noodle* if ya ask me.

VIC: Ed is . . .

SADE: *You're* not gonna do this, Vic.

VIC: If I decide . . .

SADE: Not a *word* about paying your *expenses*.

VIC: My expenses, of course, are . . .

SADE: A trip 'way up there by Canada'd run you a million dollars.

VIC: Naw. I'm . . .

SADE: You'd hafta buy railroad tickets back an' forth from here to Chicago. An' railroad tickets back an' forth from Chicago to Saint Paul. An' *sleeper* tickets. An' *meals.* An' nickels an' dimes for the porters that shine your shoes an' carry your valise. Besides that long long train ride. It might even be a fancy church wedding where you'd need *morning* coat an' pants.

VIC: That's true, but . . .

SADE: An' for *what?* To be best man to a fella ya haven't seen in twenty years that thinks your name is *Arch.*

VIC: As I have pointed out, Ed is . . .

SADE: Ed is *crazy.* That's what *Ed* is. He's gettin' married on *Saturday.* How comes he writes an' asks ya to be his best man on *Thursday?* People don't make up their mind two days before they get married who their best man's gonna be. An' selecting a fella he hasn't laid eyes on in twenty years. "Regards to Irene an' little Gus" . . . fssst!

VIC: Sade, I . . .

SADE: He must be awful hard up for friends in Saint Paul if he hasta send clear down here for *you.*

VIC: That angle is . . .

SADE: I've heard all I wanta hear about this business.

VIC: [*coldly*] O. K.

RUSH: Mom, how about the meat?

SADE: I think it's done now.

RUSH: Swell.

SADE: You can pull up chairs.

RUSH: Yeah.

SADE: [*to Vic*] C'mon, we're going to eat—Arch.

Which concludes another brief interlude at that small house half-way up in the next block.

First broadcast 1937.

22

Mr. Gumpox Has Lost His Dentures

Well sir, it's late afternoon as our scene opens now, and here walking along Virginia Avenue toward the small house half-way up in the next block we discover Mr. Victor Gook and Mr. Rush Gook. The gentlemen are returning from a matinée movie performance at the Bijou Theatre and at this moment the picture is under discussion. Listen:

RUSH: Yessir, I don't hesitate to say that was the worst picture show I ever saw in my life.

VIC: Pretty bad all right.

RUSH: They never have anything but "love" any more. Love, love, love. I get so sick of movies about love I feel like going to the box-office an' demandin' my money back.

VIC: Thomas A. Edison, the Great Emancipator, usta say it's love makes the world go round.

RUSH: Boy, he can take his love an' put it in his hat an' pull his hat down over his ears.

VIC: *I* was mildly entertained this afternoon.

RUSH: *I* wasn't.

VIC: See, I'm on my vacation an' I like to squeeze every possible drop of pleasure out of each passing moment.

RUSH: Seemed to *me* you dropped off to *sleep* a couple times in the show.

VIC: I *did.*

RUSH: Wonder the whole *audience* didn't go to sleep. Shucks, why

168

don't they ever have movies like they *used* to: shootin' an' horseback ridin' an' guys fallin' off the cliff an' stuff. Last ten picture shows I've seen have been all alike. Here's Hector Harwood in the Library. He's crying. "What seems to be the trouble, sir?" says the butler. "Cynthia has given me back my ring," says Hector. [*tough*] "Cynthia"—ain't that a name for ya though? Shucks, I wouldn't name a rattlesnake "Cynthia."

VIC: I see your mother out in the backyard.

RUSH: Yeah.

VIC: She's prob'ly dishin' out a little tender care for her Panther Blood.

RUSH: I expect. No, Gov, from my viewpoint the movies have gone to pot. Remember the bang-up pictures they usta have . . . Gilmore Griswold, the four-gun cattle thief, in "Wild Western Dynamite" . . . Bill Bleatman, the carefree cowboy cavalier in "I Hate You" . . . Vincent Vance, the ruthless Romeo of the Ranch, in "Murder, Murder, Murder" . . .

SADE: [*off*] Boys.

VIC: [*to Rush*] I'm afraid we're due for a little exercise with the lawn mower.

RUSH: Looks like it.

VIC: [*calls*] Yeah, kiddo?

SADE: Come on back here, will ya?

VIC: [*calls*] Sure.

RUSH: [*to Vic*] It might not be so bad. Maybe we'll just hafta water the Panther Blood with the sprinklin' can or somethin' easy like that.

VIC: It might pay us to keep our fingers crossed. The two hours I spent in the theatre sleeping have sapped my vitality to where the idea of pushin' a lawn mower around makes me vaguely ill.

RUSH: What's Mom *doin'*? She don't seem to be foolin' with her Panther Blood.

VIC: She acts like she's *lookin'* for somethin'.

RUSH: [*calls*] What'd ya lose, Mom?

SADE: [*off a little*] C'mere an' I'll tell ya.

VIC: [*to Rush*] I bet she lost a ten-thousand-dollar bill.

RUSH: Well, you know *Mom*. She wouldn't look any harder for a ten-thousand-dollar bill than she would for a *dime*.

VIC: You figure your mother's close-fisted, huh?

RUSH: Well, *ain't* she?

VIC: [*chuckles*] All women are, I guess.

RUSH: Known fact. Smelly Clark usta carry suitcases for people down at the Union Depot an' he says the ladies never tipped more'n a nickel. [*raises voice*] What'd ya lose?

SADE: [*almost up*] *I* never lost anything, but somethin's been lost.

RUSH: Who lost it?

SADE: [*up*] Mr. Gumpox. How was the show?

RUSH: Punk.

SADE: [*to Vic*] I bet you slept.

VIC: I'll say I did.

SADE: Ya might as well take your picture show money an' throw it in the street.

VIC: Oh no. I had a good time. My dreams were pleasantly embroidered with the speeches of the people talkin' on the screen. "I adore you, Everett." "Try to understand, mother, that I can't live without Cynthia." "Hands off that girl, Bernard Breen, or I'll forget you only got one leg."

SADE: [*giggles*] I wouldn't call that gettin' my money's worth.

VIC: Oh, I'm not kickin'. The theatre was dark, my chair was comfortable, an' the sweet breezes from electric fans bombarded me deliciously. *I* got value for my twenty-five cents.

RUSH: What is it you're lookin' for, Mom?

SADE: Somethin' Mr. Gumpox lost.

RUSH: What'd he lose?

SADE: [*giggles*] His false teeth.

VIC AND RUSH: Aw.

SADE: [*giggles*] Yeah.

VIC, SADE, AND RUSH: [*laugh*]

SADE: [*straightening up*] 'Course it's nothin' to *laugh* at. It's his upper plate he lost an' he paid I don't know how much for it in Decatur. They had to make it special for him.

RUSH: *All* artificial teeth got to be made special. It's like buyin' a pair of shoes.

SADE: Do you have your shoes made special?

RUSH: No, but I hafta buy shoes that fit my feet. Same way with false teeth. Ya got to get 'em to fit your *mouth*.

SADE: Then you could send away for some that fit whatever size mouth ya *got*. But Mr. Gumpox had his made extra-special by an outfit in Decatur. I think he said they cost over a hundred dollars.
RUSH: You still don't get the point I'm attempting to put across. Take a pair of shoes, for instance. All right, say you wear size nine an' a half. All right, say . . .
SADE: C'mon, let's try an' find those teeth.
VIC: Gumpox think he lost 'em in our yard?
SADE: He don't know *where* he lost 'em. He thinks in some yard along the alley here between Kelsey Street an' Wallis Avenue. What happened was he rapped on the door about an hour ago an' told me how he lost his teeth sometime this morning an' would I mind lookin' around a little. He asked that of *all* the neighbor ladies.
RUSH: I see Mis' *Harris* out by her woodshed lookin' around.
SADE: Uh-huh—an' there's Mis' Corkle too.
VIC: Well, look, were the teeth in his *mouth?* Did they just drop *out* somewhere?
SADE: [*giggles*] 'Course not, foolish. Person'd certainly know it if their *teeth* fell out.
RUSH: Rooster Davis had an *uncle* that's teeth dropped out under mysterious circumstances without his knowledge. It was on a Saturday night an' he was out late with some various friends an' all of a sudden . . .
SADE: [*giggles*] Look, there's Mis' *Drummond* out huntin'.
VIC: Mis' Snyder also. See her pokin' around with a stick?
SADE: [*giggles*] Whole neighborhood out lookin' for false teeth. [*laughs and stops suddenly*] Person shouldn't laugh. It's a real serious *thing* to lose teeth worth a hundred dollars.
RUSH: [*wisely*] Prob'ly worth a *million* dollars to Mr. Gumpox.
SADE: Why?
RUSH: [*not prepared to be challenged*] Why . . . a . . . because . . . a . . . [*chuckles*] I don't know.
SADE: What'd ya say that for then?
RUSH: I guess I was thinkin' about kids. You've heard people with kids say, "I wouldn't take a million dollars for Billy, but I wouldn't give a nickel for another one like him."
SADE: I don't get the connection. Ya mean Mr. Gumpox wouldn't

take a million dollars for his teeth an' he wouldn't give a nickel for another pair?

RUSH: Another pair of teeth?

SADE: Yeah.

RUSH: Teeth come in *sets*, Mom, not in *pairs*. Same thing as when ya . . .

SADE: Oh, such pointless chit-chat. C'mon, let's hunt around.

VIC: Kiddo, I still don't understand how Gumpox lost his teeth. You say they didn't fall out of his mouth?

SADE: *'Course* they never fell out of his mouth. *He'd* certainly know if his teeth fell out of his mouth.

VIC: What in thunder *did* they fall out of? His hair?

SADE: His *pocket*. He had 'em in his *pocket*.

RUSH: *That's* a fine place for teeth, *I* must say.

VIC: What were they doin' in his *pocket?*

SADE: He slips 'em out of his mouth quite often, he says, in order to rest his jaws. He prob'ly slipped 'em out, stuck 'em in his pocket, an' they jounced loose an' got lost.

RUSH: Maybe they worked their way *through* his pocket. Maybe they *bit* their way through. If they're hundred dollar teeth they're prob'ly extra sharp an' . . .

SADE: Look, Mis' Corkle's got the whole *family* lookin'. Curtis an' everybody.

VIC: I see Mis' Drummond's got Bulldog sharin' in the search.

RUSH: *I* don't see any false teeth anywhere.

SADE: Person hasta *hunt* if they wanta find something.

RUSH: You'd think false teeth'd be *easy* to find. Gleaming *fangs* sparklin' in the grass.

VIC: Kiddo, Gumpox don't come *this* far up in the yard when he collects our garbage, does he?

SADE: No, why?

VIC: I was just thinkin' they'd be near the *garbage* box if they'd be *anywhere*.

SADE: Let's go *there* an' hunt then.

VIC: O. K.

RUSH: [*humorously*] Maybe Mr. Gumpox was *robbed*. [*laughs*]

SADE: What's comical about *that?* Maybe he *was*.

RUSH: Take a pretty slick burglar to steal a fella's teeth out of his mouth.

SADE: [*crisply*] I've already told you eleven times they were in his pocket.

RUSH: Makes me think of a humorous story as told by Smelly Clark. A certain hen-pecked husband went down to the river swimmin' in spite of his wife's orders. When he was putting his clothes back on he discovered some dog had run away with his underwear. Well, at the dinner table that day his wife noticed through his shirt he wasn't wearin' any underwear so she says, "Where's your underwear?" He says, "Holy Smoke, I've been robbed." [*laughs*]

SADE: Well, he *was* robbed, wasn't he?

RUSH: *No.* A *dog* took his underwear.

SADE: *I* call that bein' robbed.

RUSH: You miss the climax of the *joke,* Mom. What *he* was doin' was tryin' to give his wife the impression somebody stole his underwear while he had it on. Look at it from *this* slant. You're a guy that . . .

VIC: [*off a little*] This them?

SADE: [*to Rush*] That ain't false teeth he's got, is it?

RUSH: [*chuckles*] Naw—that's an ol' busted clothes-pin.

VIC: [*closer*] This them, Sade?

SADE: [*not amused*] Throw that clothes-pin away an' be some help. Look how everybody *else* in creation is tryin' to find Mr. Gumpox's teeth.

RUSH: I see Mis' Harris's roomer Mr. Overholt is on the job.

SADE: Yes, an' down on his hands an' knees too.

RUSH: Don't see what he wants to do *that* for. Human teeth are sparkling fangs that gleam in the grass.

SADE: These ain't human teeth; these are false teeth.

RUSH: They're still *fangs* though. They oughta gleam in the grass. I don't wanta split hairs with ya, Mom, but . . .

VIC: This them?

SADE: Where?

VIC: Here in my hand.

SADE: Oh my, aren't you just havin' a picnic for yourself though. C'mon . . . look . . . maybe you'll be the one that *finds* 'em.

VIC: I'd be a mighty happy man if I did.

SADE: Throw that ol' cigar butt away an' get busy.

RUSH: *I* have a little theory about what might of happened.

SADE: Keep it to yourself.

RUSH: No, but this is red-hot. Listen, have you ever heard about elderly people lookin' around all day for their spectacles an' all the time they got 'em on their forehead?

SADE: No.

VIC: *I* have, George.

RUSH: Well, could the same thing of happened to Mr. Gumpox?

VIC: He's got his teeth in his forehead?

RUSH: No, in his *mouth*.

VIC: Ya mean he's got 'em in his mouth an' *still* thinks he lost 'em?

RUSH: I guess that ain't such a red-hot theory at that. He could feel his teeth with his *tongue*.

VIC: Yeah. However, if they *were* on his forehead he couldn't feel 'em with his tongue.

RUSH: [*chuckles*] No, sir.

VIC: I'll give anybody in this crowd a silver dollar that can touch their forehead with their tongue. No, I'll boost that to *four* silver . . .

SADE: [*low tones*] Vic.

VIC: Uh-huh.

SADE: Mis' Fisher's lookin' out her kitchen window.

VIC: Yeah . . . I noticed her there a minute ago.

SADE: Ain't that mean? *She* knows what we're huntin' for. *She* knows Mr. Gumpox lost his false teeth. But will she go out in *her* backyard an' hunt? Not a bit of it.

VIC: Um.

SADE: Just look at the *other* neighbors doin' their best to find 'em. Mis' Corkle, Curtis, an' the kids. Mis' Drummond an' Bulldog. Mis' Harris an' Mr. Overholt. Mis' Snyder. *Us* three. But Mis' *Fisher* sits in the kitchen an' peeks out the *window*.

VIC: Um.

SADE: Some people are just as mean as they can be. *It* wouldn't hurt her to step out by her garbage box an' . . .

RUSH: Hey, there's some excitement up the alley.

SADE: Where?

RUSH: Mr. Overholt's found something.

SADE: He's wavin' it around over his head.

RUSH: I bet it's Mr. Gumpox's false teeth.

SADE: Vic, looks like Mr. Overholt's found the teeth.

VIC: Catch me. Rush, bring Papa a cold glass of water an' a few . . .

SADE: [*calls*] Teeth. Ya find the teeth?

RUSH: He found 'em all right. He's noddin' his head very proudly.

SADE: [*delighted*] Ain't that nice.

Which concludes another brief interlude at the small house half-way up in the next block.

First broadcast 1936.

23

Preparing for a Visit from the Brimmer Family

Well sir, *it's early evening as we enter the small house half-way up in the next block now, and here in the living room we discover Mr. and Mrs. Victor Gook and their son Mr. Rush Gook. Mr. Victor Gook occupies his customary chair under the floor lamp; Mrs. Victor Gook sews quietly on the davenport; and Mr. Rush Gook sits at the library table, his school books open before him. There has been silence for some little time, but now the head of the family says:*

VIC: *Well.*
SADE: Readin' about Hal Keefer an' Dorothy Lodge?
VIC: Yeah. They're gonna get married.
SADE: Uh-huh. Ain't that the limit?
VIC: He's been engaged to that Finely girl for fifteen years, ain't he?
SADE: More'n that.
VIC: Wonder what happened.
SADE: Search me.
VIC: Maybe Hal didn't like the *looks* of the Finely girl since she had all her teeth pulled out.
SADE: Maybe not.
RUSH: She's got *false* teeth. They're classier lookin' than real ones.
SADE: You're s'posed to be studyin', ain't ya?
RUSH: This ain't really studyin'.
SADE: Whatcha workin' on? Algebra?

RUSH: No. I'm lookin' up words in the dictionary. Nothin' to it, I can talk an' work at the same time.

SADE: Seems to me it'd be better to keep your mind on your business.

RUSH: Oh, no. See, all I gotta do is look up a word an' then write it down on a piece of paper.

SADE: What words ya lookin' up?

RUSH: Lookin' up "ferocity" now.

SADE: [*approvingly*] Uh-huh. That's a nice word.

RUSH: Yeah.

VIC: *I* didn't know Hal Keefer was forty-seven years old, did you?

SADE: Oh, yes.

VIC: Don't *look* it.

SADE: *I* think he does. Hasn't got a hair on his head.

VIC: Neither has Joe Heeney down to the Plant an' Joe's only twenty-six.

SADE: Well, but he's just a *young* fella.

VIC: That's the *point*. Joe's just a young fella an' he's bald-headed. Hal's an *old* fella an' *he's* bald-headed. How ya gonna tell the difference?

SADE: The difference between Joe an' Hal?

VIC: No, the difference between a young fella an' an old fella.

SADE: By their hair. You can tell Hal is old because he's bald-headed.

VIC: So is *Joe* bald-headed.

SADE: Yes, but he's just a young fella.

VIC: [*grunts*]

SADE: Ain't that right?

VIC: [*giving up*] I guess so.

RUSH: I just looked up "ferocity," Mom. Wanta know what it means?

SADE: Yes.

RUSH: Means: "Savage cruelty of disposition; untamed fierceness."

SADE: Goodness. Almost a swear word, ain't it?

RUSH: [*laughs*] Uh-huh. "I just ate supper with ferocity."

SADE: [*laughs*] Hear that, Vic?

VIC: [*looking up*] Huh?

SADE: Rush just looked up the word "ferocity" in his dictionary an'
. . . [*phone*] *I'll* get it, son. You go on an' study.

RUSH: I got an idea it's Rooster.

SADE: I'll see.

RUSH: He's probably worried about the seven cents I owe him. I
just *borrowed* it this afternoon. That guy . . .

SADE: [*at phone*] Hello. Yes. Oh, *hello*, Mis' Brimmer.

RUSH: It's Mis' Brimmer callin' up.

SADE: [*at phone*] Oh, just fine. How are *you* all? Uh-huh. What?
This evening? Why, *yes*. No, we're not goin' anywhere. No. Rush is
here studyin' an' Vic's readin' the paper. I been sewin' an' . . . why,
sure, c'mon over. Certainly. Oh, no, bring 'em all. Sure. Well, we'll
be expectin' you then. In about half an hour? Surely. All right, Mis'
Brimmer. See you pretty soon. Yes. Good-bye, Mis' Brimmer. [*hangs
up*] [*to the others*] Oh, heavens!

VIC: What's the matter?

SADE: The whole tribe is comin' over.

VIC: Tonight?

SADE: In just a few minutes.

RUSH: Is Orval comin'?

SADE: *All* of 'em are comin'.

VIC: How long they gonna stay?

SADE: All evenin', I s'pose.

VIC: Oh, thunder.

SADE: Ya know what we gotta do, don't ya? We gotta move all the
breakable things outa this room. You know what terrors them kids
are.

VIC: I got a pair of busted glasses an' a cracked pocket watch to
remind me. Are they bringin' the baby?

SADE: They're bringin' *everybody*. Well, let's get busy. Lands, I
wish we could tell 'em we were plasterin' this room or somethin' an'
had to have it closed off. I hate to think what'll happen with that
tribe loose in here.

RUSH: Let's tell 'em the whole *house* is bein' plastered. Take 'em
down cellar.

SADE: Only wish I could. They're nice folks . . . nobody in the
world is nicer than Verna Brimmer, but the way they let them kids

run over other people's property is a downright shame. Vic, ya wanta help me?

VIC: Whatcha want me to do?

SADE: Well—first of all, let's take the fancy plates off the top of the bookcase. I'd shiver in my shoes every minute with 'em out in plain view.

VIC: Them little kids couldn't get 'way up there to the top of the bookcase.

SADE: Oh, couldn't they? They'd get a chair.

RUSH: Maybe we better take out the chairs.

VIC: Where would we sit down?

RUSH: On the floor, Indian fashion. We could tell 'em we had to sell our chairs to get somethin' to eat. That way we'd . . .

SADE: Let's not talk. Let's get busy. Rush, you better finish your homework. Won't have a chance after the Brimmers get here. Listen, Vic, will you disconnect the floor lamp an' take it out in the kitchen? Better put it behind the pantry door. I'll take the fancy plates down an' hide 'em in the bottom bookcase drawer. C'mon, let's kinda hurry. They might be here any minute. Don't take ten seconds to get here on the streetcar.

VIC: It'll be dark in here without the floor lamp, Sade.

SADE: We can turn on the top lights. Lands, even the *top* lights ain't safe. Remember what little Kennedy did last time the Brimmers was here?

VIC: No.

SADE: Took a broom, reached up, an' battered two globes out slick as you please. A minute later he rammed that broom in my stomach. I like to died.

RUSH: Maybe what we oughta do is take out the top lights, hide the broom, an' you wear a chest protector, Mom.

VIC: [is amused at this]

SADE: Don't fool, Vic. Hurry an' get that floor lamp outa here. Rush, don't bother us. Do your studyin'.

RUSH: I can't find "duodenum" in this dictionary. What's it mean?

SADE: What's the word?

RUSH: Duodenum.

SADE: How ya spell it?

RUSH: D - U - O - D - E - N - U - M.

SADE: Oh, I don't know.

RUSH: I'm stuck then. Might as well quit.

SADE: Go on to the next word.

RUSH: The next word is "dynamic."

SADE: That means gunpowder.

RUSH: Thank you. The next word is . . .

SADE: Look 'em *up*, son. Don't ask *me*.

RUSH: I'd get *done* quicker if you'd tell me the definitions to . . .

SADE: No, I'm busy. Got that disconnected, Vic?

VIC: Yeah. What'd ya say to do with it?

SADE: Put it behind the pantry door. Here, ya better take your little ashtray along too. You don't want *that* to get broke.

VIC: [*on his way*] Heck, you'd think a herd of buffaloes was comin'.

SADE: Not much difference. Lands, I hope Orval ain't got on them shoes with the nails in 'em. The floor there by the davenport is *still* all criss-crossed from his feet. Rush, ya wanta get a chair an' hand me down the fancy plates?

RUSH: You said for me to study.

SADE: This won't take a second. C'mon.

RUSH: Ya don't happen to know what the word "percussion" means, do ya?

SADE: Somethin' ya stick pins in?

RUSH: Not "pin-cushion," "percussion."

SADE: No, I don't know. Get up on the chair now.

RUSH: [*getting up*] D'ya think Stobo Brimmer'll come too, Mom?

SADE: Mis' Brimmer said the whole family. Guess that means Stobo along with the rest. I hope he don't bang his head against the wall an' knock down the plaster like he did last time.

RUSH: What'd he bang his head for?

SADE: He'd been swimmin' that afternoon an' had water in his ear. Tryin' to knock it out.

RUSH: Ya do *that* with your *hand*, Mom.

SADE: Stobo did it with the wall. Plaster fell like rain. Hurry up an' hand 'em down, son. I wouldn't want 'em to walk in while we were hidin' things. Lands, I . . . handle that gentle!

RUSH: Here y'are.

SADE: Take the olive an' pickle plate next. It *does* seem kinda mean to treat people's children like they were wild tigers but I don't see how else . . .

VIC: [*back again*] What else ya want done, Sade?

SADE: Listen: why doncha run upstairs in the closet an' get that auto robe.

VIC: What for?

SADE: Put on the davenport. You know what the baby done last time.

VIC: Oh, uh-huh. Which closet is it in?

SADE: It's . . . a . . . Oh, I don't know. Hafta look for it. Here . . . you take the fancy plates as Rush hands 'em down. *I'll* run up an' get the auto robe.

VIC: Hand me a plate, Roscoe.

SADE: [*going*] Handle 'em gentle now.

RUSH: Have a fancy dish on *me*, Gov.

VIC: Delighted. Where they go? . . . Here in the drawer?

RUSH: Yeah.

VIC: I wonder if that young wildcat *Foster* Brimmer will be among our guests.

RUSH: Mom said *everybody*.

VIC: It's a real treat to have young Foster on the premises. I'd just as soon entertain a sick rhinoceros.

RUSH: Here's the meat platter. Heavier'n the dickens.

VIC: I'll say.

RUSH: Foster *shaves* now, Gov.

VIC: Indeed. I'll be all the more thrilled when I see him.

RUSH: He started shavin' the first of the year, an' he's shaved five times a day ever since.

VIC: Whiskers grow fast?

RUSH: No, but Foster believes in doin' a thing up brown. Here's a bean dipper.

VIC: Foster Brimmer was the chap who doctored up our picture of William McKinley with colored crayons.

RUSH: [*chuckling*] Did he do that?

VIC: Yessir. He made President McKinley look very much like Santa Claus. Your mother was somewhat excited. I remember . . .

SADE: [*reappearing*] Got 'em all down?

RUSH: There's just a couple more.

SADE: Well, hurry. I got the auto robe. It'll be *some* protection. Say, Vic, I'll finish here with Rush if you'll go out in the bottom drawer of the cupboard an' get that strip of oilcloth that's under the towels.

VIC: Whatcha want *that* for?

SADE: Put it under the auto robe. Our davenport is just too good to be ruined. That baby is . . . say, Vic, before ya do that, why doncha take the photograph album an' hide it in the cupboard drawer? Remember William McKinley?

VIC: I was just regaling Rush here with that anecdote.

SADE: Well, do that. [*to Rush*] What else is up there, son?

RUSH: Salt an' pepper shakers an' celery splasher.

SADE: Hand 'em down.

VIC: [*going*] Ya say that oilcloth is in the bottom cupboard drawer?

SADE: Under the towels. You'll find it.

RUSH: That's all, Mom.

SADE: All right. Jump down.

RUSH: [*jumping down*] Want me to do anything else?

SADE: No, you can go back to your studyin'.

RUSH: How about Gov's little footrest? Wanta hide that?

SADE: No, it's substantial enough so nobody can hurt it. I wish *everything* we had was . . . say, I guess we *had* better hide that footrest. Alvin always trips over it.

RUSH: [*giggles*] He does?

SADE: Last time he was here he fell over it three times. Once he clawed at my table scarf an' tore a big chunk of embroidery off. I *tell* ya, just push it under the davenport. No, better not. Eugene'll be sure to crawl under there. Take it out an' put it under the sink.

RUSH: Won't Eugene be crawlin' under the sink?

SADE: I'm gonna try to keep 'em *out* of my kitchen. Go on, take it. [*raises voice*] Find it, Vic?

VIC: [*appearing*] Yeah.

SADE: Give it here.

RUSH: [*going*] I'll put the footrest behind the wastebasket, Mom.

SADE: All right. [*to Vic*] Wanta take one end of this oilcloth?

VIC: O. K.

SADE: It won't reach all the way. It'll just cover this end.

VIC: Why not put it in the middle?

SADE: No, let's put it like this. Then we'll remember to sit on *that* end of the davenport. If the baby crawls over there, move him an' sit down.

VIC: All right.

SADE: [*regretfully*] I guess we can't do anything about the curtains.

VIC: What's the matter with 'em?

SADE: Hobart is sure to have a pocketful of sticky candy. Remember what he did to the curtains last time?

VIC: Oh, that's right.

SADE: Well, the davenport's fixed. [*giggles*] *Looks* kinda funny. That ol' robe. I hope Verna don't catch on. She's very sensitive even if she *don't* seem to care what her children do.

RUSH: [*returning*] I put the footrest out on the back porch, Mom.

SADE: Good.

VIC: What's the matter with the footrest? Nobody can damage *that*.

SADE: You know how Alvin always trips over it.

VIC: Oh.

SADE: Well, I guess we done all we can do.

VIC: Yeah.

SADE: Rush, you better finish your studyin', hadn't ya?

RUSH: Yeah.

VIC: Through with *me*, Sade?

SADE: I guess so.

VIC: I'll finish readin' my paper then.

SADE: I'm goin' out in the hall an' see how things are. I wouldn't dare leave any good clothes hangin' around. [*goes*]

RUSH: Gov.

VIC: Yeah?

RUSH: Happen to know what "flotsam" means?

VIC: Why, yes. Flotsam is a disease that afflicts the nether limbs of cuttlefish, making their oil useless in the manufacture of shoe polish.

RUSH: Will you write all that down for me?

VIC: Gladly.

RUSH: Here's pencil an' paper.

VIC: I'll fix you up after a while. Right now I . . . [*doorbell*]

RUSH: There's the Brimmers.

VIC: Yes, indeed.

RUSH: I bet . . .

VIC: Listen . . .

SADE: [*in distance*] Hel-lo there. Hello, Verna. How are *you*, Mr. Brimmer? Come on in. Hello there, Orval. How are you, *Alvin?* Well, well, well . . . an' the *baby*.

VIC: [*to Rush*] C'mon, son, we got company.

Which concludes another brief interlude at the small house half-way up in the next block.

First broadcast 1937.

24

·——·••·——·

Is Charley Dead?

Well *sir, it's late afternoon as we enter the small house half-way up in the next block now, and here in the living room we discover Mr. Victor Gook and his son, Mr. Rush Gook. This latter individual is reading aloud from the works of one of his favorite authors, while his father attends with no great enthusiasm. Listen:*

RUSH: [*reading*] "It was a tender leave-taking between the young captain and his aged father. Tears rolled down the old soldier's face as he wrung the hand of the boy an' said, 'Charles, when you're on the field of battle slayin' the wild native bushmen, bear in mind that in your veins flows the blood of courage. I myself as a youth was cited for bravery, an' upon my breast were placed eleven medals for extraordinary valor. Charles, I cannot *believe* that you were once a golden-haired baby, lisping at my knee, an' sayin', "Daddy, tell about . . ."

VIC: Aw, that's enough of that junk.

RUSH: No, wait. Pretty soon it takes us to the sweltering jungles of darkest Africa.

VIC: I got my *own* book to read.

RUSH: I'll skip over to where Captain Chalmers hides inside a dead elephant an' takes pot-shots at . . .

VIC: Naw.

RUSH: It's the most exciting thing ya ever heard of.

VIC: I can get enough excitement outa this Kitchenware Dealers' Quarterly.

RUSH: Let me just read ya about where Captain Chalmers pulls out his front teeth to put in his rifle to use for bullets because he's run outa ammunition an' hasta . . .

VIC: Naw. Anyway there's somebody on the porch.

RUSH: [*looking*] That's Mom.

VIC: Read your story-book to *her.*

RUSH: You're missin' somethin' *good,* Gov. A few pages further along here Captain Chalmers trips over a boa constrictor an' at the same time falls into a lagoon alive with crocodiles. By gosh, he . . .

SADE: [*off*] Rush?

RUSH: [*calls*] Yeah, Mom.

SADE: [*closer*] Your *father's* not home, is he?

RUSH: [*calls*] Sure. In here.

SADE: [*closer*] Vic?

VIC: [*raises voice*] Uh-huh?

SADE: [*closer*] Have you *heard?*

VIC: No.

SADE: [*almost up*] Haven't heard *anything?*

VIC: No. What's the matter?

SADE: [*up*] Anybody telephone?

VIC: Not since *I* been here.

RUSH: Phone ain't rung since I been home either.

VIC: What's the excitement, kiddo?

SADE: [*in a dither*] You'll hafta give me a chance to catch my breath. Here, Rush, take my coat an' hat.

RUSH: Hang 'em up in the hall?

SADE: Yes. When'd ya get home from school?

RUSH: Oh, half an hour ago, I guess.

SADE: Come through the alley?

RUSH: Uh-huh.

SADE: Never saw anything going on?

RUSH: Nothin' outa the *ordinary.* Mis' Fisher was lookin' out her kitchen window an' Mr. Drummond was sittin' on the back porch but there wasn't any other signs of human life except Mr. Gumpox's horse that was . . .

SADE: Run along with my hat an' coat.

RUSH: Has somethin' happened that . . .

SADE: *I'll* tell ya when I get my breath.

RUSH: [*moving off*] O. K.

SADE: [*to Vic*] My heart's just *pumpin'* away.
VIC: What the dickens . . .
SADE: I guess I'm not *built* for excitement. Why, I found myself just *runnin'* home.
VIC: Well, spit out what's happened. I . . .
SADE: Charley Razorscum.
VIC: What about him?
SADE: *Dead.*
VIC: Charley *Razorscum* is dead?
SADE: Passed away not over half an hour ago.
VIC: Holy Smoke.
SADE: Ain't it awful?
VIC: Well, tell me . . .
SADE: I gotta get *hold* of myself. Just a second while I breathe in some air.
RUSH: [*approaching*] Who'd you say was dead, Mom?
SADE: [*raising voice*] Talk to your father. My nerves are jumpin' up an' down like a house afire.
RUSH: [*closer*] Who's dead, Gov?
VIC: Charley Razorscum.
RUSH: [*in disbelief*] Aw. When'd he die?
VIC: I don't know. Your mother's kinda upset an' can't give any details. She says . . .
RUSH: Charley Razorscum's over in his backyard changin' a tire on his automobile.
VIC: Aw.
RUSH: I *saw* him. When I come home from school.
VIC: You saw somebody *else* prob'ly.
RUSH: I saw *Charley.* In fact I *spoke* to him.
VIC: Hear that, Sade? Howard here claims . . .
SADE: Let me sit here with my eyes closed a minute an' try to get myself settled.
VIC: Rush says Charley's over in his backyard changin' a tire.
SADE: It's the last tire he'll ever change on *this* earth. He fell down an' died in Yamilton's store only half an hour ago.
RUSH: *I* saw him *less'n* half an hour ago. I hollered, "Nice job ya got there, Mr. Razorscum," an' he hollered back, "*Next* time I want transportation I'm gonna buy a *horse.*" I says . . .

SADE: Vic, *you* wanta call Ruthie?

VIC: Why?

SADE: *I'm* not quite up to it. Nerves are janglin' together like Pat an' Mike. An' *she'll* wanta know about this. Just tell 'er Mr. Razorscum passed away this afternoon.

VIC: Yeah, but are you sure he *did* pass away? Albert claims he's alive an' feelin' fine.

RUSH: He wasn't feelin' so fine when *I* saw him. He'd just banged his leg with a jack-handle an' he was doin' some talkin' I wouldn't care to repeat in . . .

SADE: Watch your tongue, Rush. Mr. Razorscum was awful good to *you* before he died.

RUSH: He never *died*, Mom. I saw him with my own *eyes*. I . . .

SADE: [*to Vic*] Go call Ruthie.

VIC: Let's check *up* on this. If the guy's *alive* . . .

SADE: He's *not* alive. What's the *matter* with you? Mis' Appelrot wouldn't lie.

VIC: What's Mis' *Appelrot* got to do with it?

SADE: She's the one that *told* me about . . . Don't go 'way, Rush, I'll prob'ly need you for *lots* of things. We'll hafta bake cakes an' pies for Mis' Razorscum an' the relatives an' . . .

RUSH: [*moving off*] I'm only going to the kitchen. Wanta take a look out the window.

SADE: [*after him*] What for?

RUSH: [*off*] See if Mr. Razorscum's still changin' that automobile tire.

SADE: [*vexatiously to Vic*] What *ails* that child?

VIC: He thinks you're *wrong* about this. He says he saw Charley . . .

SADE: Oh, "he saw Charley." He saw his *grandmother*. *Boy,* how my heart thumps. I'm not *up* to things like this.

VIC: Did Mis' Appelrot say Charlie . . .

SADE: A man fell dead on the second floor of Yamilton's. Charley Razorscum. They think it was heart trouble.

VIC: I never heard of *Charley* havin' heart trouble.

SADE: Ya never can *tell* about that stuff. Lands, this all happened so quick I don't know *what* to think. Poor ol' Charley Razorscum. Only forty-four years old. Why, just *yesterday* we had a nice long chat out by the garbage box. An' a funny, funny *thing* happened. I'm not superstitious or anything like that, but Charley says to me, "Mis' Gook, did you ever see the sky so blue?"

VIC: Well, what did you . . .

SADE: "Did you ever see the sky so blue, Mis' Gook?" he says. *He* knew somethin' was comin'. He *felt* . . . oh, I'm not the kind that dreams up wild *notions,* but Vic, that man had a strange look in his eye. Seems to me I kinda shivered. An' *another* peculiar . . .

RUSH: [*off*] Hey.

SADE: . . . thing was when he walked away from our garbage box an' . . .

RUSH: [*off*] Hey!

SADE: . . . started back to his house. I was watchin' him an' I . . .

RUSH: [*off*] Hey!

SADE: . . . noticed that his arms kinda waved back an' forth like . . .

RUSH: [*off*] Hey!

SADE: [*to Vic*] What's the *matter* with him?

VIC: Maybe he . . .

SADE: He's got to cut out that yellin' now that *this* has happened. When a person's at rest right in the neighborhood, ya hafta show respect an' . . .

RUSH: [*off*] Mom.

SADE: [*calls irritably*] What do you *want?* [*to Vic*] Phone Ruthie, will ya? Just tell her that Mr. Razorscum passed away this afternoon an' . . .

RUSH: [*off*] He's still workin' on that automobile tire.

SADE: [*to Vic*] Huh?

VIC: He's still workin' on that automobile tire.

SADE: Who?

VIC: Charley Razorscum, I s'pose. Rush says . . .

SADE: Oh, "Rush says." Go ahead, phone Ruthie.

VIC: I think I'll check *up* on this, kiddo.

SADE: Where ya going?

VIC: To the kitchen an' look out the window. C'mon.

SADE: I couldn't get up off this davenport to save my life.

VIC: Aw, c'mon, you wanta be *sure*, doncha? . . . before ya start callin' up people on the phone.

SADE: [*getting up*] Do you think Mis' Appelrot would *lie?*

VIC: It's possible she was *mistaken.*

SADE: [*tough*] How ya mean?

RUSH: [*closer*] I never saw Charley Razorscum look any healthier in my life.

SADE: [*tough, to Vic*] How ya *mean* it's possible she was mistaken?

VIC: Did she *see* Charley kick the bucket?

SADE: Vic, I'd be ashamed.

VIC: Why?

SADE: Sayin' kick the bucket about a man that's been a close neighbor for years.

VIC: [*little chuckle*] Well, shucks, it . . .

SADE: An' *laughin'.*

VIC: *I'm* not laughin'. I only . . .

SADE: What do you *mean* did she see him?

VIC: Did she personally see him pass away in Yamilton's store?

SADE: *No.* A clerk told her.

VIC: Well, perhaps . . .

SADE: An' the name was Razorscum. Charley Razorscum. If you know any *other* Charley Razorscums . . .

RUSH: [*almost up*] Take a look at your dead man, Mom.

SADE: Where?

RUSH: Up the alley by the telephone pole.

SADE: Get outa the way.

RUSH: He's kneelin' down beside the rear wheel of his car now. But you can see his legs.

SADE: *This* is a fine time to be hammerin' an' clangin' around automobiles . . . with a *body* only six feet away. Who *is* that?

VIC: [*suppressing a chuckle*] Don't *hit* me, Sade, but I think it's Charley Razorscum.

SADE: [*ignoring Vic*] Who is that man, Rush?

RUSH: Charley Razorscum.

VIC: Them are certainly Charley's *legs.* I'd recognize them . . .

RUSH: *There*, he's standin' up. You can see his face.

VIC: Charley Razorscum.

RUSH: If *he's* dead I'll throw in with ya.

VIC: Satisfied, kiddo?

SADE: I can't *understand* it.

VIC: The guy that fainted in Yamilton's prob'ly just *looked* like Charley. Charley's one of these people that kinda fall into a *class*. I've mistaken *lotsa* fellas for Charley. Why, one time in Chicago I was havin' lunch with Mr. Buller an' I'd of bet my last dime the waiter was Charley Razorscum. Same face an' walk an' . . .

SADE: I just can't *understand* it.

VIC: Are you satisfied that that man over there fixin' the auto tire is Charley?

SADE: Yeah, he's Charley all right.

VIC: Will you admit he's alive an' not dead?

SADE: Um.

RUSH: *I'll* cover everything that's laid on the line he's alive.

VIC: If I put up a nickel that says he's dead, will you give a thousand to one odds?

RUSH: I'll give *two* thousand to one odds.

SADE: I just can't *understand* it.

VIC: Why?

SADE: Mis' *Appelrot* wouldn't lie.

Which concludes another brief interlude at the small house half-way up in the next block.

First broadcast 1937.

25

Stembottom's Invitation to Drive 35 Miles to a Double Feature

Well sir, *the murkiness of eventide has descended upon peaceful Virginia Avenue as our scene opens now, and as we approach the small house half-way up in the next block we see Mr. Victor Gook and his son Mr. Rush Gook ascending the front porch steps. And the one is saying to the other:*

VIC: Your mother in the house?
RUSH: Living room.
VIC: You were cruel to drag me away from my game of indoor horseshoes.
RUSH: Mom told me to trot over to Kneesuffers' basement an' bring you home. I had to obey orders.
VIC: Open the screen door then.
RUSH: [*opening the screen door*] Were you winning when I dragged you away?
VIC: Had Ike looking like thirty cents.
SADE: [*off a little*] Hi-de-hi.
VIC: [*as screen door slams*] Ho-de-ho. What's the idea sending disreputable characters to drag me away from my pleasure?
RUSH: I left that for *you*, Mom.
VIC: I bet some beautiful woman heavily veiled an' greatly agitated is hiding under the davenport. I bet . .
SADE: [*up*] Ruthie just telephoned.

VIC: She objects to me pitchin' indoor horseshoes over in Ike Kneesuffer's . . .

SADE: Invited us to go for a spin in the car.

VIC: [*disconsolate*] Aw.

SADE: Such a lovely evening an' all, they thought we'd enjoy . . .

VIC: Ya accept?

SADE: I felt like I *had* to. Ruthie knew we didn't have any *other* engagements.

VIC: I'd rather take a *lickin'* than bump around in that roller skate of Fred's.

SADE: Well, *I* didn't know what to say.

VIC: [*a suggestion*] "Victor is tired."

SADE: Oh, *that's* no excuse.

VIC: You could have said . . .

SADE: I've already accepted the invitation an' they'll be around honkin' the horn out in front pretty soon.

VIC: [*unhappy*] Shucks.

SADE: I laid your hat an' top-coat over the hallway bannister. Soon as they pull up to the curb an' toot we'll run right out. May not be for quite a while yet. Fred hasta pump up three of the tires.

VIC: *That's* cheerful. A tiny fear gnaws at my heart *I'll* be pumpin' up tires later on. When we're out on the hard road.

SADE: [*undisturbed*] Oh, maybe not.

VIC: [*discontented*] I wanted to go to bed *early* tonight.

RUSH: [*chuckles*] I *am* going to bed early.

VIC: You're not joining us?

RUSH: [*negative*] Uh-uh.

SADE: Makes it a little too *late* for *boys*. He's got to be wide awake for school tomorrow.

RUSH: [*giggles*] Tomorrow's Saturday.

SADE: Makes it a little too late *anyway*.

RUSH: [*chuckles*] *I* don't care. *I'd* just as leave go to bed.

VIC: What's this "too late" business? Ain't gonna take all night to drive to *Chenoa* an' back. Even if Fred *does* drag along like a snail.

SADE: We're not *going* to Chenoa. Going to *Hopewood*.

VIC: What's the big new glorious idea? I *thought* Fred never went anywhere but Chenoa.

SADE: [*hesitant*] We're invited to . . . the picture show.

VIC: In Hopewood?

SADE: Yeah.

VIC: [*exasperated*] Sade, *you* know I hate . . .

SADE: [*quickly*] Listen now an' don't get hot under the collar. It was Fred's notion an' he's so pleased an' proud about it he's dancing a jig.

VIC: *I'll* dance a jig if . . .

SADE: Ruthie called up an' said, "What you people doin'?" I thought she was going to suggest Five Hundred so I said we were just sittin' here with our teeth in our mouth. She says, "This great big crazy spendthrift Fred Stembottom here at my elbow wants to pile you sports in the automobile an' drive up to Hopewood an' take in the motion pictures." Well . . . what could I answer to *that?*

VIC: "Victor's tired."

SADE: [*contempt*] Oh—"Victor's tired." I said, "Why, Ruthie, how wonderful!" That's all in the wide world I *could* say.

VIC: Bumpety-bumpety-bump. All the way to Hopewood.

SADE: [*agreeing*] *I* know. But that's the way it is. An' we hafta make out to Fred like we're all delighted. He thinks it's the cutest idea since the bullet that choked Billy Patterson. [*quotes Fred's probable thought*] "Vic and Sade are most likely dying to take in a movie show an' the Bijou is closed for repairs. By George, Ruthie, let's run 'em up to Hopewood an' give 'em a treat."

VIC: [*mild groan*]

SADE: So don't you behave grumpy and sour. Act like you're grateful as a horse.

VIC: Wish I could go to bed.

RUSH: I *am* going to bed.

VIC: Thunder, kiddo, it's thirty-five *miles* to Hopewood. The way *Fred* nurses that garbage-wagon along the road it'll take us an hour an' a half to get there.

SADE: [*I can't help it*] Um.

VIC: An' it's eight o'clock now. Great guns, we *will* be out late. Say we get started at eight-thirty. All right, add an hour an' a half to eight-thirty an' ya got ten o'clock. Movie show takes about two hours. *Twelve* o'clock. Another hour an' a half to get home makes it one-thirty. We won't be in bed till *two!*

RUSH: Double feature.

VIC: [*to Sade*] *Think* of it . . . two o'clock. An' I wanted to be in the hay by eleven.

SADE: Oh well, missin' *one* evening's sleep won't kill ya.

RUSH: They got a double *feature* on at the Hopewood theatre, Gov.

VIC: Naw.

RUSH: [*chuckles*] Yeah.

VIC: Have they, Sade?

SADE: That's what Ruthie told me.

VIC: Will we hafta sit through *both* pictures?

SADE: I'm afraid so. When Fred puts out his good money an' buys *tickets* for a thing he stays till the last dog dies.

VIC: [*appalled*] But Holy *Smoke!*

SADE: We're in for it an' can't get loose so let's make the *best* of it.

VIC: [*appalled*] But *look*. Another moving picture makes another two hours tacked onto . . . what time did I say we'd . . .

RUSH: [*chuckles*] One-thirty.

VIC: Yeah—one-thirty. Two hours tacked onto one-thirty . . .

RUSH AND VIC: *Three*-thirty.

VIC: [*dismal groan*]

SADE: I don't think . . .

VIC: We'll all get to bed around *four*.

SADE: [*giggles*] Oh, that's crazy.

VIC: It's *not* crazy. It's . . .

SADE: Is *too* crazy. Right now the clock says quarter till eight. Fred and Ruthie'll drive up in the next few minutes an' we'll be on our *way* by eight. An' it don't take any hour an' a half to drive to Hopewood.

VIC: The way *Fred* drives?

SADE: He certainly can get to a place thirty-five miles away in an hour no matter *how* slow he drives.

RUSH: I disagree.

VIC: So do I.

SADE: Say a little *over* an hour. All right, we'll be in the theater a little bit past nine o'clock. The two movies together don't last more'n three hours. I bet we'll be home in bed by midnight.

VIC AND RUSH: Oh, go on. You didn't figure in the . . . [*ad lib*]

SADE: [*laughing*] There's no use in a lot of fuss an' *feathers*. I told 'em we'd go, an' we're going. Let's make the best of it an' try to enjoy ourselves.

VIC: [*unhappily*] Oh my, my. An' just a few minutes ago I was a gay light-hearted man.

RUSH: [*mischievously*] Tell him the *picture*, Mom.

SADE: [*sharply*] I don't see as *you're* concerned in this, Rush. *You're* not going. Trot along an' read your book.

VIC: What is the picture, Sadie?

SADE: [*blankly*] Picture?

VIC: What are they *showing* at the playhouse in Hopewood?

SADE: [*timidly*] I'm afraid it's the one you've already seen.

VIC: [*coldly*] Yes?

SADE: We saw it last month or sometime at the Bijou.

VIC: [*coldly*] You propose to drag me to a . . .

SADE: Ruthie an' Fred were so *delighted* with their idea, Vic. Just happy as *larks* they were givin' us a treat. I didn't have the *heart* to dampen their enthusiasm. Should of heard Ruthie over the phone. [*quotes*] "This great big crazy spendthrift of a Fred Stembottom here at my elbow wants to pile you sports in the automobile an' drive up to Hopewood an' take in the motion pictures." I *had* to act overjoyed.

VIC: [*coldly*] Reveal the name of the motion picture.

SADE: What is it, Rush?

RUSH: "You Are My Own Wonderful Husband, Subaltern Gleek."

VIC: [*explosive*] *No.*

SADE: [*timidly*] I *told* you you'd already *seen* it.

VIC: I seen it an' I hated it. It was rotten.

SADE: Never cared much for it myself. But Fred and Ruthie . . .

VIC: So I hafta bump an' lurch thirty-five miles in that broken-down rattletrap of Stembottom's to go up in the sticks in Hopewood Illinois an' watch that halfwit Gloria Golden go through the same halfwit antics I saw her go through before. So I hafta . . .

SADE: Now, Vic, *please.*

VIC: *I'll* say, "Now Vic please."

SADE: You'll get all flushed in the face.

VIC: It's a wonder I don't turn *purple*.

SADE: Get all flushed in the face an' they'll think something's wrong.

VIC: An' they'll be perfectly right.

SADE: Any *second* the horn'll honk out in front. You don't wanta look upset an' peculiar to where everybody feels uncomfortable.

VIC: Ump.

SADE: [*giggles*] Think of the *funny* side of it.

VIC: [*chuckles*] Maybe that *is* a good stunt.

SADE: Sure.

VIC: [*chuckles*] Shucks.

RUSH: [*innocently*] Quite a co-incidence. Gloria Golden's also in the *other* picture.

SADE: [*sharply*] Rush, go upstairs an' read your book. This business don't in any way concern . . .

VIC: [*to Sade*] What *is* the other picture?

SADE: [*blankly*] Other picture?

VIC: [*coldly*] I understood we were attending a double feature. Double feature, unless I'm misinformed, means two pictures. One of 'em is Gloria Golden in "You Are My Own Wonderful Husband, Subaltern Gleek." What's the other?

SADE: [*timidly*] I guess Gloria Golden's in it.

VIC: [*gently and politely*] Something I've seen before?

SADE: I . . . believe you *did* see it when they had it at the Bijou.

VIC: [*gently*] An' the title?

SADE: I forget.

VIC: Rush . . . the title?

RUSH: [*timidly*] Mom'd prefer I never said nothing.

VIC: She'll forgive you this time.

RUSH: Um.

VIC: [*gently*] The title, please?

RUSH: "Yours Is A Magnificent Love, Petty-Officer Griswold."

VIC: [*low moan of anguish*]

SADE: [*after a moment*] Let's go out on the porch, Vic. They'll be along any second an' we might as well be ready to hop in the machine . . .

VIC: [*in pain*] "Yours Is A Magnificent Love, Petty-Officer Griswold." Absolutely the rottenest movie that ever was given out to a suffering people. The rottenest, rottenest, rottenest, rottenest . . .

SADE: Let's go out on the porch.

VIC: [*piteously*] What?

SADE: Let's put on our wraps an' go stand on the front porch so we'll be all set to trot out to the curbing as soon as the machine . . .

VIC: [*piteously*] Sadie, you *couldn't* make me go through this. You wouldn't have the *heart* to . . .

SADE: [*briefly*] We're stuck an' that's all there is about it.

VIC: [*moan of anguish*]

SADE: [*briefly*] We're stuck an' that's all there is about it.

VIC: [*piteously*] I am a miserable wretched . . . [*auto horn*]

RUSH: There they are.

VIC: . . . abused, grief-stricken . . .

SADE: Fred an' Ruthie's out in front honkin'. C'mon.

VIC: [*low moan*]

SADE: C'mon . . . [*auto horn again*]

VIC: [*low moan*]

SADE: [*briefly*] Straighten up an' get that look off your face. An' don't you dare in any way let on to Fred and Ruthie.

VIC: [*low moan*]

SADE: [*briefly*] C'mon. [*auto horn*]

RUSH: Good-bye, Mom.

SADE: [*briefly*] 'Bye.

RUSH: 'Bye, Gov.

VIC: [*low moan*]

RUSH: [*cheerfully*] Have a dandy time.

Which concludes another brief visit at the small house half-way up in the next block.

First broadcast 1939.

26

Schoolmate Telephones Sade from the Bus Station at 4:20 A.M.

W*ell sir, we're visiting our friends who live in the small house half-way up in the next block at a very, very odd time today. It's past four o'clock in the morning, and Mr. and Mrs. Victor Gook and young Mr. Rush Gook are all in their beds fast asleep. But . . . listen:*

[*Telephone rings steadily a few seconds. There's a pause, and it rings again . . . and again . . . and again.*]

SADE: [*wakes up suddenly and calls*] Yes? [*telephone again*] [*pokes her husband*] Vic.

VIC: [*makes guttural noises*]

SADE: *Vic.* [*phone again*]

RUSH: [*off*] Mom.

SADE: *Vic.* [*calls*] Yes?

RUSH: [*off*] Telephone's ringing.

SADE: [*calls*] I know it. *Vic.*

VIC: [*gradually coming to life*] Huh? [*telephone rings*]

SADE: *Telephone.*

VIC: Who?

RUSH: [*off*] Want me to answer it?

SADE: [*calls*] What?

RUSH: [*off*] Shall I answer it?

SADE: Yeah. [*telephone again*]

VIC: [*to Sade*] What's going on?

SADE: Telephone's ringing.
VIC: Where?
SADE: [*calls*] Who is it, Rush?
RUSH: [*off*] I haven't answered yet.
VIC: [*to Sade*] What time is it?
SADE: *I* don't know.
VIC: Hand me my watch there on the table.
RUSH: [*off a little ways*] Hello? Yeah. Who?
VIC: [*to Sade*] Hand me my watch there on the . . .
SADE: *Listen.*
RUSH: [*at telephone*] Mister Gook? *Missus* Gook? One second, please. [*calls*] Mom.
SADE: [*calls*] Who is it?
RUSH: [*approaching*] They never said.
SADE: Man or lady?
RUSH: Lady.
SADE: [*excited*] Oh, goodness, somebody sick. Who'd it sound like?
RUSH: [*up*] Didn't recognize the voice.
SADE: See if you can see my other slipper.
RUSH: Can't see *nothin'*. It's dark.
SADE: Vic, turn on the light.
VIC: Huh?
SADE: Turn on the light.
VIC: Who is it on the telephone?
SADE: [*irritably*] *I* don't know. Hurry up: switch on that lamp.
VIC: [*switching it on*] That you, Rush?
RUSH: [*chuckling*] Sure. I was sound asleep when that telephone started to ring. There was a little dream about bein' on the Sahara Desert going on in my brains an' that doggone bell . . .
SADE: Rush, *will* you find my other slipper?
RUSH: It's right here by the foot of the bed.
SADE: Well, *hand* it to a person. There's people waitin' on the phone.
VIC: Wonder who the heck it is.
SADE: Somebody *sick.* [*to Rush*] Never sounded like Aunt Bess, did it?
RUSH: I can't trust my own judgment, Mom. See, I was only half awake when I answered it an' the sound of a human voice . . .

SADE: [*moving off*] Keep quiet in here now so I can hear what they say.

VIC: [*to Rush*] What's the time?

RUSH: Search *me*.

VIC: Well, look at my *watch* there.

RUSH: An individual's brains are very foggy when they're awoke out of a deep sleep. Under different circumstances . . .

VIC: What's it say?

RUSH: Ah . . . four-twenty.

VIC: Holy Smoke.

SADE: [*off—at phone*] Yes? Yes, this is Sadie. Who?

RUSH: [*to Vic*] Twenty minutes past four in the morning. If I was *guessin'* at it I would of said . . .

VIC: Pipe down.

SADE: [*off—to phone*] I'm sorry . . . I didn't quite catch the name. Mrs. Shuggle? Myrtle? Myrtle Frummer. [*remembers Myrtle*] Oh— sure. Well forevermore! [*cordial, but not gushingly so*] How *are* ya, Myrtle? My stars! Oh, fine an' dandy. Well, where *are* ya, Myrtle? Oh. Oh, uh-huh. Yes.

RUSH: [*to Vic*] Who's Myrtle Frummer?

VIC: I don't know.

RUSH: No sir. *I* wouldn't of guessed it was four-twenty in the morning. If I'd been called upon to approximate the time I would of said . . .

VIC: Be still.

SADE: [*off; she's been ad libbing yesses and uh-huhs*] Well, think of that. Lands, I'd just about thought you'd dropped off the face of the earth. Oh sure, *often* think of ya. I expect you're still located in Sioux City, Iowa? Oh, it's Niles, *Michigan* now, huh. *Well.* My, my. Yes, I guess work like that *does* take ya around the country a good deal.

RUSH: [*to Vic*] Don't *sound* like anybody's sick.

VIC: Ump.

RUSH: Who'd ya say Myrtle Frummer was?

VIC: I never said. I don't know.

SADE: [*to phone*] Oh, he's big as a house now. Oh sure—going on fifteen years old. Well, some says he looks like me an' some says he looks like his father. Vic? Fine as silk. Uh-huh.

RUSH: [*to Vic*] Must be some dear old *friend* of Mom's. I don't set myself up as the eighth wonder of the world or anything but give me a set of facts an' I can deduce . . .

VIC: Go on back to bed. I'm in no mood for light chit-chat at five o'clock in the morning.

SADE: [*to phone*] Why . . . a . . . of *course. Surely,* Myrtle.

RUSH: [*to Vic*] I bet she wants to come an' stay all night.

SADE: [*approaching*] Vic.

VIC: [*raises voice*] Yeah?

SADE: [*closer*] I guess you'll hafta get up an' talk over the phone.

VIC: Who is it?

SADE: [*closer*] Myrtle Frummer—girl I went to school with back in Dixon.

VIC: *I* don't know her, do I?

SADE: No. But she wants to hear the voice of the man I married.

VIC: Aw, for gosh sakes. Do you realize what time it is?

SADE: Midnight?

VIC: It's going on five o'clock in the morning.

SADE: Really?

VIC: What the heck is her half-wit idea of . . .

SADE: They're takin' a trip on a bus. On their way to Saint Louis. Bus stopped at the bus station outside of town where the people get out for a bite to eat an' coffee an' freshen up in the bathroom. Myrtle remembered this is the town we live in an' thought it'd be nice to telephone.

VIC: [*bitterly*] At four-thirty in the morning.

SADE: She never *was* an awful *bright* kid. Wasn't ever any particular friend of mine either.

VIC: *I'm* not gonna get up.

SADE: You *got* to.

VIC: Tell her I just died.

SADE: She's *waitin'*, Vic. Ya got to treat people *civilized.*

VIC: People ain't treatin' *me* civilized. Ringing the doggone telephone at dawn like a nitwit that don't . . .

SADE: C'mon—here's your slippers.

VIC: Oh my, my, my, my.

SADE: Rush, *you* go to talk to her . . . till your father gets there.

RUSH: What the heck'll I say?

SADE: I don't know, but she said she wanted to hear my little boy's voice too.

RUSH: [moving off] Shall I say I hope she has a peachy bus ride to Kansas City?

SADE: It's Saint Louis they're going to. An' her name is Myrtle Frummer. "Shuggle" is her married name.

RUSH: [off a ways] What'll I call her?

SADE: [raising voice] Mrs. Shuggle.

RUSH: [calling back] "Mrs. Shuggle, I hope you have a peachy bus ride to Saint Louis"?

SADE: [calls] Yeah. [to her husband] Vic, don't just sit there on the edge of the bed. Let's get this over with.

VIC: What kind of a lunatic is the woman?

SADE: She prob'ly never stopped to think about the time. Always was kind of a scatterbrain. C'mon.

VIC: [groaning] Oh, my, my, my.

RUSH: [off] Hello? No, this is Rush. Huh? Yeah, I was named after my mother's maiden name. Uh-huh. That so?

SADE: [to Vic] Talk nice now. I don't want her to think I married a mean old bear.

VIC: Why deceive her? I am a mean old bear.

RUSH: [closer] I'm fourteen. Uh-huh. Yeah, first year. Hundred an' eleven pounds stripped. Five feet three inches. Eyes? Blue. Hair? I part it on the side.

SADE: [to Rush in low tones] All right, let Gov talk.

RUSH: [to phone] Thank you, Mrs. Buggle.

SADE: Shuggle.

RUSH: [to his mother] Huh?

SADE: Shuggle.

RUSH: How ya mean?

SADE: Her name is Shuggle—not Buggle.

RUSH: [to phone] Yes, Mrs. Shuggle. Well, I hope you have a peachy trip to Kansas City. Now I'll connect you with my father. [to Vic] She'll wanta know what color your hair is an' how much ya weigh an' how tall . . .

SADE: [hissing] Be still. She'll hear ya.

VIC: [to phone] Hello? Yeah. Just fine. No. I guess we never met. [negative] Uh-uh. I'm in the kitchenware business. No, I'm in the manufacturing end of the game. Yeah. No. Yeah. Oh, that so? Yeah, like to meet him some time. What? Well, don't bother *now*. Listen, if he's asleep let him *sleep*. Some *other* time . . . [*to Sade*] Oh, thunder, thunder, thunder.

SADE: She want ya to talk to her husband?

VIC: Yeah . . . an' he's out in the bus asleep.

SADE: [*irritated*] Lands.

VIC: She's gone out to wake him up an' bring him in.

SADE: What time'd ya say it was?

VIC: Must be a quarter to five or so.

RUSH: *I'd* say it was in the neighborhood of . . .

SADE: You hop back to bed, Rush. Liable to catch cold standin' around in your . . . [*doorbell*]

RUSH: Front doorbell.

VIC: *Now* what?

RUSH: Shall I go answer it? [*doorbell again*]

SADE: Who on earth can it *be?*

RUSH: I'll go answer it, huh?

SADE: Yeah. [*to Vic*] Nobody on the phone yet?

VIC: No. An' if this ain't the most ridiculous, outrageous . . .

SADE: [*quickly*] Where you going, Rush?

RUSH: [*off a little*] To my closet to get my baseball bat. *I'm* not gonna open the front door at this time of the night where maybe murderers an' cut-throats are prob'ly . . .

SADE: Come back here.

VIC: [*viciously to phone*] Hello, hello, hello.

SADE: He there?

VIC: No.

SADE: Well, when he answers don't you talk like that. [*doorbell again*]

RUSH: Mom, *I'm* not gonna go downstairs without a weapon. It's almost five o'clock in the morning an' . . .

SADE: *You* go, Vic.

VIC: How *can* I? I've got to wait for this other nit-wit to come to the telephone.

SADE: Rush, go in our bedroom an' look out the front window. You can see who's on the porch from there.

RUSH: [*moving off*] O. K. [*doorbell is heard again in the distance*]

SADE: [*to Vic*] Who on earth can that *be*?

VIC: Prob'ly some dear old schoolmate of yours droppin' around with a box of fudge. Prob'ly some darling sweet cuddlesome . . . [*to phone*] Hello? *Hello.*

SADE: He there?

VIC: Yeah, but he's so sleepy he don't know what he's doin'.

SADE: That Myrtle Frummer always *was* a ninny.

VIC: [*to telephone*] Hello. [*to Sade*] He keeps mumblin' "Who is it?"

SADE: Well, *tell* him who it is.

VIC: [*to phone*] Hello, this is Vic Gook. Your wife is a friend of . . . What? No, not *my* wife—*your* wife. No, *I* don't wanta speak to your wife. I . . . [*to Sade*] Oh, what a swell time I'm havin' tonight.

SADE: What's he tryin' to . . .

VIC: He's gone to get his doggone wife.

RUSH: [*off*] Who's there? Who? Oh. Hello. [*calls*] Mom.

SADE: [*calls*] Yes?

RUSH: It's Mr. *Donahue* on the front porch.

SADE: What's he want?

RUSH: [*off*] He just got in off'n a freight run an' he saw our light on an' thought somebody might be sick.

SADE: [*calls*] Well, *tell* him.

RUSH: [*calls to Donahue*] We're all O. K., Mr. Donahue. Some people are callin' us up on the telephone. Yeah. *That's* all. Thanks for stoppin' by. O. K. Good night, Mr. Donahue.

VIC: [*viciously to phone*] Hello, hello, hello.

SADE: Vic, stop that.

VIC: No half-wit son-of-a-gun is gonna . . . [*to phone*] Hello? [*to Sade*] Oh thunder, it's the *husband* again. [*to phone*] What?

RUSH: [*approaching*] Pretty *nice* of Mr. Donahue to take such a friendly interest, huh, Mom? He said he saw the light burnin' in our bedroom an' was apprehensive . . .

VIC: [*to phone*] Well, *listen. I* don't wanta . . . [*to Sade*] If I ever see that guy I'm gonna choke him to death.

SADE: What's he . . .

VIC: He says he can't get a-hold of his wife because she's in the ladies . . . [*to phone*] Hello. *I* don't wanta talk to your wife. No.

Why don't I? Just because I *don't*. I never *said* I was too good to talk to your wife. Hey, look here, brother, I don't *know* you, but if you think I'm gonna stand for that kind of talk you're badly mistaken. You've got me outa bed at . . . hello . . . hello. [*clicks telephone*] . . . hello . . . [*to Sade*] The big fat-head.
SADE: He hang up on ya?
VIC: Yeah.
SADE: Mad?
VIC: Yeah.
SADE: Maybe we can all go back to bed then.
RUSH: Mom.
SADE: What?
RUSH: This has been kinda *fun*.

Which concludes another brief interlude at the small house half-way up in the next block.

First broadcast 1937.

27

Sade Thinks Baseball
Is Just a Game

*W*ell *sir, it's late afternoon as we enter the small house half-way up in the next block now, and here in the kitchen we find Mrs. Victor Gook and her son, Mr. Rush Gook. This latter individual has just entered from out of doors and at the moment is lightly tossing his cap underneath the sink. Listen:*

SADE: All right; go pick that up.

RUSH: I plan to *leave* again pretty soon.

SADE: Go pick it up. Call *that* civilized?—a monstrous big high school boy throwin' his hat on the floor like a pigpen? *We* got hooks.

RUSH: Yeah, but hooks is way off in the front-room hall an' you hate to have people tramp over your rugs so I should think—

SADE: *You* know I don't mean the front-room hall hooks. Your hat can hang on the hooks in the cellarway.

RUSH: Yes'n a guy's liable to miss his step an' fall down the stairs. Sixty-nine fatal accidents of that nature occurred in Cleveland, Ohio, during the month of—.

SADE: Oh, scoot. Argue, argue, argue.

RUSH: [*moving off*] Certainly been a fine day outside.

SADE: Hasn't it though?

RUSH: [*moving off*] Around noon it was just plain hot.

SADE: Uh-huh. Mr. Gumpox came through the alley an' I noticed he had his coat folded up an' layin' beside him on the seat of the garbage wagon.

RUSH: [*off a way*] Mom, *I* don't see any hook. They're all full of overalls an' aprons an' junk.

SADE: *You'll* find a place if ya look. There's squillions of nails there. Hey, what's your father an' Mr. Drummond doin' so much talkin' about?

RUSH: Where are they?

SADE: Garbage box. Just *more'n* wavin' their arms around.

RUSH: [*returning*] They weren't there when *I* come past just now.

SADE: Prob'ly walked home together an' stopped by the garbage box to finish their talk.

RUSH: [*almost up*] If they're talkin' about baseball they never *will* finish.

SADE: [*giggles*]

RUSH: What they doin'?

SADE: [*giggles*] Glarin' at each other an' makin' signs an' doublin' their fists all up. See out the window?

RUSH: [*chuckles*] Uh-huh.

SADE: Looks like they're almost *yellin'!*

RUSH: Let's raise the window an' listen.

SADE: Naw.

RUSH: They're talkin' *baseball* all right. I could tell that with my *hands* tied behind me—

SADE: Why do they get so *excited?*

RUSH: [*chuckles*] I don't know.

SADE: Person'd think one had stole the other one's pocketbook or bumped into his *automobile* or something.

RUSH: Yeah.

SADE: Baseball's only a *game* ain't it?

RUSH: Well, yes an' no. It's kind of a business, too. Professional baseball players go down to the diamond after dinner just like Gov goes down to the office. They got wives an' children an'—

SADE: Guess the argument's all over. Here comes Gov toward the house.

RUSH: He acts like Mr. Drummond got the best of him. See the little quick steps he takes an' the way his face is?

SADE: [*giggles*] Uh-huh.

RUSH: That's the expression he gets when he comes home an' you tell him you've made arrangements for you an' him to go with Mr. an' Mrs. Stembottom to the Bijou an' see Gloria Golden.

SADE: [*laughs*] Yeah.

RUSH: Let's rap on the window an' give him a jolly wave of the hand.

SADE: You just wanta aggravate him some more?

RUSH: [*chuckles*] No.

SADE: [*giggles*] Ya do, too. Lands, "baseball." What is there *to* it to get upset about?

RUSH: Oh, there's *thousands* of ins an' outs.

SADE: Maybe for *kids*. But grown-up men like Gov an' Mr. Drummond—what do *they* care?

RUSH: You just don't *comprehend* the National Pastime, Mom.

SADE: I guess I don't.

RUSH: See, it's the *Big* Leagues that interest Gov and Mr. Drummond. Here we got a whole bunch of large cities all represented by baseball teams. New York, Chicago, Boston, Philadelphia—[*door opens*]

SADE: [*raises voice*] Hello there, mister.

VIC: [*cheerily enough*] Hi, everybody. How's tricks?

SADE: All right.

RUSH: [*as door closes*] I must of missed ya along the alley some place, Gov. I got home about two minutes before you did.

VIC: Drummond an' I saw you up ahead. We didn't holler an' ask ya to join us because we were in no mood for crude company.

RUSH: I see.

VIC: [*to Sade*] Paper come yet?

SADE: I doubt it. Boy very seldom shows up this early. What were you an' Mr. Drummond havin' such a to-do about?

VIC: When?

SADE: Just now by the garbage box. We saw you through the window.

VIC: What makes ya think we were havin' what you are pleased to call a "to-do"?

SADE: Never saw so much arm wavin' in my life.

VIC: The arm wavin' you saw through the window will in no wise unbalance the equilibrium of the world. Life will go on as before.

SADE: No, but a person watchin' would get the idea you fellas were about to have a fight.

VIC: That may come to pass one of these days. [*to himself*] The big boob.

SADE: Who—Mr. Drummond?

VIC: Yes, Mr. Drummond.

SADE: Are ya mad at him?

VIC: I wouldn't *condescend* to get mad at a creature so handicapped. Mr. Drummond is short the normal quota of brains. Mr. Drummond moves helplessly in a fog of stupidity. Mr. Drummond, in short, is a halfwit.

SADE: [*giggles*] Did you *tell* him that?

VIC: I intimated as much—an' *more*—only I couched my barbs with such subtlety they went over his head like soft summer clouds.

RUSH: Baseball, huh, Gov?

VIC: How's that?

RUSH: You an' him were discussin' baseball?

VIC: One could hardly refer to it as a *discussion*. I'd vouchsafe a thoughtful opinion an' Drummond'd come back with a splatter of meaningless words boorishly strung together.

RUSH: But it was baseball you were talkin' about?

VIC: Yes.

RUSH: [*chuckles*] See, Mom?

SADE: I was just askin' Rush, Vic, how grown-up men can work theirself into a frenzy about such stuff.

VIC: Am I worked up into a frenzy?

SADE: You acted like you were worked up into *something* out by the garbage box just now. You an' Mr. Drummond both.

VIC: What did Master Rush *reply* when you quizzed him?

SADE: [*giggles*] He said he didn't know.

VIC: That would be his rejoinder when quizzed on *any* topic, I believe.

RUSH: [*chuckles*] Aw, c'mon, Gov, don't take it out on *me*.

SADE: [*to Vic*] No, but *really*. If there was a baseball eleven in *this* town an' your brother was in it or somebody an' a fella run *down* your brother an' his baseball eleven, I could halfway see why you might let yourself be *upset*. But these baseball elevens in Chicago an' around. What do *you* care?

VIC: Baseball, Sade, is a strong American institution.

SADE: Is it?

VIC: Baseball is a wholesome vent for excess nervous energy.

SADE: [giggles] Prob'ly is if you're fullback on the team or somethin'. But all you an' Mr. Drummond can do is *talk* about it. *I* always think of baseball as a game Rush an' the kids play over in Tatman's vacant lot. Can't understand why grown-up *men* should lose sleep because New York beats Pontiac.

VIC: You can understand why grown-up men would be interested in *science*, can't ya?

SADE: Is baseball science?

VIC: Certainly.

SADE: I never knew it.

VIC: I expect not. However, baseball *is* a science an' a mighty fascinating one.

RUSH: He's right *there*, Mom. You take when, say, there's a man on first base an' no outs. O. K., the next batter'll attempt to bunt. That means hit the ball easy. In cold blood this batter's cuttin' his own throat. He *wants* to be put out. He's desirous of advancing the man on first to second, see?

SADE: No. The whole business is Greek to me.

RUSH: I could make it clear in a few minutes' time.

SADE: Don't bother. [to Vic] Is that what you an' Mr. Drummond were arguin' about—the science of it?

VIC: Not exactly, no. We were tryin' to get together on a little investment but we couldn't reach an agreement.

SADE: [quickly on the alert] Money?

VIC: How ya mean "money"?

SADE: You're not gonna put *money* on the baseball.

VIC: I still don't get your point.

SADE: You're not gonna—send money to Chicago—to hire a baseball fella to—kick a home run or somethin', are ya?

VIC AND RUSH: [laugh]

RUSH: You don't know the first *thing* about baseball, Mom.

SADE: I know it.

RUSH: [to Vic] Imagine sendin' a dollar to Lou Gehrig an' tellin' him to knock one over the fence?

VIC: [negative] Uh-uh. [laughs]

SADE: Well, what *was* that about money?

VIC: I don't recall *mentioning* money.

SADE: You said you an' Mr. Drummond something.

VIC: Oh. Well, since him an' I both are interested in the old apple an' also because we could use a little exercise now an' then, it was my idea for us to go in cahoots an' buy a pitcher's glove for me an' a catcher's mitt for him an' we'd play catch evenings after supper out in the alley.

SADE: Oh.

VIC: See, summer's comin' on an' we'll have lotsa time to play before it gets dark nights.

SADE: Uh-huh. Do baseball gloves cost much?

VIC: Oh, depends on what quality ya buy. I expect we could pick up the pitcher's glove an' the catcher's mitt both for less than ten dollars.

SADE: There's baseball stuff of Rush's down in the basement by the bushel.

VIC: *Kid's* junk. What *we* want is regular standard big-league equipment.

SADE: Um.

VIC: Won't that be kinda nice for me? Give me a chance to exercise an' loosen up the old arm.

SADE: I should think you could play with *Rush* as well as with Mr. *Drummond.*

VIC: Rush couldn't *catch* me.

SADE: Couldn't what?

VIC: *Catch* me. He couldn't hold onto the ball when I threw it. I've got a steamer that'd tear his arm off if I ever let loose with it.

RUSH: *I* never witnessed that steamer you brag about.

VIC: No. Because I never endangered your life by throwin' it at ya. They usta say, back in Dixon, my steamer would go through a half-inch solid oak board.

RUSH: I'm from Missouri.

SADE: Well—what was it you an' Mr. Drummond argued about?

VIC: That boob.

SADE: Didn't he wanta put up his share of the money?

VIC: *He* wants to wear the pitcher's glove.

SADE: Huh?

VIC: *He* wants to wear the pitcher's glove. Wants *me* to do the *catchin'*. *Imagine* that? Drummond posin' as a hurler?

SADE: I don't know what you're talkin' about.

RUSH: *I* do.

VIC: Explain to your mother.

RUSH: [*chuckling*] Mom, here we got Gov an' Mr. Drummond.

SADE: Yes?

RUSH: They decide wouldn't it be dandy to buy a pitcher's glove an' a catcher's mitt an' play catch out in the alley evenings.

SADE: I caught on to *that* much.

RUSH: But here's the *rub*—[*chuckles*] . . . both of 'em wanta *pitch.*

SADE: Throw the ball?

RUSH: Yeah.

SADE: Well, *lands,* when ya play catch ya throw the ball back an' *forth,* don't ya?

RUSH: Sure—only the guy that's wearin' the pitcher's glove gets to whirl around fancy an' wind up an' let loose with all he's got. While the guy with the catcher's mitt only has the privilege of catchin' the ball an' tossin' it back.

VIC: The point *is,* kiddo, that Drummond has neither the mentality or the physique to work on the mound. He hasn't got the arm an' he hasn't got the brain.

SADE: [*helpless*] I don't get it.

RUSH: May I put it in a nutshell for ya, Mom?

SADE: Yeah.

RUSH: It's simply this. [*chuckles*] Gov an' Mr. Drummond each want to wear the pitcher's glove. Neither one will even *think* of wearin' the *catcher's* mitt.

SADE: [*to Vic*] Is that right?

VIC: Yeah.

SADE: Well, if you're gonna buy both things, can't ya take *turns* wearin' the pitcher's glove an' the catcher's mitt?

VIC: [*obstinately*] No.

SADE: You mean to tell me that two great big grown-up men with offices an' families can jump at each other's throat over a thing like *that*—who gets to be pitcher?

VIC: [*stubborn*] Sure.
SADE: Is that baseball, Rush?
RUSH: [*chuckles*] Uh-huh.
SADE: Is that science?

Which concludes another brief interlude at the small house half-way up in the next block.

First broadcast 1938.

28

Rabbit Hunting from the Back Porch

Well sir, *it's late afternoon as our scene opens now, and here in the living room of the small house half-way up in the next block we discover Mr. Victor Gook. Mr. Victor Gook has just descended the stairs from the attic and is greeting Mrs. Victor Gook, who has just come in the front door with an armload of groceries. Listen:*

SADE: *Well—you* home?
VIC: *Been* home about half an hour.
SADE: Whatcha been doin' up in the attic?
VIC: How ya know I've been up in the attic?
SADE: There's a streak of dirt along your eyebrow.
VIC: [*chuckles*] Can't fool *you*, can I? I *have* been up in the attic.
SADE: Find what you were looking for?
VIC: Yep. Found this. My rabbit-hunter's cap.
SADE: Gonna hunt some rabbits?
VIC: I *may* sometime soon. Me an' Ed Hill.
SADE: Oh. Well here: take some of my packages, will ya? My arm's so tired it's about to drop off.
VIC: Gonna put your stuff on the kitchen table?
SADE: Yes. C'mon.
VIC: [*as they go*] I sure had to do some tall diggin' around to locate my rabbit-hunter's cap. Know where it was? 'Way in back of the trunk layin' on the plaster.
SADE: Hope you didn't muss things up. I *straightened* that attic just the other day.

VIC: Guess I didn't hurt anything. I knocked that pile of portières off on the floor an' tripped over the popcorn popper but I'll clear away the stuff next time I'm up there.

SADE: Should of waited till *I* got home.

VIC: I wanted my rabbit-hunter's cap.

SADE: When ya gonna hunt rabbits?

VIC: I'm *not* gonna hunt rabbits. That is I'm not gonna hunt 'em for some time yet. But it won't do any harm to get *ready* to hunt rabbits. How's this rabbit-hunter's cap *look* on me?

SADE: Dirty.

VIC: Huh?

SADE: It looks dirty. Did you wipe out the inside before you put it on?

VIC: No.

SADE: Now, you'll have a ring around your head. Here—just lay the things on the oilcloth. Lands, I'm tired. Been in every store in town this afternoon. Did get some nice bargains though. Lovely big batch of washrags for fifty-nine cents. You can unwrap 'em an' have a look if ya want. They're in that little package there on top.

VIC: I think I'll wait till some other time. I'm gonna be busy for a little while right now.

SADE: Whatcha gonna do?

VIC: Guess.

SADE: Guess?

VIC: I'm going out in the backyard.

SADE: You guess you're going out in the backyard?

VIC: No. *You* guess. Guess what I'm gonna *do* out in the backyard.

SADE: How would *I* know?

VIC: Well, you figured I'd been up in the attic. Thought maybe you could figure what I'm gonna do out in the backyard.

SADE: I haven't the slightest idea.

VIC: Look at my head.

SADE: What?

VIC: I say look at my head.

SADE: Vic, I'm tired. Been on my feet all day. I don't believe I want to . . .

VIC: I'm giving you a *hint*.

SADE: What for?

VIC: So you can figure out what I'm gonna do in the backyard. What's on my head?

SADE: Don't you *know?*

VIC: Sure I know. What's on my head?

SADE: Rabbit-hunter's cap.

VIC: Good. Now what am I gonna do out in the backyard?

SADE: Oh, Vic.

VIC: Can't figure it out, huh?

SADE: Honest, I'm tired. Haven't sat down since one o'clock. I can't stand around an' . . .

VIC: O. K., kiddo. I won't keep you in the dark. I'll *tell* ya what I'm gonna do out in the backyard. Take a look over there.

SADE: Where?

VIC: By the sink. Leaning against the wall.

SADE: [*looking*] A *gun!*

VIC: Uh-huh. B'longs to Ed Hill. Wait a second: I'll bring it over an' show ya.

SADE: What have I said a million times about bringing things that shoot inside this house?

VIC: I know you're apprehensive about fire-arms but . . .

SADE: Is it loaded?

VIC: Naw. Safe as a baby. Take hold of it once.

SADE: I certainly will not.

VIC: [*superior laugh*] Uh-huh—that's the way it is with women. They don't know the *luxury* of guns. Take a man—there's nothin' he likes better than the feel of good metal.

SADE: You better get that good metal *out* of here . . . an' quick too.

VIC: How do I look?

SADE: All right. Why?

VIC: I mean how do I look holding this gun with my rabbit-hunter's cap on?

SADE: [*puzzled*] All right.

VIC: [*kindly*] I guess you're tired.

SADE: I am.

VIC: Tell ya what ya do: Go lay down on the davenport a while.

SADE: Where *you* going?

VIC: Out in the backyard.

SADE: Whatcha gonna do?

VIC: Can'tcha guess?

SADE: No.

VIC: Sure ya can. What have I got on my head?

SADE: Vic, don't ask me that any more. I *am* tired.

VIC: [*chuckles*] Go on, kiddo. See if you can't figure it out. Ask me what I got on my head.

SADE: [*wearily*] Whatcha got on your head?

VIC: I mean *tell* me what I got on my head.

SADE: [*wearily*] Rabbit-hunter's cap.

VIC: Good. Now what have I got here in my hand?

SADE: Rabbit-hunter's gun.

VIC: No, just a *gun*. *Now* can't ya figure out what I'm gonna do in the backyard?

SADE: No.

VIC: *Sure* ya can. Look: now here I am a fella.

SADE: What?

VIC: Here I am a fella.

SADE: [*wearily*] Oh my.

VIC: Here I am a fella wearin' a rabbit-hunter's gun . . . I mean wearin' a gun-hunter's rabbit . . . rabbit-gunner's . . .

SADE: I'm gonna go lay down.

VIC: [*chuckling*] O. K. I'll be in after a while. I'm going outside for a half hour or so.

SADE: [*going*] All right. If Rush shows up send him in. I'll need him to help pretty soon.

VIC: Yeah. An' listen, if ya hear any shots don't be scared. It's only me doin' a little shootin'. I'm gonna . . .

SADE: [*returning*] What? Whatcha gonna do?

VIC: Gonna do a little shootin'. [*laughs*] That's what I wanted you to figure out. I had this gun an' my rabbit-hunter's . . .

SADE: You're not gonna shoot off any *guns*.

VIC: Sure, I got a pocket full of bullets. I'm gonna . . .

SADE: No.

VIC: Yes.

SADE: No.

VIC: Why not?

SADE: The idea!

VIC: What's the matter with the idea? I wanta get in some practice. I'm gonna put some targets on the garbage box an' . . .

SADE: Oh no, you're not.

VIC: What's the harm?

SADE: Nobody's gonna shoot off any guns around *here*.

VIC: Think I'll *hit* anybody?

SADE: Nobody's gonna shoot off any guns around *here*.

VIC: *I* won't make much noise. This is just a *little* gun. It don't make a big bang. It just makes kind of a bang.

SADE: Vic, you're positively *not* gonna do any shootin'.

VIC: *I'm* gonna have my rabbit-hunter's cap on.

SADE: I don't care if you're gonna have your elephant-hunter's cap on.

VIC: The neighbors'll know I'm not crazy. They can tell by my rabbit-hunter's cap I . . .

SADE: I mean just exactly what I said, Vic.

VIC: All I'm gonna do is go quietly out in the backyard an' put an ol' shingle or something on top of the garbage box an' . . .

SADE: Here comes Rush.

VIC: What?

SADE: Rush is home.

VIC: Listen: I come home early to get a little target practice. *I'm* no infant. *I* can handle fire-arms. *I* know what . . .

SADE: Hello there, son.

RUSH: [*coming up*] Hi, Mom. Hi, Gov.

VIC: [*briefly*] H'lo. [*impassioned again*] Sade, if you can show me what harm there is in going out in your own backyard an' . . .

SADE: No.

RUSH: Whose gun?

VIC: I made a special effort to come home *early*.

SADE: No.

RUSH: Lemme see the gun, will ya, Gov?

VIC: Get outa the way, Sade.

SADE: No, no, no, no, no.

VIC: *I* ain't gonna shoot anybody. All I'm gonna do is put some kind of a target on the garbage box an' . . .

SADE: Might as well save your breath. I'm tellin' ya once an' for all there's gonna be no gun-shooting around this house. *You* know how

I feel about guns. I'm surprised you brought one home here in the first place. Besides it's against the *law* to shoot off guns inside city limits. Besides Mr. Donahue's asleep next door. Besides I'm not gonna have the neighbors see my husband actin' like a crazy man. Besides it's the innocent gun that does the damage. Remember Petie Brainfunny there in Dixon? *He* took a gun out in his backyard to shoot off an' his mother-in-law happened to be walkin' across . . .

VIC: I don't care nothin' *about* Petie Brainfunny. All I'm sayin' is . . .

SADE: I'm going in an' lay down on the davenport. Don't you go 'way, son. Gonna need ya after a bit. [*goes*]

RUSH: O. K., Mom.

VIC: [*to himself*] Thunder!

RUSH: [*to Vic*] Ya mighta *known* Mom wouldn't stand for *guns* around here, Gov.

VIC: Go 'way an' quit botherin'.

RUSH: [*after a pause*] Gonna shoot some rabbits sometime? [*pause*] I see you got your rabbit-hunter's cap on. [*pause*] I guess the last time I saw you wear that rabbit-hunter's cap was when . . . Where ya going?

VIC: Out on the back porch.

RUSH: Guess I'll go along.

VIC: [*grunt*]

RUSH: May I carry your gun for ya?

VIC: No.

RUSH: Whose gun is it?

VIC: [*opening door*] B'longs to Ed Hill.

RUSH: By gosh, *I* never knew he had a gun. Knew he had a fifteen-dollar fishin' pole though. One time me an' Smelly Clark was carryin' out Mrs. Hill's ashes for fifteen cents split 'er two ways an' we noticed there in the basement . . . . Gonna sit down on the steps?

VIC: Yeah.

RUSH: Guess I'll sit down myself.

VIC: [*to himself*] Shucks.

RUSH: Mad because Mom won't let ya shoot off your good ol' gun, huh?

VIC: [*grunt*]

RUSH: Well, ya mighta *known* . . . . There goes Buffalo Kurtz.

VIC: Who?

RUSH: Buffalo Kurtz. Kid in my algebra class. He's gazing at you in admiration, Gov. He sees your gun an' your rabbit-hunter's cap.

VIC: Um.

RUSH: [*chuckles*] Look at him look.

VIC: Ask him if he sees anything green.

RUSH: I bet he thinks you look swell.

VIC: Um.

RUSH: You *do* look like a regular rabbit-hunter, Gov. I guess it's that rabbit-hunter's cap turns the trick.

VIC: [*warming up a little*] It's my nose too. Fella has to have a certain kind of a nose to go with a rabbit-hunter's cap.

RUSH: Uh-huh.

VIC: You take some fellas they couldn't wear a rabbit-hunter's cap five minutes.

RUSH: I expect.

VIC: That is an' get *away* with it.

RUSH: [*flattering him*] Heck, Gov, you oughta wear a rabbit-hunter's cap all the time.

VIC: [*modest chuckle*]

RUSH: I betcha Buffalo Kurtz tells it all over town how good you look holdin' a gun an' wearin' a rabbit-hunter's cap.

VIC: [*modest chuckle*] Naw.

RUSH: *Sure. Buffalo* knows a rabbit-hunter when he sees one. Hey, can I examine that gun a minute?

VIC: [*won over*] Help yourself.

RUSH: Ain't loaded, is it?

VIC: No. Wish to thunder it was.

RUSH: Got some bullets in your pocket?

VIC: 'Bout sixty of 'em.

RUSH: Certainly tough Mom entertains such a hatred for various fire-arms. Gov, see the hinge on the door of Mis' Fisher's chicken coop?

VIC: Yeah.

RUSH: I bet if this good ol' gun was loaded with a good ol' bullet I could knock that hinge six ways from Sunday.

VIC: Uh-huh.

RUSH: Here's how I'd do it. I'd take good aim like this, see? An' I'd get a bead on 'er, see? An' *bang!*

VIC: [*interested*] Yeah.

RUSH: That hinge'd go fifty miles up in the air.

VIC: Yeah, but wait. You don't *hold* the gun right. Give 'er here.

RUSH: O. K.

VIC: Now watch. What ya wanta do is grab 'er like *this.*

RUSH: Uh-huh.

VIC: Now suppose *I'm* gonna knock that hinge off the door. I grasp the barrel firmly. I close my eye. I take deadly aim. An' *bang!*

RUSH: [*pleased*] Uh-huh.

VIC: I bet there ain't much left of *that* hinge.

RUSH: No, sir.

VIC: If this'd had a bullet in it you'd never see a *trace* of that hinge.

RUSH: Let *me* try again, will ya?

VIC: Hold your weapon *right* this time. Get your left hand 'way down there.

RUSH: Yeah.

VIC: Let's see what you can do now. Tell ya what . . . see if you can knock that can off Drummond's shed.

RUSH: It's a pretty long ways off.

VIC: *You* can do it if ya try.

RUSH: Gov.

VIC: What?

RUSH: Can I wear the rabbit-hunter's cap?

VIC: Sure.

RUSH: Thanks.

VIC: Prob'ly be a little large.

RUSH: That's O. K.

VIC: Wear it *back* on your head.

RUSH: Uh-huh. All right now: whatcha want me to hit?

VIC: That can on Drummond's barn.

RUSH: O. K.

VIC: Get your arm down a little farther . . . that's it.

RUSH: Now watch. *Bang.* Did I get 'er?

VIC: I think you shot too quick. Deliberation is the thing that counts in stuff like this. Give me the gun. I'll demonstrate what I mean.

RUSH: Here y'are.

VIC: This is the idea now: hold your gun steady an' don't be nervous. Very carefully take your aim. Never hurry. Count *ten* if you have to. See how I'm doin'? I act like I got all year. I close my eye very slowly. I slide my arm down the barrel of my . . . . Rush.

RUSH: Yeah?

VIC: Ah—gimme my rabbit-hunter's cap, will ya?

RUSH: Sure. Here—I'll put it on for you.

VIC: Thanks.

RUSH: Go ahead. Shoot.

VIC: O. K. I close my eye very carefully. I slide my arm down the barrel of my gun. I take deliberate aim. I wait half a second to coordinate my muscle with my brain. An' *Bang!*

RUSH: Got 'er!

VIC: I'll say I did. If this gun'd had a bullet in it that can'd gone a mile in the air.

RUSH: Mile an' a half.

VIC: Sure.

RUSH: Heck, Gov, *we* don't need any bullets.

VIC: [*chuckles*] Naw.

RUSH: Give *me* the gun now, will ya?

VIC: Here.

RUSH: *An'* the rabbit-hunter's cap. Now look: see that nail stickin' up there in the fence? Well, I'm gonna shoot that good ol' nail . . . [*fade*]

Which concludes another brief interlude at the small house half-way up in the next block.

First broadcast 1936.

29

A Porch Collapses: Rotten Takes the Blame

Well sir, *it's a few minutes past nine o'clock in the evening as we enter the small house half-way up in the next block now, and here in the living room we find Mr. and Mrs. Victor Gook abiding quietly at home. They've been playing rummy for the last hour or so and the game has begun to take on a sluggish, lack-luster quality. Listen:*

SADE: [*listlessly*] I win?

VIC: Let's see your cards.

SADE: [*displaying them*] Um.

VIC: *Sure* ya win. Got three queens, three deuces, an' the four, five, six, an' seven of hearts.

SADE: I lose *interest* in rummies after about so long a time. The spades start resembling clubs.

VIC: Wanta quit?

SADE: Would you just as soon?

VIC: [*chuckles*] All right. Not much kick to the game when your opponent's half asleep.

SADE: I *am* a little bit tired. Too early to go to bed?

VIC: Courthouse clock struck nine about five minutes ago.

SADE: [*yawns luxuriously*] I bet I sleep so sound tonight you could send my undershirt to Detroit Michigan parcel post.

VIC: Paper states showers sometime before morning. I hope they hurry along an' cool things off.

SADE: [*I hope so too*] Um. Deal out a few more rummies: might as well be doin' something.

VIC: O. K.

SADE: Kinda funny that Davis boy storming in here this evening, wasn't it?

VIC: I've learned that there's nothing extraordinary in the most un-understandable behavior on the part of fourteen-year-old boys. Being the *father* of a fourteen-year-old boy I am tutored in all . . .

SADE: Here's your fourteen-year-old boy now. [*calls*] Rush?

RUSH: [*off*] Hi.

VIC: [*to Sade*] There's a beautiful bouquet of tickets for ya, Charley.

SADE: Thanks. I hope I can tell the hearts from the clubs.

VIC: The hearts are red, the clubs black.

SADE: I mean the diamonds from the spades. After so many rummies I get so I can't keep my mind on what I'm doin' an' . . .

RUSH: [*almost up*] Rooster Davis didn't disturb ya when he come after Rotten's suitcase a while ago, did he?

VIC: Not too much. 'Course I hadda climb upstairs *after* it.

RUSH: [*up*] Well, it helped along the excitement. [*with satisfaction*] By George, I never enjoyed such high-class excitement in my life.

VIC: What excitement do you have reference to, Sunburn?

RUSH: *Center* Street.

VIC: Has there been excitement on Center Street? [*to Sade*] I'm discarding the six of clubs.

SADE: I can use it in my business. [*to Rush, giggling*] I beat your father three times in a row.

RUSH: Didn't Rooster *explain?*

SADE: Explain what?

RUSH: About Center Street.

SADE: No. What about it?

RUSH: Rooster never said a *word?*

SADE: He come to the door all outa breath an' wanted that big ol' imitation leather suitcase you borrowed off'n his brother. Gov went after it an' he grabbed it an' was gone.

RUSH: [*amazed*] Well, I'll be darned.

SADE: Why? What happened on Center Street?

RUSH: A *house* collapsed.

SADE: [*mildly*] Aw.

RUSH: You tellin' the *truth* ya don't know about it?

SADE: We've been sittin' here playin' cards ever since around seven-thirty.

RUSH: Never heard no noise? Never heard no people yellin'?

SADE: Never heard a sound. *Telephone* hasn't even rung. Except for Rooster storming in it's been quiet as my thumb.

RUSH: Beats the Dutch.

VIC: [*little chuckle*] A house collapsed you say, Temple-bells?

RUSH: Yeah.

VIC: *I* collapsed one time *myself*. I was on the outskirts of Cleveland Ohio where I'd just officiated at a wedding ceremony. After kissing the bride I pocketed the five-dollar bill given me by the bridegroom an' prepared to . . .

RUSH: [*rapidly*] Ya know that place in the three hundred block on South Center with the second-story porch that runs clear around the whole house?

VIC: Has it got fragile hedgerows of morning glories an' a solid gold belfry which catches the dazzling rays of the . . .

RUSH: [*tough*] Give me *show*, Gov. That place *collapsed* this evening.

VIC: Here's the nine of spades, Sadie. I trust it will . . .

SADE: [*to Rush*] You talkin' about that big boarding-house lookin' place, Willie?

RUSH: Sure. It collapsed at eight o'clock.

SADE: Whatcha mean by "collapsed"?

RUSH: Fell down.

SADE: [*incredulous*] Aw. A great big monstrous . . .

RUSH: The whole *thing* didn't fall down. Just that second-story *verandah* fell down. But to look at it you'd think the entire house'd been hit by a cyclone.

SADE: That's the *truth?*

RUSH: If it's *not* the truth you can send my undershirt to Saint Paul Minnesota, cash on delivery. If it's not the truth . . .

SADE: [*interested at last*] Was anybody *hurt?*

RUSH: Not a soul. An' it's the luckiest thing since the bullet that choked Billy Patterson. Why, that second-story verandah weighs tons an' *tons*. It crashed like thunder. Busted the first-floor porch into smithereens. Broke every window in the house. There's chunks of lumber an' splinters of wood scattered up an' down Center Street for half a block.

VIC: You're not exaggerating, are ya? You're not making a mountain out of some trivial accident that . . .

RUSH: [*sincerely*] No sir. I hope to *die* if I've twisted the facts. Hey, why don't you people put on your hats an' stroll *over* there? See for *yourself*. It's just like I say: Center Street is cluttered up with debris for half a block in both directions.

SADE: Well, what *happened*?

RUSH: The doggone second-story verandah collapsed from old *age*. The *pillars* were weak.

SADE: I believe *that*. Ruthie an' I noticed the place just last week when we were walking past. That upstairs porch that circles the house was saggin' in half a dozen places.

RUSH: Sure. It was *bound* to happen sooner or *later*. An' it happened *tonight*. I'm surprised you individuals never heard the *crash*.

VIC: Where were *you* when it happened?

RUSH: Standin' out in front of the Bijou Picture Show. I was in the society of Blue-tooth Johnson. By George, we were in the three hundred block on South Center in two seconds.

SADE: [*to Vic*] Looks like we *did* miss some excitement.

RUSH: Missed half your *life*. C'mon . . . slap on your hats—we'll go *over* there.

SADE: [*reluctant to exert herself*] Aw . . . it's all over an' *done* with now.

RUSH: Prob'ly still a crowd of *people* hangin' around though. No foolin', to look at that house you'd think it'd got caught between nine cyclones.

SADE: Um.

RUSH: C'mon, Gov, you an' *me'll* hike to Center Street.

VIC: I'd like to beg off, Arthur. It's too warm an evening to work myself up over a porch fallin' off a house.

RUSH: [*it's your loss*] O. K.

SADE: Certainly a good thing nobody got injured.

RUSH: Yes, indeed.

SADE: I remember the place you're talking about *very* well. Just last week Ruthie an' I walked past. Seems to me she passed some *remark*. "Look how that ol' upper-story porch sags," or something.

RUSH: Peculiar Rooster didn't give ya the details when he came after Rotten's suitcase. Guess he was too excited.

VIC: What was his big hurry for his brother's suitcase when there was so much free entertainment going on over . . .

RUSH: Oh gosh, I haven't told ya about *Rotten* yet.

VIC: What'd Rotten do?

RUSH: [*seriously*] Rotten Davis, Gov, had the most magnificent evening of his entire career.

VIC: How so?

RUSH: He made off to the crowd it was *his* fault the house collapsed.

VIC: Yeah?

RUSH: You should of *seen* him. He was runnin' back an' forth in front of the ruins *screaming*. "I lost my temper," he kept yellin', "I lost my temper."

VIC AND SADE: [*incredulous*] Aw.

RUSH: *Yes.*

VIC AND SADE: You mean he was . . .

RUSH: . . . makin' a public spectacle out of himself; *yes*. Five minutes after the big crash about two hundred *people* were on the spot. *They* didn't know what'd happened. They just saw this house all busted to pieces an' lumber layin' around every place. An' here was Rotten Davis tearin' his hair an' rushin' around crazy. "I lost my temper!" he kept screamin', "I lost my temper."

SADE: The people . . . got the notion . . . Rotten'd lost his temper . . . an' torn a whole *house* down?

RUSH: *Sure* they got that notion.

SADE: [*distaste*] Oh my.

RUSH: [*happily*] It was a *magnificent* thing to witness. People stood around with their mouths hangin' open to where you could send your undershirt to Somerset Kentucky railway express. The crowd opened up an alley for Rotten to run back an' forth in. An' he run back an' forth in it till who laid the chunk. "I lost my temper," he hollered, "I lost my temper an' look what I've done!" Remember now, the house looked like it'd been hit by a cyclone. Why, an innocent bystander would guess it'd take nine men eight days to do that much damage.

SADE: [*distaste*] Oh my.

RUSH: Rotten Davis seen his opportunity an' grabbed it. He had that enormous throng of people in the palm of his hand. If he'd looked tough at any of 'em they'd of started for home ninety miles an hour. [*happily*] Oh, it was wonderful! *Wonderful*, I tell ya!

SADE: If I had a boy that was such a smarty show-off I bet I'd . . .

RUSH: Hey, an' Rooster worked hand in glove with him. Rooster deserves fifty percent of the credit for his brother's sensational hoax.

VIC: I was gonna inquire: what did Rooster want with the suitcase? I . . .

RUSH: Wanted it to take back to *Rotten*. It's all plastered up with foreign *labels*, ya know. Foreign labels *impress* the general public. Soon as Rotten got a-hold of that suitcase he started runnin' between the divided crowd of *people* with it. I told you they separated an' left him space to run back an' forth in, didn't I?

VIC: Yeah.

RUSH: Made kind of a *lane* for him. Well, he'd run from one end of the lane to the other. When he got to one end he'd stop an' set down his suitcase. That'd give the people a chance to read the foreign labels. Nome Alaska, London England, Paris France, Rotterdam Holland, Brussels Belgium, Stockholm Sweden an' so on. All the time he kept hollerin' he'd lost his temper an' torn down a house. Then he'd pick up his suitcase an' run to the *other* end of the lane. Do the same thing *over* again. "I lost control of my temper," he screamed, "I lost control of my temper an' tore down this house in three minutes with my bare hands."

SADE: His mother oughta take him by the coat collar an' . . .

RUSH: Let me tell ya *another* trick he used to heighten the effect. He was wearin' *goggles*. When he sent Rooster after his suitcase he also had him stop by home an' pick up an aviator's helmet an' goggles that usta belong to some friend of his that owned a motorcycle. Oh, it was magnificent, Gov!

VIC: I *bet* it was . . .

RUSH: Carryin' his suitcase all plastered up with foreign labels an' wearin' an aviator's helmet on his head with the goggles pulled down over his eyes an' runnin' back an' forth like he'd gone crazy!

VIC: [*mildly*] "I lost my temper; I lost my temper."

RUSH: *Yeah.*

SADE: For a boy that's almost a grown-up man I'd say . . .

RUSH: [*to Vic*] An' every once in a while he'd holler to Rooster. "Hey," he'd holler. "How many bodies have they found so far?" An' Rooster—he was back in the shadows—would put on a deep voice an' answer, "Six—so far, seven—so far, eight—so far." *You* know.

VIC: Uh-huh.

SADE: Ain't he going on twenty-one years old, Rush?

RUSH: Rotten? Yeah.

SADE: *Imagine* a boy twenty-one years old behavin' like . . .

RUSH: Mom, he had the most magnificent evening of his entire career.

SADE: *I'd* give him the most magnificent . . .

RUSH: Oh, an' *another* feature that was dandy. Three young *ladies* he likes were in the crowd.

VIC: Yeah?

RUSH: Three very handsome young ladies he's ambitious to escort to the *picture* show an' places were present.

VIC: I bet he's their hero *now.*

RUSH: [*yes, sir*] Oh, *boy!*

VIC: You seem to have had just about as satisfactory an evening as *Rotten* did.

RUSH: [*happily*] I had a *delightful* evening.

VIC: Um.

RUSH: A *delightful* evening!

Which concludes another brief interlude at the small house half-way up in the next block.

First broadcast 1939.

30

———————

Uncle Fletcher Drops by for a Visit at 5:30 A.M.

W*ell sir, it's early morning as we enter the small house half-way up in the next block now, and we find Mr. and Mrs. Gook upstairs in their bedroom. Vic is wrapped in deep majestic slumber, but Sade is wide awake and listening intently, having been disturbed a few moments ago by a distant hammering. Listen:*

[*We hear someone pounding on the door in the distance.*]

SADE: [*after a time, softly*] Vic. [*after a pause, more sharply*] Vic.

VIC: [*sleepy unintelligible vocables*]

SADE: [*sharply*] Wake up!

VIC: [*sleepy unintelligible vocables*]

SADE: Sounds like somebody's tryin' to knock our front door in.

VIC: [*sleepily*] What's the matter?

SADE: Listen.

RUSH: [*in the distance, calls*] Who is it?

VIC: [*sleepily*] What's the matter, Sade?

SADE: [*sharply*] Listen.

RUSH: [*off, calling*] Who is it down there?

VIC: [*to Sade, sleepily*] What's *he* yellin' about?

SADE: Somebody's on the front porch.

RUSH: [*off, calls*] Hey!

VIC: [*to Sade*] Who's on the front porch?

SADE: [*Irritated*] I don't know.

RUSH: [*off, calls*] Hey, you on the porch.

VIC: [*to Sade*] What in thunder *time* is it? My gosh, a man . . .

SADE: [*briefly*] Listen.

FLETCHER: [*in the distance*] That you, Rush?

SADE: [*to Vic*] Oh, my.

RUSH: [*off, amused, calls*] Hello, Uncle Fletcher.

VIC: [*to Sade*] Uncle Fletcher?

SADE: Yeah.

VIC: [*irritated*] For Pete's sake.

FLETCHER: [*off*] Good morning, Rush.

RUSH: [*off*] Good *morning*.

FLETCHER: [*off*] Glorious day.

RUSH: [*off*] Yeah. Just a second. I'll come down an' let you in.

FLETCHER: [*off*] Fine.

VIC: [*to Sade, irritated*] What half-wit *time* is it?

SADE: Five-thirty.

VIC: [*irritated*] Holy smoke.

SADE: What on earth can *he* want at this time of the night?

VIC: Pop some popcorn maybe. I'm going back to sleep. I hope you'll see to it that our different relatives don't disturb me further. I . . .

RUSH: [*in the doorway, cheerfully*] Everybody awake?

SADE: Hello, sonny.

VIC: [*grunts*] Go 'way, sonny.

RUSH: [*chuckles*] Good morning, Gov.

VIC: Unk.

RUSH: [*chuckles*] Hear all that racket?

SADE: Yes.

RUSH: It was Uncle Fletcher pounding on the front door. I'm going down an' let him in.

SADE: Ya suppose anything's the matter?

RUSH: [*chuckles*] No. I leaned out my bedroom window an' he was standin' down there screamin' what a glorious day it is.

VIC: [*grouchily*] How about you guys takin' your jolly conversation someplace else? At this uncivilized hour a man objects . . . [*the hammering in the distance begins again.*]

SADE: [*disturbed*] Goodness, there he goes *again*.

RUSH: [*hastily*] I'll run down an' let him in.

SADE: Yeah.

VIC: [*grouchily*] Don't bring him up *here*.

RUSH: [*moving off*] O. K.

VIC: [*to Sade, grouchily*] Why don't he use the lamebrain *door*bell?

SADE: Just Uncle *Fletcher* for ya. Why don't he do a *lot* of things other people . . .

VIC: [*summarily*] Fine, fine, fine, fine. And now if you'll excuse me I'll sink back into the arms of Morpheus. I will seal the hushed casket of my soul.

SADE: [*puzzled*] What in *goodness* name can he want at five-thirty o'clock in the morning?

VIC: [*I don't know and I don't care*] Um.

SADE: I was just on the edge of waking up when that pounding started. *You* know how you are. You're not quite awake and you're really not asleep. I got the peculiar dreamy notion I was working for the Chicago and Alton Railroad an' was down in the roundhouse with nine million locomotives chuggin' an' puffin' back an' forth an' . . .

VIC: I'd like to hear all that another *day*, Doctor Sleetch. Do you mind terribly?

SADE: Going back to sleep?

VIC: [*emphatically*] I most certainly *am*.

SADE: Maybe you ought to wait a minute. Maybe Uncle Fletcher's got something important up his sleeve an' . . .

VIC: [*tough*] Hey, what's *this* now?

FLETCHER: [*approaching*] . . . my shoe box full of lunch an' some other odds and ends.

RUSH: [*approaching*] Yeah.

VIC: [*horrified, to Sade*] They're coming up *here!*

SADE: *I* can't help it, can I?

VIC: [*bitterly*] Ecstasy, ecstasy!

FLETCHER: [*approaching*] Papa and Mama both awake, are they, Rush?

RUSH: [*approaching, chuckling*] *Mama* is, I think. I don't know about *Papa*.

FLETCHER: [*approaching*] Fine.

VIC: [*to Sade, bitterly*] Isn't this delicious?

SADE: [*little giggle*] Well, goodness.

RUSH: [*coming up*] Here's Uncle Fletcher, people. He's leaving town in a little while.

FLETCHER: [*coming up, brightly*] Good morning, Sadie.

SADE: [*cheerfully*] *Well.* Good *morning*.

FLETCHER: Glorious day, Vic.

VIC: [*without warmth*] Yeah. [*significantly*] What *time* is it?

FLETCHER: *Yes.* I look for the thermometer to hit around eighty or so by *noon.*

VIC: [*without warmth*] That's just dandy.

SADE: [*briefly, low tones*] All right.

RUSH: Uncle Fletcher's taking the train for *Dixon* after a bit.

SADE: [*with interest*] Oh?

FLETCHER: [*importantly*] I'm taking the train for *Dixon* after a bit, Sadie.

SADE: [*interested*] Well.

FLETCHER: [*importantly*] Got my shoebox full of lunch here an' a few other odds an' ends. Train pulls out of the station at six-forty-five.

SADE: How long you plan to be gone?

FLETCHER: *Yes.* I just made up my mind last *night.* I told my landlady about it. I had something in my tooth an' was whittlin' a kitchen match into a toothpick there in the living room. "Mis' Keller," I said, right out of a blue sky, "I believe I'll run up to *Dixon* in the morning."

SADE: [*cheerfully*] Uh-huh.

VIC: [*bitterly, low tones*] Can't this happy roundtable discussion be moved downstairs?

SADE: [*briefly*] Don't see how.

VIC: [*bitterly, low tones*] It's five-thirty in the *morning.*

FLETCHER: Glorious day, Vic.

VIC: [*fervently*] Yes *sir,* a *glorious* day.

FLETCHER: Reason I stopped by, Sadie, I knew you people generally got up around this time of the morning an' . . .

VIC: [*tough*] You knew *what?*

SADE: [*low tones, soothingly*] All right, all right.

FLETCHER: . . . I thought I might as well look in a minute.

SADE: Uh-huh.

VIC: *We* don't get up at any five-thirty in the morning.

FLETCHER: Beg pardon, Vic?

VIC: Where in the world you ever got the idea we make it a practice to get out of bed at any five-thirty o'clock in the . . .

SADE: [*hastily*] We *heard* you pounding on the front door, Uncle Fletcher.

FLETCHER: Fine.

RUSH: Why didn't you use the *bell?*

FLETCHER: Bell, Rush?

RUSH: *Door*bell.

FLETCHER: Doorbell's on the *blink*, ain't it?

RUSH: *No.*

FLETCHER: I *pressed* it, but I never *heard* nothing.

RUSH: That's because you were *outside. We* would of heard it if you'd rung it a few more times. It rings *quite* loud.

FLETCHER: [*agreeing*] *Yes.* Better get it *fixed.*

RUSH: Um.

FLETCHER: [*generously*] *I'll* fix it one of these times.

RUSH: Um.

FLETCHER: [*chuckles*] I expect you wondered why I hammered on the door again after you stuck your head outa your bedroom window.

RUSH: Yeah, I did.

FLETCHER: [*chuckles*] Figured you'd most likely jumped back in *bed.*

RUSH: [*little chuckle*] Oh, uh-huh.

FLETCHER: [*chuckles*] Boys'll do that, Sadie.

SADE: Um.

FLETCHER: Wake 'em up out of a sound sleep and talk to 'em an' give 'em directions an' everything else an' the minute your back is turned they'll fall right back in *bed* again.

SADE: Um.

RUSH: [*chuckles*] *I* didn't do that.

FLETCHER: [*chuckles*] *Yes.* Been a boy *myself.* Remember Henry Fedrock, Sadie?

SADE: No-o.

FLETCHER: [*somewhat surprised*] *He* was a Belvidere fella.

SADE: Was he?

FLETCHER: Sure. Oh, wait though, maybe he was before your *time.*

VIC: [*sourly to Rush*] What *you* gonna do?

RUSH: Sit down on the bed.

VIC: [*sourly*] You're sittin' on my *feet.*

RUSH: *Move* your feet a little.

VIC: [*moans piteously*] Oh, my.

FLETCHER: [*pleasantly*] Got something in your tooth, Vic?

VIC: [*sourly*] No.

FLETCHER: [*pleasantly*] Had your face all screwed up there; it give me the notion you had something in your tooth.

VIC: [*bitterly*] Five-thirty in the morning.

FLETCHER: [*agreeably*] Yes.

VIC: [*to Rush, tough*] You gonna lay *down?*

RUSH: Why *not?*

VIC: Go lay down on your *own* bed.

RUSH: *That* wouldn't be very polite, would it? Here we got company and . . .

VIC: [*tough*] Ouch!

RUSH: Oh, excuse me.

FLETCHER: [*to Sade, informatively*] He's got something in his tooth.

SADE: *Yes*, must have.

FLETCHER: No, but this Henry Fedrock there in Belvidere was a good deal like *Rush*. Wake him up out of a sound sleep an' tell him something an' he'd agree with ya an' talk back intelligent as a horse an' the minute your back was turned he'd fall right back on the *bed* again.

RUSH: [*chuckles*] *I* never done that.

FLETCHER: [*chuckles*] Yes, you scalawag. Glad to hear you own up.

RUSH: [*chuckles*] Um.

FLETCHER: [*to Sade*] Henry Fedrock *left* Belvidere there in nineteen-aught-*nine*. He moved to Albuquerque Colorado, married a woman twenty-eight years old, went bail for his brother-in-law that skipped the country, invented a fingernail file that run by electricity, an' later died.

VIC: [*to Rush, bitterly*] Get off my feet.

RUSH: *Move* your feet a little.

VIC: [*piteous moan*]

SADE: [*politely*] How long you plan to visit in Dixon, Uncle Fletcher?

FLETCHER: *Just* today. Coming back tomorrow.

SADE: [*polite interest*] *Well*. [*tough*] Oh, *Rush*.

RUSH: Sorry, Mom.

SADE: Get *up*.

RUSH: There's room for me on the bed if you an' Gov'll *move* three-quarters of an inch.

SADE: [*distaste*] Ish.

FLETCHER: No, reason I stopped past, Sadie, I knew you people had a habit of gettin' up around this time of the morning an' I thought I'd look in a minute an' tell you my *plans*.

SADE: Uh-huh. Well, glad you did, but you made one little mistake. [*little giggle*] We don't as a rule get up this early.

FLETCHER: That's what I *say*. An' then on top of that I figured there's people in Dixon you an' Vic would like to have me say hello to for ya.

SADE: Uh-huh.

FLETCHER: Mrs. T. K. *Hoygawper* for one.

SADE: I don't guess I *know* anybody by that name.

FLETCHER: *I'll* tell her hello for ya.

SADE: All right.

FLETCHER: Wait a second. I'll jot *down* the different ones.

SADE: Um.

FLETCHER: Got a pencil stub an' scratch paper right here *on* me.

SADE: Um.

FLETCHER: Mrs. T. K. Hoygawper. I'll make it a special point to tell her you wanted to be remembered to the family.

SADE: Um.

FLETCHER: [*cheerfully*] Here we are, a pencil stub an' scratch paper.

SADE: Um.

RUSH: [*little chuckle*] Gov's gone to sleep.

SADE: Has he?

RUSH: Sure. Uncle Fletcher, Gov's gone to sleep.

FLETCHER: Fine. Got something in his tooth likely. [*to Sade*] *Now.*

SADE: Um.

FLETCHER: [*importantly*] Mrs. T. K. *Hoygawper.*

SADE: [*sleepily*] Um.

FLETCHER: *Walter* Hoygawper *left* Dixon a year or so ago, ya know.

SADE: [*sleepily*] Um.

FLETCHER: Moved to Richmond, North Carolina, married a

woman sixteen and three-quarters years old, bought a dry-goods store an' sold it twenty minutes later at a profit of eleven dollars, grew chin-whiskers to spite his landlord and later died.

SADE: [*sleepily*] Um.

FLETCHER: I've got Mrs. T. K. Hoygawper wrote down here. Who *else* ya want me to say hello to?

SADE: [*sleepily*] Um.

FLETCHER: [*thinks of somebody*] Oh? Myrtle *McAnderson*.

SADE: [*no comment*]

FLETCHER: Myrtle McAnderson still makes the bakery goods an' sells 'em there in Dixon. Best apple pies in the world. [*writes*] Myrtle McAnderson. [*brief pause*] Now, who *else* ya want me to say hello to?

SADE: [*no comment*]

FLETCHER: Jim Fashrope?

SADE: [*no comment*]

FLETCHER: No, come to think of it Jim Fashrope don't *live* there any more. Some gives it out he moved to Tallahassee Georgia, married a woman thirty-nine years old and later died an' others give it out he moved to Fargo Minnesota, married a woman *forty*-nine years old an' later died. You can search me which story is true. In *any* case he's not in *Dixon*.

SADE: [*no comment*]

FLETCHER: [*after a pause*] Oh, . . . I bet you want me to say hello to Doctor *Klackgummer*.

SADE: [*no comment*]

FLETCHER: Sadie, shall I tell Doctor Klackgummer hello for ya?

SADE: [*no comment*]

FLETCHER: [*after a pause, softly*] Sadie? [*pause*] Sadie? [*after a longer pause*] Vic? [*pause*] Vic? [*after another longer pause*] Rush? [*pause*] Rush? [*after a long pause, to himself*] Fine. Fine.

Which concludes another brief interlude at the small house half-way up in the next block.

First broadcast 1942.